VILLAGE
OF EDINBURGH

To my younger daughter
Karen
the clarinettist
who has never been asked
to play second fiddle

VILLAGES OF EDINBURGH

Volume 2

MALCOLM CANT

With maps by

BRYAN RYALLS

Foreword by

THE RT. HON. DR. JOHN McKAY, C.B.E.
Former Lord Provost of Edinburgh

JOHN DONALD PUBLISHERS LTD
EDINBURGH

© Malcolm Cant 1987

Reprinted 1989
Reprinted 1991

ISBN 0 85976 186 X

British Library Cataloguing in Publication Data
A catalogue record for this book is available from the British Library.

Printed and bound in Great Britain by
Courier International Limited, East Kilbride

Foreword

Edinburgh is a City with a momentous history. As the capital of Scotland it was the locus for hundreds of years of major events in the history of Scotland. The City has also at several periods in its history exercised a considerable influence on the international scene.

Behind this magnificent facade of national and international affairs lies the life of the City and of the small communities and villages which make up present-day Edinburgh. I am sure that this second volume of histories of these communities will be as well received as the first. Both Edinburgh residents and visitors will find much to interest them in these accounts of life in the villages and small towns which have been absorbed into Edinburgh.

Mr Cant paints vivid pictures of the separate communities. This is based on meticulous research, the results of which are presented in a very readable style with highly appropriate illustrations. Altogether, this second volume of *Villages of Edinburgh* will, I am sure, fill a gap in many bookshelves both in Edinburgh and in the home towns of our most welcome visitors.

THE RT. HON. DR.
JOHN McKAY, C.B.E.,
FORMER
LORD PROVOST
OF EDINBURGH

Contents

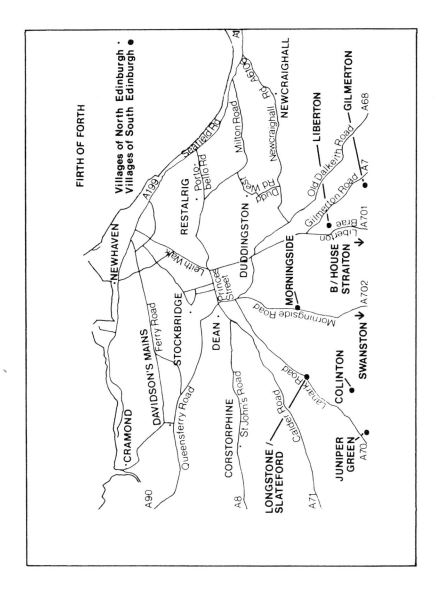

FIRTH OF FORTH

Villages of North Edinburgh ·
Villages of South Edinburgh ●

NEWHAVEN

RESTALRIG

CRAMOND

DAVIDSON'S MAINS

Ferry Road

Queensferry Road

STOCKBRIDGE

DEAN

CORSTORPHINE

St John's Road

A8

A90

Leith Walk

Princes Street

Seafield Rd

A199

Porto-
bello Rd

Milton Road

DUDDINGSTON

Dudd Rd West

Newcraighall Rd

A6095

NEWCRAIGHALL

LIBERTON

GILMERTON

Old Dalkeith Road

A68

Gilmerton Road

A7

Liberton Brae

A701

MORNINGSIDE

Morningside Road

B/HOUSE
STRAITON

A702

SWANSTON ↓

COLINTON

Lanark Road

Calder Road

JUNIPER
GREEN

A70

A71

LONGSTONE /
SLATEFORD

Introduction

In my Introduction to Volume 1 of *Villages of Edinburgh* I explained how the idea of researching Edinburgh's village communities emerged from an earlier study of the district of Marchmont. This second volume, dealing with the villages on the south side of the City, follows substantially the same pattern as that set in the first volume, which dealt with the north side of Edinburgh. I found that there were many similarities, and a few, quite pronounced, differences. The basic composition of each village—church, school, pub and cottages—remained fairly constant, regardless of its geographical position. On the other hand, some villages on the south side appear to have taken longer to be fully integrated with the City, as in the case of Swanston, which still retains some geographical separateness. Again, each northern village was very compact and easily identified, whereas, on the south side, an element of grouping has been necessary for Burdiehouse, Straiton and Old Pentland in Chapter 1, and for Longstone and Slateford in Chapter 6. In doing this I hope that I have succeeded in presenting the complete picture, without losing the identity of any one community. In some villages, the original dominance of one trade was again obvious, particularly the mills at Colinton and Juniper Green, the quarries at Longstone, and the limestone and shale at Burdiehouse and Straiton.

I have again found the research interesting and rewarding. As the title suggests, the book deals generally with the villages of Edinburgh and does not claim to be an exhaustive study of any one aspect, be it architectural or sociological. The reason is simply that in studying each village I found that it was not divided up into little boxes in the way that might be suggested.

There is one major addition in Volume 2 which unfortunately was not available in Volume 1, and that relates to the excellent street maps prepared by Bryan Ryalls, Principal Teacher of Geography at Liberton High School. I am sure that these maps, inserted at the beginning of each chapter, will help to orientate readers, even if their knowledge of the locality is already comprehensive.

It remains for me to thank the many people who assisted me at various stages in my research.

BURDIEHOUSE; STRAITON; OLD PENTLAND. The geological perplexities of limestone and shale were expertly unravelled for me by Dr W.B. Heptonstall of the Grant Institute of Geology, Edinburgh University. I also made extensive use of maps and plans held by the British Geological Survey at Murchison House. J.H. Trotter assisted with Mortonhall and David Dick, O.B.E., with Broomhills. I gained an insight into the old villages of Burdiehouse and Straiton during my frequent discussions with Mrs Mabel Adamson, Mr & Mrs Anderson and several members of the Denholm, Mathison and Robertson families. My account of Old Pentland owes much to the research already done by J.C.H. Gibsone.

COLINTON. My initial contact was with members of Colinton Local History Society and Miss E.D. Robertson. School logs and records were made available to me by Miss. M.W.J. Ferguson, Headteacher at Colinton School, and Mrs Irene A. McCulloch, Headteacher at Bonaly Primary School. In my study of the churches, similar assistance was provided by the Very Rev. William B. Johnston, of Colinton Parish Church, and the Rev. D.R. Cole of St. Cuthbert's Episcopal Church. My references to James Gillespie were strengthened by reference to Maurice Berrill of the Company of Merchants of the City of Edinburgh. Information on Merchiston Castle School was provided by the Headmaster, Mr D.M. Spawforth.

GILMERTON. My first reference was to the Rev. Donald M. Skinner of Gilmerton Parish Church and the various members of Pioneer Tec. Later I discussed particular topics with Mary McLean, A.G. Muir and Miss E. Waldie. Assistance was also obtained from Mrs C. Bennett, Headteacher at Gilmerton Primary School, Mrs Carol M. Cameron, Headteacher at Fernieside Primary School, and the staff of Dr Guthrie's Girls' School with whom I lost contact when the school closed. Valuable information was also supplied by Moredun Research Institute, The Murray Home, Gilmerton Bowling Club, and G.A. More Nisbet of The Drum. I thank particularly James M. Turner for allowing me access to the Gilmerton Cove.

JUNIPER GREEN. My starting point was Juniper Green Village Association who put me in touch with many residents with particular knowledge of the village, including Juniper Green Church and Juniper Green Primary School. In my study of the mills I thank Mr &

Mrs Downie of Upper Spylaw Mill and Mr & Mrs Carmichael of Mossy House for their hospitality, and also the various commercial undertakings who took the trouble to answer my enquiries. Information was also gladly supplied by D.M. McBain of Baberton Golf Club and M.R.A. Matthews of Baberton House. I also learned much from my walks round the district with Sqn. Ldr. John P. Wilson.

LIBERTON. The Rev. John W.M. Cameron, minister at Liberton Parish Church, and his predecessor, the Rev. Campbell Ferenbach, were both very helpful in my research into the church and the general history of the village. Specific information was added by Mrs J. Forrest, Mr & Mrs Laverick and Mr & Mrs Philp. I also thank Alex Forall for allowing me access to Liberton House.

LONGSTONE; SLATEFORD. My introduction was to read a school project by Kirsty Pollock which highlighted many of the early historical associations of the area. To this I added more detailed information from Longstone Parish Church, LANCAS, and Miss Patricia McCall, Headteacher at Longstone Primary School. Particular aspects of village life, old and new, were gleaned from Miss C. Fleming, Stuart Harris, Dr Mary G. Thow and the Royal Society for the Prevention of Accidents.

MORNINGSIDE. Many churches, of various denominations, contributed to the fairly lengthy account in this chapter. Additional assistance was given by Charles J. Smith and William R. Smith. School logs were made available to me for South Morningside School by the Headteacher Mrs J. Perry, and for St. Peter's School by the Headteacher, Miss M.T. Dunne. The section on entertainment was completed after discussion with Derek M. Cameron on the Dominion Cinema, Mrs E. Casciani on the Plaza Ballroom and Bill Robertson and others on the Church Hill Theatre. Access to various plans and maps was given by Maurice Berrill of the Company of Merchants of the City of Edinburgh and Douglas F. Stewart, principal partner with the solicitors J. & F. Anderson. Other pieces in the jigsaw were completed by Mrs J. Crawford, Mrs S. Durham and Mrs E.C. Mackenzie.

SWANSTON. As almost the entire population of this small village made some contribution to my research, it would be unfair to single out any specific person. I thank everyone together. My contacts with the golf clubs were Alex R. Roxton of Lothianburn Golf Club and Sid Berry of Swanston Golf Club. Visits to the Pentland Hills Ranger Centre and Hillend Ski Centre were also most rewarding. Further afield I was also made very welcome at Morton House by Lord and Lady Elliott and at Morton Mains Farm by Jim and Angela Brass. My section on Robert Louis Stevenson would have been much more difficult to compile without the guiding hand of Robin A. Hill who has made an exhaustive study of Stevenson, both at home and abroad.

My final acknowledgements go to the group of people whose help was not confined to any one village. These include the staff, librarians and archivists of Edinburgh City Libraries, Edinburgh District Council, Lothian Regional Council, the National Library of Scotland, the Royal College of Physicians, the Royal Commission on the Ancient and Historical Monuments of Scotland, the Royal Observatory, *The Scotsman* Publications Ltd and the University of Edinburgh. Photography has been acknowledged throughout the text, but my special thanks go to Malcolm Liddle who again undertook reproduction of many old photographs.

It is a great privilege for me to have my work prefaced by the Rt. Hon. Dr. John McKay, C.B.E., Former Lord Provost of Edinburgh. My appreciation goes to Dr. McKay and also to his secretary, R.J. Freeman-Wallace, who dealt so expertly with the very demanding timetable.

I have tried to keep the text as accurate as possible, but inevitably mistakes will have arisen. In accordance with tradition, and good sense, I accept responsibility now: the errors would have been much greater had it not been for the very careful proof reading, again undertaken by Morag Sinclair.

Finally I thank my wife Phyllis for typing and checking the script and for undertaking numerous other tasks associated with the book. Our family, who took Volume 2 in their stride, will be pleased to know that the pace is now much reduced.

MALCOLM CANT

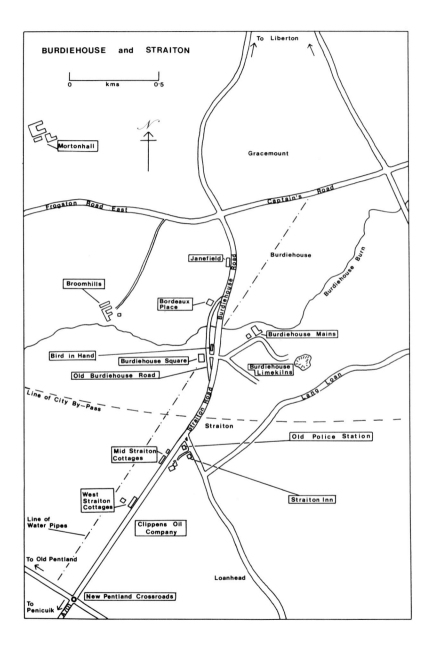

BURDIEHOUSE and STRAITON

0   kms   0·5

N

Mortonhall

Gracemount

To Liberton

Captain's Road

Frogston Road East

Janefield

Burdiehouse

Burdiehouse Burn

Broomhills

Burdiehouse Road

Bordeaux
Place

Burdiehouse Mains

Bird in Hand

Burdiehouse Square

Old Burdiehouse Road

Burdiehouse
Limekilns

Lang Loan

Line of City By-Pass

Straiton Road

Straiton

Old Police Station

Mid Straiton
Cottages

West
Straiton
Cottages

Straiton Inn

Line of
Water Pipes

Clippens Oil
Company

To Old Pentland

Loanhead

To
Penicuik

New Pentland Crossroads

CHAPTER 1

Burdiehouse; Straiton; Old Pentland

Burdiehouse and Straiton lie within a few hundred yards of one another on the A701 road between Edinburgh and Penicuik. At the beginning of the twentieth century the ability of Burdiehouse and Straiton to remain as distinct communities was inextricably linked to the future prosperity of the shale oil and limestone workings. When the natural resources became exhausted, or uneconomic to mine, the district entered a long period of industrial decline from which it did not recover. In the 1960s, after the shale oil and limestone era had ceased to have any influence on the community, the old villages were dealt an almost lethal blow by the construction of the dual carriageway from Kaimes crossroads to New Pentland. This broad elegant sweep of tarmac completely dissected Burdiehouse and Straiton, leaving the remnants of each stranded on either side of the new A701. On completion of the City Bypass the separation will be even more definite with Burdiehouse lying to the north of it and Straiton lying to the south. Despite their somewhat truncated appearance, history records an interesting story, though perhaps not immediately obvious on the surface.

The neighbouring village of Old Pentland lies just outside the Edinburgh city boundary on the road between New Pentland cross-roads on the Penicuik Road and Lothianburn on the Biggar Road. By its position, therefore, Old Pentland cannot be claimed as a village of Edinburgh but its strong historical links on both sides of the city boundary justify its inclusion. The barony of Pentland can be traced from at least the twelfth century, through the Sinclairs of Roslin, to the great Covenanting period in the mid-seventeenth century, by which time Old Pentland was owned by the Gibsones of Durie in Fife.

Burdiehouse and its Environs

With so little of the old village of Burdiehouse remaining, it is necessary to look further afield to get some idea of how and when the village was first established. Although the contention is not without its critics, the most prevalent theory is that the name Burdiehouse is a corruption of

The former Broomhills Farmhouse, dating from 1817, built close to the sixteenth-century Broomhill House, long since demolished.
Courtesy of David Dick, O.B.E.

Bordeaux House, so called from some of the French ladies-in-waiting who settled there while in service to Mary Queen of Scots at Craigmillar Castle in 1561. Whilst there is no evidence of the extent of the community in the mid-sixteenth century, considerable information is available on the existence and ownership of the mansionhouses, some of which remain, whilst others exist only as street names in a changed locality.

One of the earliest and most comprehensive accounts of the district is by the Rev. Thomas Whyte in *Transactions of the Society of Antiquaries of Scotland,* 1792. It is difficult to be precise about the exact location of each hamlet in relation to modern street names, but some idea of the relative importance of each area is given by the Rev. Whyte's census of the parish population in 1786: Morton Hall 37; Morton 61; Bordeaux 128; South Kaims 22; North Kaims 42; Houden's Hall 26.

The earliest recorded owner of the lands of Mortonhall is Sir Henry St. Clair of Rosslyn in the fourteenth century, whose desendants were in occupation for several generations. After the St. Clair family, Mortonhall was owned for a short time by Alexander Ellis, and in 1635 the estate was acquired by John Trotter who became the first Baron of Mortonhall. It was, of course, the Trotters whose name became synonymous with ownership of Mortonhall over a period of more than three hundred and fifty years. When John Trotter acquired the estate in 1635, the principal building was a fortified keep, with a drawbridge and surrounding moat, but in 1765 Thomas, the 9th Baron, pulled down the old fort and built the present house, designed by John Baxter, and completed in 1769. It is a most handsome building designed in a rather austere Palladian style of three main storeys, attic and sunken basement. The centre is advanced and pedimented, containing three broad bays, flanked on each side by a single bay completing the alternate triangular and segmental pediments above the windows. Only marginal alterations have been made to its external appearance over the years: a low service wing to the east has been added; and in 1835 a Greek Doric porch was built over the north-facing consoled doorway. The original interior is also considered to be of outstanding quality, the square entrance hall leading to two cantilevered stone staircases side by side. The main stair is set in a square well with wooden balusters alternately straight and serpentine. The principal rooms display a wide variety of fine craftsmanship on the chimneypieces, dados and friezes, with leafy sprays and foliage in abundance.

At the present day, Mortonhall is entering a new phase of development in its long history. The house has been skilfully divided into separate apartments, retaining many of the original features, and the policies, although extensive and heavily wooded, are showing signs of commercial development along the boundary on West Frogston Road. Mortonhall Garden Centre was established by Mortonhall Park Ltd in 1975 and acquired by J. Trotter in 1983 on land immediately to the west of the main driveway to the house.

Broomhills Farm, lying to the south of Frogston Road East, is one of a dwindling number of farms within the Edinburgh city boundary. Although nothing now remains of Broomhill House, fairly modern maps show the site of it as being a few hundred yards south-west of the present farmhouse and steadings. It was described as a ruin in Whyte's report of 1792, having previously been a fortified keep surrounded by water, and reached by a drawbridge. The earliest recorded owners, from 1508, were the ancestors of Sir John Henderson of Fordel, who sold Broomhill in 1709 to Sir John Baird of Newbyth, who in turn sold it to the Trotters of Mortonhall in 1827. Broomhills was tenanted to various members of the Allan family for well over two hundred years. From 1818 to 1876 the tenant was John Allan whose father farmed Paradykes, and whose brother was George Allan, author and poet.

George Allan, born on 2nd February 1806, qualified as a Writer to the Signet in Edinburgh, but instead of pursuing a legal career he turned to the world of literature. In addition to being editor of the *Dumfries Journal* and later literary assistant with Chambers in Edinburgh, he made several contributions to Peter MacLeod's *Original National Melodies of Scotland* and wrote a *Life of Sir Walter Scott* before the more comprehensive work by Lockhart. He died on 15th August 1835 at Janefield near Leith before his thirtieth birthday.

There is an unexplained coincidence between the name Janefield, near Leith, where George Allan died, and the long narrow strip of land east of Broomhills Farm, bordering the A701 road, south of Kaimes crossroads. Maps as early as 1812 refer to part of this area as Five Houses, and Good in *Liberton in Ancient and Modern Times* uses the location of 'the hamlet of the Five Houses' to describe the extent of old seams of coarse parrot coal, so called from its tendency to burn with a bright chattering flame. Successive Ordnance Survey maps between 1855 and 1914 identify Five Houses as a small group of buildings to the south end of this narrow strip of land, but the 1931 Ordnance Survey map shows the same location as Janefield. Five Houses appears to have changed its name to Janefield prior to 1926 when Mr & Mrs Adamson Snr. moved into a small house on the east side of the A701. At that time Janefield was occupied by a family who ran the Janefield Dairy at Silvermills near Stockbridge as the retail outlet for their dairy herd at Burdiehouse. In 1930 Janefield (Five Houses) came up for sale and was bought by Mr & Mrs Adamson Snr., who continued the small farm tradition with cattle, pigs, goats, hens, ducks, and geese, and later a sizeable orchard of soft fruit managed by Mrs Adamson Jnr. Produce was sold at the door to neighbours, whilst customers further afield had the benefit of door-to-door deliveries from a high, covered, platform lorry, with spoked wheels and long running boards. Before the involvement of the Adamsons, part of the land, nearest to Kaimes crossroads, was sold for the erection of bungalows on what became Burdiehouse Road. On the death of Mrs Adamson Snr., in 1955, Janefield was acquired by her son Bill Adamson who spent much of his youth cultivating the ground and building up the business. He continued to combine these activities with a successful career in insurance until his death in 1980. Shortly thereafter, his widow, Mrs Adamson Jnr., sold the plot of land for housing development. The small group of houses, one of which is owned by Mrs Adamson, still retains the old name Janefield.

Bill Adamson of Janefield on his door-to-door delivery service in 1932.
Courtesy of Mrs Mabel Adamson.

The village of Burdiehouse lies a few hundred yards to the south of Janefield, its main street now bypassed by the higher level of the dual carriageway which sweeps past on the east side. Even before the transformation of Burdiehouse in the 1967 road improvement scheme it was a village which shared many of its services and facilities with Straiton, or further afield. Today only a handful of old buildings remain, although many others have been replaced by bungalows in a quiet modern setting.

The west side of the main street has a row of old terraced houses with the name Bourdeaux Place cut into the stonework of the corner house. Immediately to the north of this house is a curious niche of old masonry which contained one of the village wells until piped water was introduced about 1925. Maps prior to 1850 show a ruined building situated between the old terraced houses and Burdiehouse Burn, but no identification has yet been made of it. The garage to the south is the site of an old tenement building which was demolished many years ago, and Burdiehouse Square was built in the mid-1930s to house the residents of Oakbank Cottages on Lang Loan Road which had been declared unfit for further habitation.

On the east side of the main street many of the old cottages have disappeared along with the mill buildings, weir and sluice gates which took advantage of the natural water power from Burdiehouse Burn. The most dominant building remaining is the large two-storeyed, pitched-roof construction of the Bird in Hand, converted to licensed premises in recent years from its former use as a private house. To the south, in the triangular piece of ground formed by the main street, and the road to Burdiehouse Mains, was the village school and the schoolmaster's house. This school served the children for many years, with a headmaster and three teachers, until it was closed in the early 1960s and demolished a few years later. The school building was also used as a community hall with evening classes for sewing and woodwork, and the Sunday School on Sunday mornings.

The old road to Burdiehouse Mains is now dissected by the dual carriageway. Burdiehouse Mains farmhouse dates from about 1830, beside which is a most interesting farm courtyard of elaborate symmetry, with remnants of its former reliance on water power from the burn. This road also gives access to the old limestone kilns, and one or two detached properties formerly connected with the limestone industry.

Straiton and its Environs

The sister village of Straiton also straddles the A701 road, half a mile south of Burdiehouse. Like Burdiehouse, its relative importance was closely allied to the success of the shale and limestone industries. Its history, however, comfortably precedes either of these important industrial eras, and is reviewed in some detail by Good in *Liberton in Ancient and Modern Times*.

Straiton and Brownhills (Broomhills) were owned by a family of the name of Straiton under a charter of David I. The barony was of considerable value and included the village of Straiton, Straiton Mill (at Broomhills), Burdiehouse and Fantasy, the last mentioned of which is shown north-east of Straiton on Laurie's Map of 1766 and Knox's of 1812 but does not appear on the first Ordnance Survey Map of 1855. There is an interesting charter which also throws some light on the origin of the hamlet of Frogston which was at Frogston Brae (now West Frogston Road). The charter refers to confirmation of an indenture made at the burgh of Aberdeen on 5th February 1447 by Lady Christian of Straiton where she grants to Alexander Frog, his sons, and Marion his wife, to farm the lands of Straiton and Straiton Hall for a period of nineteen years with full power 'to big ane mill' within the said lands, and to work coals and stone to their best advantage, at a yearly

Bourdeaux Place (now Burdiehouse Road) named after the area where the French ladies-in-waiting stayed when Mary Queen of Scots resided at Craigmillar Castle.
Photograph by Phyllis Margaret Cant.

rent of twenty-six merks. There are also several references to Straiton in the sixteenth century. In 1534 David Straiton was burned at the stake for heresy at Greenside on the north side of Calton Hill, and in 1508 James Henderson of Fordel, King's Advocate, and later Lord Justice-Clerk, secured a charter of the lands of Straiton. James was killed in action in 1513, but was succeeded by his son who died at the Battle of Pinkie in 1547. The Hendersons appear to have been a family of mixed fortune: after the untimely deaths of James and his son George, relative calm returned for Sir John Henderson of Fordel, who found favour with James VI from whom he received a knighthood. But the family were again dogged by misfortune. A sister of Sir John was apprehended for being a witch and was imprisoned in the Tolbooth in Edinburgh in 1648 for almost five months awaiting her fate at the burning fire. The exact cause of her sudden death was not established. In the evening she was well but by the following morning she was dead with evidence of having taken poison. It is assumed that rather than face being publicly burned she took the advice of her friends, and ended her own life.

Straiton in the late nineteenth and early twentieth centuries had close links with Burdiehouse and Loanhead, but, in common with many other outlying villages, had very little affinity with Edinburgh. Many of the inhabitants lived in long rows of cottages built of stone and roofed with slate, on either side of the road to Penicuik. The larger houses tended to be concentrated in the centre of the village near the junction with the road leading to Loanhead. The early maps show a large part of the village to the east of the old A701 road, lying between the Straiton Inn and the steadings of Straiton Farm. On the west side of the A701 three separate ranges of cottages were named East Straiton Cottages, Mid Straiton Cottages and West Straiton Cottages. At West Straiton Cottages a long line of buildings, running westwards at right angles to the main road, was built by the Pentland Oil Works, and named Meadow Bank Cottages.

The village was not entirely self-sufficient in services. The school was located at Burdiehouse and there was a small Mission Station on the east side of the A701 about opposite Meadow Bank Cottages. For the most part, however, adult churchgoers walked to Liberton Parish Church, although the children had the advantage of the Sunday School at Burdiehouse. A few shops stocked everyday commodities, and a few luxuries, but the daily papers came out from Edinburgh on the bus. Mary Hodge ran a small confectioner's, whilst her father ran the Post Office next door, and Mrs Kelly sold oil, paraffin and kindling wood. In a small whitewashed and thatched cottage, quaint but rudimentary, Mary Myles, an Irish immigrant, brought up her family without the luxury of tap water and electricity. The licensed trade was adequately represented by the Straiton Inn, and conveniently situated opposite the police station where the occasional reveller restored his flagging spirits. The police station and police house was the northmost cottage occupied in the 1920s and '30s by the village policeman, Alexander Smith. In addition to the living accommodation there were two cells reached by a side door. The cells had no outside windows but were lit by a small skylight in the roof. The walls were bare and whitewashed, the only source of comfort being a coarse red and black blanket on a low wooden bunk on which the prisoner lay within sight of the small square peep hole in the metal-lined door. Immediately adjacent was the small office which provided almost equally scant accommodation for P.C. Smith. The only available equipment was a small sloping desk, a high stool, and a slate and pencil hanging on a nail in the hallway on which to record important telephone messages.

The Bird in Hand, one of the few remaining substantial properties in the old village of Burdiehouse.
Photograph by Phyllis Margaret Cant.

In view of the limited resources available, prisoners were seldom, if ever, detained overnight, but it was necessary for the duty officer to wait up until the Black Maria arrived in the early hours of the morning to transfer the accused to the Police Headquarters in the High Street of Edinburgh.

The apprehension of wrongdoers was of course only part of P.C. Smith's duties which were frequently associated with the general welfare of the community. One of his proudest moments was to lead the long procession of local people who assembled each year for Straiton Gala Day. All the local children and many of the adults joined in, to follow the Pipe Band of Dr Guthrie's Boys' School at Liberton as the procession made its way from Burdiehouse School to Kaimes crossroads, and then back for sports and games at Straiton Park.

The Limestone and Shale Industries

Limestone and shale were mined at Burdiehouse and Straiton for a very long time, yet there remains little tangible evidence, on the surface of the earth at least, of this long period of economic dependence on mining. The rusting machinery, the corrugated iron sheds, and the unsightly bings have long since disappeared, as well as many of the families whose menfolk spent a lifetime cutting the seams hundreds of feet below ground level. Geologically, limestone and shale occur for different reasons but economically they have frequently been mined by the same companies, and by the same workforce. The limestone industry is very much older than the shale industry, and endured for a much longer period.

The Lime Works of Burdiehouse are described in detail by the Rev. James Begg, minister at Liberton Parish Church, in the *New Statistical Account of Scotland,* 1845. According to Begg's analysis the importance of limestone was discovered at Burdiehouse about 1760, when it was worked by tirring (open-cast mining) until about 1800 when a satisfactory attempt was made to work it by means of a mine. Even then, working methods were rudimentary and fraught with difficulties. At Burdiehouse these problems related primarily to the constant threat of water flooding the mines, and the angle (frequently more than 45°) at which the seams dipped in relation to the surface of the earth. The problem of water flooding the mine was tackled firstly by cutting a level to allow the water to run by gravity to the burn at Burdiehouse Mains, and then, when the mine was sunk deeper, by the introduction of a steam engine to pump the water to the surface. The limestone was almost thirty feet thick in places, but the angle of dip made extraction very much more difficult, particularly for the team of asses which was used to lift the limestone to the surface. In 1822 two gins, or lifting gear, with inclined planes, were erected which greatly increased the output of the mine, so that by 1825 about fifty men were able to produce almost a thousand bolls (a boll was a dry measure equivalent to approximately forty-eight gallons) of limestone every week during the summer months. In subsequent years that high production rate fell on account of exhaustion of the limestone at a depth within the pumping capacity of the steam engine. A new quarry was therefore opened to the west in 1829, with the stone being lifted by a gin and conveyed to the kilns by rail. Despite improved technology, the high production rates did not return, and by 1845 up to thirty men were needed to produce three hundred bolls per week.

Between 1850 and 1900 Burdiehouse Lime Works went through a period of comparative stability, operating from their main base south-

Straiton Inn, an old coaching inn, at the heart of the old village of
Straiton.
Photograph by Phyllis Margaret Cant.

east of Burdiehouse Mains. The 1855 Ordnance Survey map shows
clearly the position of the main shaft and kilns, served by numerous
pit-head buildings to the east, and a light railway affectionately known
as 'the Pug', running south-eastwards towards Straiton. The railway
was later realigned to the south-east of the kilns to serve a new shaft at
Mortonhall Pit, and had a connecting loop serving the Shale Pit
opposite Oakbank Cottages on Lang Road. By 1907, however,
Mortonhall Pit, Burdiehouse Quarry and the Shale Pit had all been
closed, and the railway had been shortened, so that it no longer served
the pit-head. Although no information is available on the trading
accounts of the Burdiehouse Lime Works for that period, there is a very
comprehensive map in the possession of the British Geological Survey
giving details of the workings up to the time they were abandoned on
2nd February 1912. A labyrinth of stoop and room workings is shown
in regular square formation extending from the kilns in the east, to
Straiton in the west. The Main Dook is shown running in a south-
easterly direction from the kilns, and at the pit-head there are several
cottages, sheds and stables. Various dates on old shafts show workings
before 1870 near Straiton, and more recent workings appear along the

line of Lang Road, starting in 1895 at the east side and working progressively westwards until 1912.

Limestone was in serious decline at Burdiehouse from the early twentieth century, despite there being ample geological evidence that other seams were capable of exploitation nearer to Straiton and the New Pentland crossroads. These seams were mined by the Clippens Lime Works until 1930 when they were taken over by the Shotts Iron Company who improved the works and installed electricity at a cost of £50,000. Output rose significantly to 50,000 tons per annum in response to increased demand, particularly for agricultural use. Unfortunately when Shotts Iron Company sold out their interest, the production of limestone ceased completely. Robertson Sutherland, writing in 1974, described the demise with more than a hint of local feeling, in *Loanhead: The Development of a Scottish Burgh:*

> Why the limeworks were discontinued is not clear. All that is known is that the working of lime followed the fate of its long-deceased partner oil-shale to the regret of many a man working there and returning home of an evening tired and very, very dusty.

Long after the dust had settled, at Burdiehouse and Straiton, the limestone industry was studied in detail by the Extra Mural Department of Edinburgh University under the guidance of B.C. Skinner, their findings being published in 1969 under the title *The Lime Industry of the Lothians*. Five kilns and quarries at Straiton were obliterated by the road improvements of 1967, but three brick-lined kilns at Burdiehouse survived reasonably intact. The University project examined and measured each of the three kilns: the east kiln is polygonal with three vents incorporated in sloping buttresses, the vents being ten feet wide, the base thirty feet by twenty feet, and the kiln diameter ten and a half feet; the middle kiln is semi-circular with a base twenty feet across, vents seven and a half feet wide and the kiln diameter ten and a half feet; and the west kiln is rectangular with a frontage of forty feet, a projection of thirty feet, vents twelve feet across, and the diameter of the kiln is ten and a half feet.

At the present day, the three kilns can be seen across the fields to the east of the dual carriageway as it sweeps past Burdiehouse village. Little else remains of the limestone industry which was at its peak at the end of the nineteenth century. Many local people were employed at the kilns making the limestone ready to be sold directly to builders in Edinburgh and elsewhere. The Burdiehouse men would take a dozen pigeons with them each day and travel into Edinburgh to seek new

The village policeman, P.C. Smith, who operated from the small police station at 9 and 10 East Straiton Cottages from around 1925 to 1935. Courtesy of Mr & Mrs Anderson.

markets wherever building work was in progress, particularly in the tenement areas of Marchmont, Bruntsfield and Morningside. When an order was received a homing pigeon was released with a note giving particulars of the quantity of limestone required and the address at which it was to be delivered by horse and cart later in the day.

In the latter half of the nineteenth century an extensive shale oil industry had been established in central Scotland in the wake of Paraffin Young's successful experiments making illuminating oils and lubricating oils.

Lothian's shale oil industry received a great boost in 1880 when the Clippens Oil Company Ltd transferred its main operations from Paisley to the new Pentland Works at Straiton. Prior to that, the main operator was the Straiton Oil Company, whose earlier work had revealed substantial deposits of high-yield shale near Loanhead. The main fields lay one mile north-west of Loanhead, and extended for a distance of almost two miles with an average breadth of six hundred yards. It was here that the famous Pentland or Dunnet shale was mined at depths of around 1200 feet, in strata almost six feet thick. Its yield was considerable: twenty-five gallons of crude oil to a ton of shale and from twenty to twenty-three pounds of sulphate of ammonia. Although Dunnet was the highest by tonnage, there were other shales which were extensively mined in the same area. Broxburn shale was cheaper to mine as its strong natural roof required fewer props, but it was less productive in oil. On the other hand, Fells shale was extremely high in yield but lay in very thin strata which made it costly to extract. These conflicting geological and economic problems were compounded by the extreme angle at which some of the seams dipped, in relation to the surface of the ground. A vertical dip located at Broomhills Farm many years ago was not exploited, partly on account of the difficulty of extraction, and partly on account of the quality of the deposits. Robertson Sutherland in his book on Loanhead includes an interesting account of how the shale was brought to the surface and subjected to various processes:

> The shale was mined to a vertical depth of 1175 feet from the surface. It was blasted by explosive, and sieved through a one-inch riddle, only the larger fragments being retained and passed through a toothed breaker. Thereafter the granulated material was conveyed in iron tubs of 10-25 cwt. on rails to the retorts. There at a temperature of 600°-800° F., it was distilled, producing ammonia water, from which sulphate of ammonia was obtained, and crude oil, which, after further treatment in the refineries, yielded naphtha, lubricating oil and solid paraffin, from which, in turn, paraffin and wax were secured.

The Clippens Oil Company Ltd reached high levels of production in its early years at Straiton, and was greatly encouraged in 1882 when a new process of distillation was invented at Straiton. A patent was taken out by the inventors, William Young of Clippens (not related to James Young—of paraffin fame) and George Thomas Beilby (later Sir George) of Oakbank Works, the central feature of the process being 'the adoption of a two-stage process of distillation, the shale passing continuously through a vertical retort, the upper portion of which was heated to a suitable temperature for the production of oil, while in the lower part, a higher temperature was maintained and, in an atmosphere of steam, a larger percentage of the nitrogen of the shale was converted into ammonia'. There is little doubt that the Young and Beilby Retort of 1882 put the Clippens Company in the forefront of the Scottish shale-oil industry, their gross profit reaching £40,000 in 1886. Success was short-lived, with failure coming from an unexpected source. To be ruined by the presence of natural water seeping into workings is a constant threat to any mining operation, but to be put out of business by piped drinking water on its apparently innocuous way to Edinburgh was a problem not envisaged by the Clippens directors when they first came to Straiton.

The Burdiehouse kilns to the east of the A701, once the centre of a thriving limestone industry which employed many local people.

Several decades earlier, Edinburgh, in its quest to improve the city's water supply from Comiston and Swanston, laid a new pipe from the Crawley Springs at Glencorse. Unfortunately the path of the Crawley pipe in 1822 and later, the Moorfoot pipe in 1879 ran through the Clippens shale field at Straiton. In 1847 Parliament had passed the Water Works Clauses Act to regulate potential disputes between Water Trustees and the owners of mineral rights in land through which the pipes passed. The 1847 Act applied to the Straiton problem but appeared to give the Water Trustees a distinct advantage in the event of the Trustees taking no action at all. The law was fairly simply stated: it said that when mineral workings approached within forty yards of water pipes, notice had to be sent to the Water Trustees. Thereafter the Water Trustees had an option: *either* they could elect within thirty days to stop the mineral workings and pay compensation; *or* they could allow the workings to go ahead, but take the risk themselves of the pipes being broken or damaged. What incurred the wrath of the Clippens directors was that if the Trustees elected to do nothing under the Act, and the pipes were fractured as a result of being undermined, the escaping water would flood the mines, drown the workforce, and put the business into liquidation. Perhaps predictably, the Trustees elected to do nothing. The Clippens directors were sorely tempted to dig on and undermine the pipes, but they were held in check by the threat of placing their own workforce in danger. In 1898, following a lengthy report by the Clippens directors to their shareholders and bondholders, the case came before the Court of Session, which ruled in favour of the Water Trustees. On appeal to the House of Lords the decision of the Court of Session was upheld, although the Clippens Company was given compensation of £27,000. The compensation may have been welcome, but the decision was the deathknell for Clippens. By 1909 the liquidators had produced a thirteen-page report extolling the virtues of Clippens' Pentland and Straiton Oilworks in a futile attempt to sell the works as a going concern:

> The properties form together a very valuable shale field already provided with railway facilities and eminently suited for the establishment of a new Scottish Oil Company.

The liquidators may as well have added the facetious comment 'fitted with running water in every room'.

Robertson Sutherland reviewed the social consequences to Straiton of losing this obvious source of employment, but, rather poignantly, observed that one hundred years' production of *all* the Scottish shale-oil industry would have satisfied Britain's demand for oil for less than sixty days at 1974 levels of consumption.

Old Pentland

According to the 1863 edition of *The Scottish Nation*, William de Sancto Claro was one of the many Anglo-Norman barons who settled in Scotland in the reign of David I (1124-1153). William obtained from the monarch a grant of the barony of Roslin, to which his descendants added Cousland, Pentland and Catticune. Other sources, however, maintain that the barony of Pentland was in the hands of the Sinclair (Sancto Claro) family as early as the eleventh century during the reign of Malcolm III (1057-1092). The Sinclairs held the barony of Pentland until 1633 when it was purchased by the ancient Scottish family of Gibsone, whose name became synonymous with that of Pentland.

The Gibsones were an established and influential family in Scotland for several generations prior to 1633. In the fifteenth century the immediate ancestor of the family was Thomas Gibsone of Durie in Fife (1488-1513) who received a grant of armorial bearings from the Pope.

In Old Pentland Graveyard, the family tomb of the Gibsones of Pentland, an imposing mausoleum by the architect Thomas Hamilton, c. 1845.

The coat of arms depicts three keys, surmounted by the crest of a pelican plucking her breast and feeding her young, with two angels as supporters, below which is the motto PANDITE COELESTES PORTAE (OPEN HEAVENLY GATES). Thomas Gibsone had two sons. The younger one, William, entered the church and became vicar of Garvock, Kincardineshire, being described rather quaintly in April 1526 as 'that venerable and circumspect man, Master William Gibsone, Dean of Restalrig'. The elder son, and heir to the estate, was George Gibsone of Goldingstones in Fife who became one of the two principal clerks of session in the College of Justice. High legal office became one of the hallmarks of other members of the Gibsone family. A few years after Alexander Gibsone graduated at Edinburgh University in 1588, he was appointed as the third clerk of session, and in 1621 he was elevated to the bench as Lord Durie, taking his title from the estate of Durie in the East Neuk of Fife which he purchased in 1614. He was made a Baronet of Nova Scotia in 1628 and in 1642 became Lord President of the Court of Session. J.C.H. Gibsone in his erudite *Family History of the Gibsones* in 1984 traces all the leading members of the Gibsone family, and recounts in fascinating detail the alleged kidnapping of the Lord President.

Of the various accounts perhaps the best known is that narrated in the ballad 'Christie's Will' by Sir Walter Scott in *Minstrelsy of the Scottish Border,* and also in Wilson's *Tales of the Borders.* According to this version, William Armstrong, known as Christie's Will, was held in custody at Jedburgh awaiting trial, charged with having stolen a cow. The trial stood to attract more than the usual attention for such offences, as the Crown had shown a determination to make an example of Will who was the last member of a notorious family of Border rievers. With the threat of the death penalty ever present, Will's wife, Margaret, sought assistance from a local landowner, the Earl of Traquair, hoping that his intervention would avert the sentence of the court. Traquair's apparent magnanimity masked malevolent intent. Will would escape with his life but in return had to agree to abduct Lord Gibsone of Durie, Lord President of the Court of Session, before he was able to give his anticipated casting opinion against Traquair in a land dispute pending in court. Traquair's evil intent is captured in a single verse from the *Minstrelsy:*

> But if auld Durie to heaven were flown,
> Or if auld Durie to hell were gane,
> Or if he could be but ten days stown,
> My bonny braid lands would still be my ain.

Will and a band of ruffians followed Lord Durie from his house in Assembly Close off the Canongate, and on a lonely part of the road to Leith they fell upon him, muffled him in a large cloak and threw a hood over his eyes. He was taken back through the city, and towards evening of the next day arrived at Graeme's Tower on Dryfe's Water near Moffat, where he was to be confined. Meantime his disappearance in Edinburgh had caused a great commotion, it being assumed that he had been drowned by the incoming tide on the sands near Leith. After a lengthy search he was presumed dead: his family went into mourning and a new President was appointed. When the case was called again, the new President gave judgement for Traquair, thereby giving him the disputed barony of Coberston. Eventually Lord Durie was released, a broken and confused man, after three months in solitary confinement. He made his way back to Edinburgh, went immediately to his town house and peered in through the window where he saw his wife and family sitting round the fire. With no thought for his dishevelled appearance he burst into the room, whereupon his family began to scream and shout, thinking that he had returned from the dead. Wilson narrates that 'the confusion, however, soon ceased, for Durie began to speak softly to them, and taking his dear lady in his arms pressed her to his bosom in a way that satisfied her he was no ghost...'

Lord Durie died in less dramatic circumstances at Durie on 10th June 1644 and was buried at Scoonie in Fife. He was followed by his son, also Alexander, who became a Senator of the College of Justice in 1646. The family lived continuously at Durie from 1614 to 1759, and although Pentland was bought as early as 1633, no mansion house was ever built on the estate.

In 1794 John Gibsone married Henrietta, daughter of James Watson of Saughton, and left one daughter Helen who succeeded to the estate of Pentland. She married Colonel David Anderson of the Royal Marine Artillery, but retained the Gibsone family name and armorial bearings. Helen Gibsone died in 1843 and is buried in the family tomb at Old Pentland churchyard. The only son of the marriage, John, also took the Gibsone name and had a long distinguished military career, retiring as General Gibsone. He also had aspirations to build a family seat on the Pentland estate but these plans were never implemented, and, instead, he lived in the Dower House of the Forresters of Corstorphine, during which time it was known as Gibsone Lodge.

The early history of Old Pentland is closely associated with that long struggle for religious freedom waged by the Covenanters, whose determination to oppose Charles I's 'corruptions of the public government of the Kirk' was embodied in the National Covenant, signed at Greyfriars Kirk in February 1638. The churchyard at Old Pentland contains the bodies of many of the brave Covenanters who were heavily defeated by government troops under Sir Thomas Dalyell at the Battle of Rullion Green in 1666. One of the most ardent leaders was Richard Cameron who died fighting for the cause at the Battle of Aird's Moss in 1680. After the death of Richard Cameron the Covenanters around Old Pentland were led by the Rev. James Renwick who persisted in holding conventicles against the law, for which he was eventually sentenced to death and executed on 17th February 1688. He died at the age of twenty-six but is remembered on the Martyrs' Monument in Greyfriars Churchyard 'first erected by James Currie, merchant, Pentland, and others, in 1706; renewed in 1771'. Not many years before his death the Rev. James Renwick presided at the marriage of James Currie to Helen Alexander, both ardent Covenanters. At great risk to her own safety Helen visited Renwick in prison before his execution and attended the body after his death. Her zeal and determination to indoctrinate the next generation was such that she became closely involved with the Children's Covenant, an organisation first established at Old Pentland in 1683. The first child to sign the covenant was ten-year old Beatrix Umpherston who later married the Rev. John McNeal, the Covenanting minister from Loanhead. Beatrix lived to be ninety years of age and was buried with her husband in Old Pentland churchyard.

At the present day few, if any, of the original buildings of Old Pentland remain but there are several interesting relics associated either with the Covenanters or the Gibsone family. By far the most important of these is Old Pentland churchyard, situated on the north side of the road, almost hidden from view by a line of old yew trees. Its long grass, broken headstones and indiscriminate graffiti seriously detract from the atmosphere of a quiet country graveyard. The entrance is flanked by two square pillars with cone-shaped capstones, but the left-hand gate is missing, and the right-hand gate is in a poor state of repair. On the outer wall near the left gate pillar there is a date stone 1728 or 1798, on the opposite side of which are the remains of a small enclosure probably used by the sexton. Although the enclosure is roofless and substantially reduced in height, there is evidence, on the long wall facing into the graveyard, of a broken recess which may have contained a memorial stone. In the churchyard the headstones are numerous and varied, spanning more than three centuries. One of the oldest is to Robert Umpherston, tenant in Pentland, who died on 2nd March 1624, close to which is a flat stone to the Rev. John Thorburn, minister of Pentland, author of *Vindiciae Magistratus*, who died on 17th August 1788. The old family name of Umpherston also occurs on a heavy square chamfered stone to Sir Charles Umpherston Aitchison, Knight Commander of the Star of India, born 20th May 1832, died at Oxford 18th February 1896. The grandest tomb is furthest into the graveyard, hemmed in by huge yew trees which are now beginning to nudge the pedimented stonework. This is the family grave of the Gibsones of Pentland, an imposing mausoleum by the architect Thomas Hamilton around 1845. The barrel-vaulted interior, protected by heavy iron gates, contains the family coat of arms and the following inscription on a raised tablet on the north wall:

SACRED TO THE MEMORY OF
THE LATE SIR JOHN GIBSONE
OF PENTLAND BART
DIED MARCH 1781

MARRIED 1774 HENRIETTA ELDEST DAUGHTER OF JAMES
WATSON
OF SAUGHTON AND LADY HELEN HOPE, DIED 8.3.1803

ALSO FOR MRS HELEN GIBSONE OF PENTLAND ONLY
DAUGHTER
AND HEIRESS OF THE ABOVE SIR JOHN GIBSONE
DIED 1843

Unfortunately nothing remains of Old Pentland Church: indeed even its exact location is a matter of conjecture. In 1892 Christopher Aitchison records in *Lasswade Parish and Loanhead in the Olden Time* that the foundations of the church were uncovered a few years previous to 1892 when the graveyard was being improved. However, no further details are given other than that three sepulchral slabs dating from the thirteenth century were found.

A few hundred yards east of the old churchyard, beside the steadings of Pentland farm, the substantial building now in commercial occupation was once the village school. High up on the north wall the mason has chiselled the salient dates:

ERECTED AND ENDOWED	REBUILT
by	by
MRS HELEN GIBSONE	LASSWADE SCHOOL BOARD
1827	1881
(East wing)	(West wing)

The *New Statistical Account of Scotland* describes the earlier building as spacious and elegant, 'erected wholly at the expense of Mrs Gibsone of Pentland who also paid the headmaster's salary of £20 per annum, and provided the schoolhouse'. This building obviously became inadequate for the number of children attending, but for reasons which are not now obvious Lasswade School Board was reluctant to take over Pentland School. The School Board Minutes for 13th May 1873 show the roll as 86, whereas less than a year later this had grown to 153, possibly on account of the expansion of the Clippens Oil Company nearby. Pentland School was eventually taken over by Lasswade School Board on 7th December 1879, and in 1881 a decision was taken to build a new school for three hundred pupils. Mr Johnstone was retained as headmaster and was later succeeded by R.S. Mackinnon at £140 per annum with a schoolhouse provided on the opposite side of the road.

To the rear of the former Pentland School building a small cottage, owned by the present Gibsone family, contains two interesting stones the significance of which has not yet been established. One is approximately square in shape, containing the initials JA, SF and the date 1797 within a raised band, roughly in the shape of an inverted horseshoe, outside which, on three sides only, are the words IN DEO EST SPES MEA (IN GOD IS MY HOPE). The other stone is a fireplace lintel bearing unknown insignia in the centre, flanked by the initials TS—AA on the left, and on the right, the date in an unusual mixture of Roman letters and figures MD CC 3. Also at the cottage is a memorial tablet removed for safety from Pentland School when it closed in 1978:

SACRED
TO THE MEMORY OF
MRS HELEN GIBSONE
OF
PENTLAND
ONLY DAUGHTER AND HEIRESS
OF
SIR JOHN GIBSONE BARONET
OF
PENTLAND
FOUNDRESS OF THIS SCHOOL
WHO DIED
24TH OCTOBER 1843
IN HER 69TH YEAR

More than three hundred and fifty years after the Gibsones came to Pentland, the family retain definite links with the old estate and hold in high regard such small pieces of evidence as still remain of the family history and its links with the Barony of Pentland.

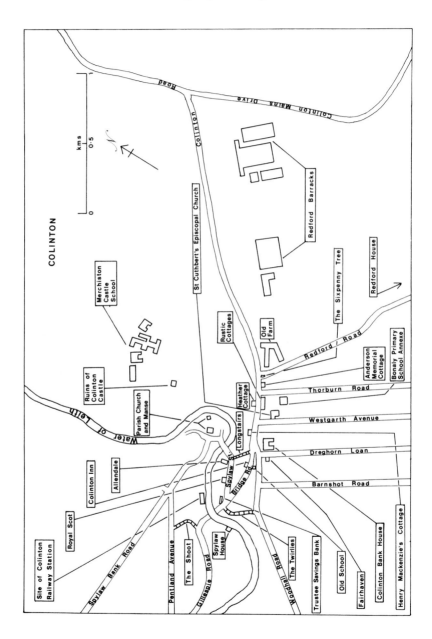

COLINTON

kms
0   0·5

Colinton Mains Drive

Colinton Road

Redford Barracks

Merchiston Castle School

St Cuthbert's Episcopal Church

The Sixpenny Tree

Redford House

Ruins of Colinton Castle

Rustic Cottages

Old Farm

Redford Road

Anderson Memorial Cottage

Bonaly Primary School Annexe

Water of Leith

Parish Church and Manse

Heather Cottage

Thorburn Road

Longstairs

Westgarth Avenue

Colinton Inn

Allendale

Spylaw Bridge Rd

Dreghorn Loan

Barnshot Road

Royal Scot

Henry Mackenzie's Cottage

Colinton Bank House

Site of Colinton Railway Station

Spylaw Bank Road

Pentland Avenue

The Shoot

Gillespie Road

Spylaw House

Woodhall Road

The Twirlies

Trustee Savings Bank

Old School

Fairhaven

CHAPTER 2

Colinton

Colinton grew up around the ancient church of Halis (Hailes) which is believed to have existed as early as the eleventh century. The village was originally settled around the Water of Leith where the natural water course was used to power the mill machinery. Like many similar rural communities nearby, its lifestyle was hardly affected by Edinburgh up to the middle of the nineteenth century. However, with the advent of public transport services by rail and by road, considerable expansion took place at the turn of the century around Woodhall Road and Spylaw Bank Road. Widespread bungalow development occurred prior to the Second World War, and in the last few decades the style of housing has become even more varied. Despite this rapid growth in the population, the old village has remained the unchallenged focal point of the community, albeit at some cost.

Colinton is an area with an unusually high number of ancient houses and castles whose earlier inhabitants, as owners of heritable property in the parish, were responsible for the maintenance of the church, the manse and the school. Whilst the era of the heritors, as they were called, has long since passed, their manor houses remain as tangible links with an earlier history.

Colinton Parish Church

Colinton Parish Church is situated near the lowest point of the village, within a hundred yards of the old ford, which was replaced, probably in the eighteenth century, by the present single-arched stone bridge. Although the picturesque square tower, rising above the old graveyard, is of relatively modern design, Colinton can trace the history of its church back to the eleventh century.

A brief, but useful, history of the early foundation of the church was compiled by the Rev. William Lockhart D.D., minister of the parish from 1861 to 1902, and inscribed in 1895 on a wooden board which hangs inside the entrance porch:

St Cuthbert's Church & Parish
Of Halis, now Colinton
were founded by
Prince Ethelred
Third son of
Malcolm III and Queen Margaret
and brother of
Edgar Alexander I and David I
King of Scotland
About the Year
1095

The ancient church which probably took the place of an older Pictish, British or Saxon foundation and which was dedicated on the 27th September 1248 disappeared about the year 1560 or was probably destroyed during the Earl of Hertford's invasion in 1544-45 in the reign of Henry VIII. This church is supposed to have stood near where Hales House now is. Another church was placed here in the year 1636
In the reign of Charles I
William Lockhart D.D. 1895

However, even this does not explain the various dates which appear on the outside walls of the church: on the angle of the entrance porch a sundial is inscribed SIR JAMES FOULLES 1630; on the west gable, a rectangular stone bears the inscription REBUILT 1771; at the north doorway the lintel stone carries the date 1907; and above the main entrance a bold inscription is framed between the lintel and the first string course:

SAINT CUTHBERT'S
PARISH CHURCH OF COLINTON
REBUILT TO THE GLORY AND DEDICATED
TO THE WORSHIP OF GOD
MCM VIII

According to the Edinburgh volume of *The Buildings of Scotland*, the church to which Dr Lockhart refers was replaced in 1771 by Robert Weir, mason, and William Watters, wright, to their own design, with further improvements done in 1837 by the architect David Bryce. The most recent major alteration was done in 1908 by Sydney Mitchell who rearranged the gables and reused Bryce's square tower over a new entrance porch. The oldest date, 1630, on the sundial remains a mystery as it pre-dates even the church mentioned by Dr Lockhart. The Foulles family of Colinton Castle, who spelt their name in a variety of ways, had a very long association as landowners in Colinton,

Colinton Parish Church, reconstructed in 1908 by Sydney Mitchell who rearranged the gables and re-used the square tower from the old church on the same site.

and the sundial could well have formed part of a much older building and been incorporated or reincorporated in the church by Sydney Mitchell in 1908. Although the dial has become weathered, it is possible to make out most of the detail. The Royal Commission on the Ancient Monuments of Scotland Report in 1929 described it as 'a tabular dial on which the gnomen springs from an incised sun: below the dial is a panel with a shield charged with three laurel leaves for Foulis and flanked by the date 1630; the top of the dial is inscribed SIR JAMES FOULLES'.

The interior of the church, redesigned in 1908, is a pleasing combination of pink sandstone pillars, dark woodwork and pastel-coloured plaster. The nave, entered under the organ and choir gallery at the west end, closes with a finely proportioned apse at the east end, flanked on either side by galleries. The pulpit is placed on the left, above which is an oak cross-beam inscribed O WORSHIP THE LORD IN THE BEAUTY OF HOLINESS. Natural light to the apse is admitted through nine windows designed and executed by James Ballantyne depicting the Fruits of the Spirit—Love, Joy, Peace, Patience, Kindness, Goodness, Fidelity, Gentleness and Self Control. The memorial panelling on either side of the apse gives access, on the left, to a small chapel originally intended for private prayer but now used for a Sunday prayer group and occasionally for weddings and baptisms. Much of the woodcarving in this small chapel was the work of the Misses Lily and Jean McEwan, lifelong members of the congregation. A small but interesting feature, the praise board stand, is the last piece of ornamental ironwork produced in Colinton Smithy before it closed in August 1960.

The 1908 organ, built by Norman and Beard, was rebuilt by Rushworth and Dreaper in 1928 and again in 1976 by Ronald Smith. It is placed centrally in the choir gallery below the window 'Christ blessing the children' in memory of Dr William Lockhart who succeeded Dr Lewis Balfour in 1861. The south aisle contains the oldest surviving stone from the graveyard:

> HEIR LYIS ANE
> HONORABIL VO
> MAN A HIRIOT
> SPOVS TO I FOVLIS
> OF COLLING TOVN
> VAS QVHA DIED
> AVGVST 1593

Some of the stones, of equal interest, though not of equal antiquity, have suffered badly from the elements in the old graveyard which surrounds the church on all four sides. A comprehensive review of the most interesting tombs was made by A. Reid and published in 1905 in the *Proceedings of the Society of Antiquaries of Scotland*. More than eighty years later some of the inscriptions, deciphered with difficulty by Reid, have disappeared altogether, whereas others appear timeless.

Two seventeenth-century stones, near the south-west angle of the church, for Thomsone 1678 and Denholm 1696, have lost much of the detail recorded in 1906, and may have been moved slightly from the original place of burial. However, the ornate pediment, skull and crossbones, and cherubs for farmer Ferguson 1771 can still be detected against the east gable of the gatehouse. Within a few yards of it an even earlier stone, 1743, displays a cherub, wings, scroll and skull for farmer Brown.

At the east end of the church the famous sower and reaper stone has been given a better position against the basement stairway railings, so that each face can clearly be examined. Reid reported in 1906 that the stone was leaning against the south-east corner of the church and that only part of the reverse could be seen. The Pitcairns of Dreghorn

St. Cuthbert's Episcopal Church, Westgarth Avenue, designed by Rowand Anderson, and opened on 10th August 1889 by Bishop Dowden.

Castle, lying nine feet to the east, have fared less well, their mausoleum long since roofless and rapidly disappearing in the undergrowth. Dr Thomas Murray noted in 1863 in the first page of *Biographical Annals of the Parish of Colinton* that the Pitcairn tomb had been covered with rubbish for as long as anyone could remember, and that the inscription was barely legible:

> Here lies Mr David Pitcairn of Dreghorn who departed this life 27th January 1709, and of his age the 60 year; leaving behind him Mary Anderson, his wife, with five sons and seven daughters by her.

In 1906 the tomb was described by Reid as roofless but in good repair, displaying three sculptured panels in the south gable, restored in 1864 by Dr Thomas Murray. At the present day only two panels are visible, the third one possibly hidden by made up ground. The plaque commemorating the restoration by Dr Murray is itself in need of restoration.

On the north side of the church a line of imposing tombs forms the boundary between the old graveyard and a later extension. The first is a pedimented mausoleum to one of Colinton's most famous residents, James Gillespie of Spylaw, who died on 8th April 1797. To the east is the family burial place of Dr Lewis Balfour, minister of the parish from 1823 to 1860, and the maternal grandfather of Robert Louis Stevenson. The most recent family stone is in memory of Lt. Cdr. David Ian Balfour R.N., killed in action aboard H.M.S. *Sheffield* in the Falklands in 1982. Three other tombs complete that side of the graveyard: an ornate stone enclosure for the Trotters of Colinton; a pedimented facade with a barely legible inscription; and the distinctive criss-cross ironwork protecting the Inglis of Redhall and Auchendinny.

Humour has hardly touched Colinton graveyard: the epitaph, believed to have been on a Colinton stone, for which the author David Shankie searched in vain, still eludes the curious:

> Here lyes the banes o' Cuthbert Denholm
> If ye saw him noo ye wouldna ken him!

The manse lies at a lower level from the old graveyard on the banks of the Water of Leith. It was built in 1783 by Robert Weir but has been altered on numerous occasions, notably in the post Robert Louis Stevenson period when the entrance doorway was moved to the south wall from its previous position facing the church. Access to the extensive garden is by a small private road past the session room and the old stables which have now been converted for use as a crèche. The Yew Tree Room, below the session room, takes its name from the yew tree which still flourishes and which featured in many of Stevenson's childhood encounters.

Colinton manse is inextricably linked with Stevenson through his maternal grandfather, the Rev. Lewis Balfour. Literary references to the manse abound, and are given further impetus in an interesting article by A.R. Davies which appeared in *Chambers Journal* for 1910-11. Mr Davies conveys some of the atmosphere of the manse as seen through the eyes of Margaret McKerrow of Ayrshire who came in 1843 to work as a servant at the manse. She was to be under no misapprehension about her conditions of employment, set out in a long letter dated 23rd October 1843 by the minister's wife: 'Mr Dalgleish mentions that you think the wages small ... I cannot promise you more than the three pounds for this half year. However if you study to please me, be sober-minded, honest, obliging and willing to do all you can to serve myself and Mr Balfour, as well as be ready to do anything in your power for the young folk, I will give you five shillings above the three pounds'. Margaret set out from Auchinleck on 14th November 1843 and travelled first by rail to Glasgow in a roofless open-sided truck and then by canal to Edinburgh in the very latest form of transport, the 'flying' boat drawn by trotting horses. When Margaret arrived at the manse she found Mrs Balfour to be kindly yet firm, but within a

The Craiglockhart to Colinton bus at Redford Barracks in September 1920.
Courtesy of D.L.G. Hunter. Photographed by the late E.O. Catford.

very few months Mrs Balfour took ill and died suddenly, leaving the running of the house to one of the daughters, Miss Jane Balfour. Around 1905 Mr Davies visited Miss Jane Balfour of Colinton and recorded many of her recollections of the manse, and her days with Margaret McKerrow. Towards the end of her life Miss Jane Balfour wrote to Margaret: 'Maggie your bridesmaid married Thomas Stevenson a civil engineer on 28th August 1848 and her only child Robert Louis Stevenson was born on 13th November 1850 and was always the delight of my heart and pride of my life'. Stevenson's appreciation can be described only in his own words:'The children of the family came to her [Miss Balfour] to be nursed, to be educated, to be mothered from the infanticidal climate of India. There must have been a half score of us children about the manse; and all were born a second time from Aunt Jane's tenderness . . .'

She died at Colinton on 15th May 1907.

St Cuthbert's Episcopal Church

Unlike the old parish church in the village, whose exact origins are lost in the mists of time, the foundation of St. Cuthbert's Episcopal Church in Westgarth Avenue is clearly documented. It was opened on 10th August 1889 following six years' campaigning and fund-raising by the Episcopalian population of Colinton and its surrounding districts. Most of the salient dates in its early history are recorded in a short account of the church compiled by C.F. Ochterlony, F.S.A. Scot.

In the summer of 1883 Sir David F. Ochterlony, Bart., responded to a suggestion made by the people of Colinton and Juniper Green to establish a local Episcopal mission. The first meeting took place on 7th October 1883 in the Liberal Reading Room in Bridge Road, the site of which was later occupied by Harwells of Colinton and then by John Menzies. It was here that monthly services were taken by the Rev. W.G. Bulloch of Dalmahoy and Balerno, until July 1885 when Colonel Trotter of Colinton House was successful in securing from Robert Andrew Macfie of Dreghorn a lease of the Iron Hall in Dreghorn Loan at an annual rent of £25. But the emerging congregation was intent on something more substantial than Mr Macfie's Iron Hall. Early in 1887 Mr Anderson (later Sir Rowand Anderson) announced to a meeting of those interested in erecting an Episcopal Church in Colinton that he had received an offer of a feu from Mr Macfie for a suitable piece of ground on which to build the church. A nominal feu duty of a peppercorn and a substantial grant from the Walker Trust ensured that work commenced in October 1888 and was completed in May 1889. The church was formally opened by Bishop Dowden on 10th August 1889 but was not consecrated until 20th July 1893, by which time the congregation, with financial assistance from Rowand Anderson and Sir Alexander Oliver Riddell, had cleared the building debt completely. The first incumbent was the Rev. Xavier Peel Massy, appointed at a meeting of the Vestry on 20th July 1893.

Within a very short time of consecration St Cuthbert's was faced with large-scale alterations funded, in part, by Sir Alexander Oliver. Riddell of Craiglockhart. In 1893 Rowand Anderson completed the tower with a lead-covered belfry instead of the intended spire, and the following year the new south transept was formed, containing the Lady Chapel and the organ chamber. The opportunity was also taken to move the tracery from the original east window to the south wall of the new transept. When the alterations were completed in 1898 the interior was handsomely decorated by Powell of Lincoln, to designs drawn by Rowand Anderson. The church hall was added to the south in 1922, but it was not until 1934 that the church took on its present-day appearance. Rowand Anderson's original four-bay nave was

The award-winning restaurant, Champany Inn Town, in Bridge Road.

expertly lengthened by the addition of three bays to the west, no external trace of this being obvious in the exactly matched stonework. The roof structure and the Ailsa Craig granite floor were also repeated to create a unified interior.

Today the church is surrounded by attractive landscaped policies situated between Colinton Road and the pre-War bungalows in Westgarth Avenue. The distinctive belfry contrasts well with the red sandstone detail of the nave and the chapel. Internally its appearance is at once joyful, yet dignified. The nave has a central aisle flanked by pews donated in memory of the church's many benefactors: Archibald MacGregor Trotter of Colinton House, born 7th September 1878, died 7th April 1925; Harry MacWatt, Advocate, Sheriff Substitute of Ross, Cromarty and Sutherland; Captain Gilbert Ralph Abercromby John Trotter, 56th Punjabi Rifles, born 28th January 1880, died 4th January 1913. The baptistery, extending into the south wall, contains a magnificent font with an ornate cone-shaped cover finely counter-balanced so that it can be raised easily to reveal the baptismal bowl. The stained-glass work has been installed at various times in the history of the church: on the north is a window to St Cuthbert; on the east, three windows depict the Resurrection; on the west a window commemorates the Riddells of Craiglockhart; and the south transept contains perhaps the finest work, dedicated to Our Lady, Saint Cuthbert and Saint George.

A concealed doorway off the chancel leads by increasingly precipitous ladders to the belfry which houses a peal of three bells bearing a quartered shield with the letters JB for Barwell, the bell founders of Birmingham. It is from this belfry that the congregation are still called to worship each Sunday by a small team of dedicated young bellringers under the supervision of an adult. The weight of the bells is such that great skill is needed to grasp the sally, or protected rope, at just the right moment before the upswing of the bell again tightens against the rope. The room was, however, equipped with its own measure of technology: leather pads could be fitted to muffle the tone when the bells were used at funerals; and heavy wooden silencers can still be fitted to the clappers during practices.

Colinton School

Colinton can trace the history of its schools back to the year 1651 when rather rudimentary accommodation was available in the parochial school beside the parish church. Unfortunately, the proximity of the church proved of doubtful value to the first schoolmaster, John Craw, who was deposed in 1655 for brewing and selling drink in the schoolhouse 'so near to ye Kirk and hard by the minister's yate'. This incident and others relating to the day-to-day running of the school are meticulously reproduced from Kirk Session Records by David Shankie in *Parish of Colinton*. The problems of frequent changes of schoolmaster, inadequate facilities and poor maintenance appear to have been largely solved by 1797 or given less credence in the *Statistical Account of Scotland* in which the Rev. Dr. John Walker commented that 'there has always been a respectable grammar-school kept in the parish . . . .well attended not only by the children of the middle and lower ranks but many gentlemen who have afterwards proved an honour to their country . . . ' The Rev. Walker came to Colinton in 1783 from the parish of Moffat with the reputation of being more of a botanist than a preacher, a reference no doubt to his intense interest in natural history. Several years earlier he had been asked by the Commission for Annexed Estates to visit the Hebrides and to report on their economic potential, his findings being contained in his Report on the Hebrides, 1764 and 1771.

The Hut, G.L. Miller's fruit store in Bridge Road, the site of which was later occupied by Harwells of Colinton and now by John Menzies, booksellers and newsagents.

By 1811 the Kirk Session Records show that the old building was too ruinous to be repaired, and a decision was taken to build a new school which was completed in 1815. This is the oldest school building still extant in Colinton, having been used in recent years as Colinton Public Library. In 1843 Robert Hunter was employed at a salary of £34 plus £40 in fees, to teach one hundred pupils English, writing, geometry, arithmetic and geography—in addition to his other duties as session clerk, clerk to the heritors, postmaster, and collector of parochial assessments. Even assuming that he had assistance from other class teachers, there must have been occasions when he wished that the blunt but salutary motto, believed to have been above the old school building, had been transferred to the new school: AUT DISCE, AUT DOCE, AUT ABI—either learn, teach, or go away.

Following the Education (Scotland) Act of 1872, Colinton, in common with the rest of the country, entered a new phase in the history of its schooling. Colinton School Board held its first meeting in the Parish Schoolroom on 14th April 1873, the members consisting of one solicitor, three ministers of religion, and three persons drawn from the local community. One of their first reports, in December 1873, provides useful information on the state of education in Colinton at the time. There were two schools under the control of the Board: the public school already referred to, built in 1815; and the female and infants' school built by the heritors in 1870 on the south-west corner of Dreghorn Loan and Woodhall Road. Out of seventy-five families in the Colinton area, there were one hundred and fifty children between the ages of five and fifteen: forty-five boys, fifty-four girls, and fifty-one infants under seven years of age. The Board Minutes between 1873 and 1896 highlight the problems of the day, and speculate on the most effective solutions: in 1874 a report dismisses the idea of closing Juniper Green School and amalgamating it with Colinton; in 1877, advice, not to be taken lightly, to William Cairns, snuffmiller, to ensure that his daughter Elizabeth attends school regularly in future; in 1878, Miss Russell the infant school mistress complains about oaths and obscene talk by a great number of men who gather to play quoits every evening at the back of her house. In the classroom the issues were no less irksome, with the schoolmaster complaining that the attendance was very low, that several children had started work before their thirteenth birthday, and that despite his efforts the school inspector's report concluded that 'the children have somewhat forgotten both how to speak out and how to be silent'.

By far the greatest issue of the day, however, was a new school building intended to replace the cramped and unsatisfactory accommodation both at the public school and the infant school. After many abortive discussions, the Board decided to ask its architect, Robert Wilson, to draw up plans, and to ascertain from Dr Rowand Anderson what offer he would make for the piece of school ground at the foot of Dreghorn Loan in which he had previously shown interest for building purposes. Dr Anderson, writing from Allermuir House on 28th March 1889, offered £650, which was later increased to £750 on condition that the Board could remove from the site the fittings, and the stones from which the school was constructed, but not the boundary walls. With disposal of the old school finalised, the Board then turned its attention to choosing a site for the new school from three options offered by the landowner Mr Macfie of Dreghorn Castle. The first location was in Dreghorn Loan to the south of Colinton Bank House, the second was a rectangular site to the east of the intended Episcopal Church, and the third was a rather awkward triangular piece of ground on the south-west corner of Redford Road and Colinton Road. The rectangular site was eventually chosen with provision made for conserving an old thatched cottage occupied by

Bridge Road through Colinton village, c 1910, showing Baillie the chemist on the left and the school shaded by trees, on the right.
Courtesy of W.B. Grubb.

James Laurie on the south side of Colinton Road. The new school, in Thorburn Road, was opened at 11 a.m. on 1st September 1891 by the Rev. William Lockhart, minister of the parish. The headmaster's log contains many diverse comments, associated with the general administration of the school rather than the day-to-day class activity: in 1899 school closed twice for outbreak of measles and scarlet fever; in 1907 an almost indecipherable report from the school inspector concedes that the pupils acquitted themselves well in written exercises; in 1909 the map of Africa is out of date and should be replaced; in 1914 'I ordered X to receive five strokes for striking Miss Bain in the face'; in 1926 the King's Own Scottish Borderers are moving into Redford Barracks and the Cameron Highlanders are moving out; in 1940 'thirty children absent today—Air Raid warning during the night requiring children to leave their beds and go to the shelters'.

In the years after the Second World War the number of families in Colinton with school-age children rose significantly, firstly from new houses in the streets of Redford and later at Bonaly and Campbell Park. This very wide catchment area resulted in Bonaly School being opened at Bonaly Grove in April 1976, after a new Colinton School had been built at Redford Place in 1967 and extended in 1969. At first it was thought that the Thorburn Road building would be surplus to requirements but it was reopened in August 1976 for the Infant Department of Bonaly School. Problems with organising such a wide geographical area are not new in Colinton: in 1874 the Colinton Infants' School Admissions Book lists pupils who walked from Bonaly, Currie Muirend, Mossy Mill, Fernieflat, Fordel, Oxgangs, Hailes Quarry, Hunters Tryst and Craiglockhart Farm.

Doon the Shoot and up the Twirlies

The traditional approach to Colinton village is by the long straight section of Colinton Road past Redford Barracks. After the construction of the Barracks by Colin Macandrew & Partners Ltd. in 1909, Colinton remained geographically isolated from the neighbouring suburbs of Craiglockhart, Firrhill and Colinton Mains. Despite that comparative isolation the old village expanded in various directions so that its exact boundaries are now difficult to define.

Approaching from the direction of Redford Barracks, the old estate walls on either side of the road have been breached in several places to give access to new development. On the south side, Colinton Old Farm with its enclosed courtyard and fruit trees was cleared to build flats for Viewpoint Housing Association in 1976, and on the north side, the boundary wall of old Colinton House screens a new telephone exchange, the doctor's surgery and several dwellings built for the masters at Merchiston Castle School. One landmark remains at the junction of Redford Road—the Sixpenny Tree which at one time shared the small island with a telephone box. Many explanations have been given for the origin of the name, some of them barely credible. The story which claims greatest authenticity, apparently by repetition alone, suggests that the tree got its name from being the approximate meeting place of members of the Guild of Papermakers. It is said that representatives from the mills on the Water of Leith met their brothers from the mills of the Esk Valley to debate the issues of the day and to pay their dues of sixpence each into a common receptacle. If the men walked all the way from the Esk Valley without a rest there may well be some truth in the comment that the cost of refreshments at Colinton accounted for a disproportionate amount of the membership fee!

To the west, the origin of the baronial-style villa on the corner of Thorburn Road is on firmer ground. A skewed stone at the ground-floor level bears the words: THE LADY ROWAND ANDERSON

Brian Rattray in his cottage workshop in Spylaw Street putting the
finishing touches to a viola da gamba.
Courtesy of *The Scotsman* Publications Ltd.

MEMORIAL COTTAGE; and above the front doorway are the
dates 1922 and the initials of Lady Rowand Anderson and her
husband Sir Rowand Anderson, the architect. Behind the Memorial
Cottage and lying between Thorburn Road and Redford Road are the
Colinton Cottage Homes run by the Aged Christian Friend Society of
Scotland, built at various times from 1891. Another famous architect
operating in Colinton was Sir Robert S. Lorimer who designed Rustic
Cottages, with the distinctive boat-shaped dormers, in 1900, on the
strip of land between Colinton School (now Bonaly School Annexe)
and the main road. Opposite Rustic Cottages is Heather Cottage,
originally a thatched single-storeyed dwelling built around 1810 as
part of the Colinton House estate but acquired by St. Cuthbert's
Episcopal Church in 1924 as the Verger's cottage. It has several
unusual features. The frontage to the street originally contained the
doorway within the pedimented stonework, but this was altered to a
window probably in 1924. Both the east and west gables project above
the line of the slates to accommodate the thatch, and there are
dripstones at the base of the chimneys.

The old village undoubtedly began where Colinton Road divides into Woodhall Road on the left, and Bridge Road on the right. It is an area which has seen many changes even since the days when the No 9 and No 10 electric tram services stopped on the level ground near the present traffic lights. On the north side the former office of John Hastie, the coal merchant, is reduced to a blocked-up door and a window, a fate which it is hoped will not befall the more historic cottage next door in which the Hasties resided. Behind an abundance of summer foliage, and lying much lower than the surrounding roadway, is Henry Mackenzie's Cottage. An iron plaque on a stone pillar is the only visible sign that Colinton recognises this important building:

IN THIS HOUSE LIVED
HENRY MACKENZIE
AUTHOR OF
THE MAN OF FEELING
BORN 25th AUGUST 1745
DIED 14th JANUARY 1831

The next building, beside the police box, has been occupied since 1984 as the award-winning Champany Inn Town whose proprietors Mr & Mrs Clive R. Davidson have their main restaurant at Linlithgow.

Another of Colinton's authors, Thomas Murray, who wrote *Biographical Annals of the Parish of Colinton,* lived for a time in Colinton Bank House, the imposing villa perched on the high ground between the bottom of Westgarth Avenue and Dreghorn Loan. The wall of this house was demolished and set back several yards in 1960 to improve the flow of traffic into Woodhall Road. Five years earlier when a similar operation was carried out on the lower wall in Bridge Road it was considered safe to reposition the pedestrian steps leading to Dreghorn Loan. By 1982, however, the steps were removed on account of the danger to pedestrians crossing Bridge Road. A commemorative seat was placed at the head of the old steps by the Colinton Amenity Association in December 1982 and a small 'tombstone' was erected to mark the right of way:

THIS STONE MARKS THE LINE
OF THE ANCIENT ROUTE FROM THE PENTLAND HILLS
TO THE FORD AND OLD BRIDGE
OVER THE WATER OF LEITH

Although this short section of steps has been lost, the Long Stairs on the north side of Bridge Road, beside the Colinton Inn, still provide access

James Gillespie of Spylaw, snuff manufacturer, and his brother John who ran the retail business in the High Street of Edinburgh.
From Kay's *Original Portraits*.

directly to Colinton Parish Church. These stairs were constructed under the direction of R.A. Macfie of Dreghorn Castle, using stones from the old Royal Infirmary.

Further down Bridge Road all development other than the original school building tended to be on the north side of the road, the south side backing directly onto the very long back gardens coming down from Woodhall Road. Although the authorities have consistently refused to allow a continuous pavement on the south side, sporadic building has eroded the rural scene. The shops with houses above, a few yards west of Colinton Inn, were built as Janefield by Mrs Johnstone, the postmistress of Colinton, and are in complete contrast to the next two houses built around 1810 in the form of pedimented lodges. At the head of Cuddies Lane an elegant restaurant in warm rustic brick has recently been built on the site of a small petrol station belonging to Waddell of Colinton whose ancestors owned the smiddy built at a lower level on the same site. At that time there were no steps, and horses were able to enter from either the top or the bottom of the lane. The long row of shops between Cuddies Lane and the Royal Bank of Scotland was not built until about 1908, the triangular piece of ground down to Spylaw Street being occupied by one cottage and its garden. Most Colinton residents will recall the detached two-storey building on the south side as the village post office, now a dental surgery. Only the senior citizens, however, will remember when the building was occupied by Harry Blyth the butcher, who kept live chickens in open boxes at the door to enable his customers to select their Christmas dinner.

Before the viaduct was built across the Water of Leith the main road through the village turned the sharp corner into Spylaw Street where the Trustee Savings Bank now is. The Bank premises were originally built for Mrs Andrew Neil as shops with her house above, in which Colinton's first telephone exchange was housed. The exchange was situated in the large front room of the house on the first floor. During the day it was operated by a full-time employee, but during the night, calls were attended to by Mrs Neil or her daughter Helen. Later, the lower part of the building nearest to the bridge was occupied by the Commercial Bank of Scotland, and the other side was occupied by Pickens Boot and Shoe Shop. But for the constant congestion caused by parked cars, Spylaw Street would still retain the appearance of a village main street. At the top end beside the Trustee Savings Bank the two-storey building with redbrick facings still has the dook holes above the doorway which carried the sign COUNTY ROADMAN, the Colinton man, William Robertson, occupying the upper floor and the Juniper Green man, Peter Stenhouse, occupying the lower floor. Both men were employed by Midlothian County Council until 1920 when Colinton came within the authority of Edinburgh Corporation. Most of the journeys were done on foot or by bicycle, to check the conditions of the roads, footpaths and drains. Many days would begin with a walk up to Torphin, Torduff and Bonaly, carrying a scythe and sickle, to cut the grass banks on either side of the road.

The adjacent stone-built house, No 24, formerly Darwal, was the village police station, the garden of which abuts onto the entrance to Spylaw House. The tiny lodge house on the lower side of the entrance gates is dwarfed by the three-storey Royal Scot, formerly the Railway Inn.

Between the Royal Scot and Allendale, the left-hand side of Spylaw Street has several commercial properties, including, until recently, Waddell's Garage run by David Waddell, the third generation of the

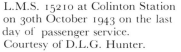

L.M.S. 15210 at Colinton Station
on 30th October 1943 on the last
day of passenger service.
Courtesy of D.L.G. Hunter.

family in the business. Only recently established is the first generation
of another successful business, run by Brian Rattray from his cottage
workshop at No 34. The craft of lute making or violin making has been
undertaken by Mr Rattray on a full-time basis for the last six years.
Before that, he worked on a part-time basis while also employed as an
architect. Most of his instruments are made to order for customers as
far afield as Shetland and Vienna, but he also has a thriving repair and
accessories service for Colinton and further afield. His compact
workshop to the rear of the cottage is equipped with a wide range of
hand tools designed to shave, plane and chisel to the most accurate
measurements. Although power machinery is occasionally used for
rough cutting on larger pieces of timber, the craft of violin making
demands that the physical skill of the craftsman identifies closely with
the piece of wood being worked upon without the intervention of
electrically driven machinery. To produce one violin requires between
one hundred and fifty and two hundred hours of work. Spruce or pine
grown on the snowline in Switzerland or Germany is used for the front,
and home-grown sycamore or maple is used for the back, sides and
neck. An interesting characteristic of many good-quality violins is the
flame effect produced naturally in the wood, running at right angles to

the direction of the grain. This is particularly attractive in home-grown timber, although the reason for its appearance in some wood but not others is not yet fully understood. The familiar ending of the violin neck is the carved scroll, although other motifs, such as a lion or other animal head, have been used. For Mr Rattray the important point is to make an instrument which is in keeping with its modern usage and yet authentic in relation to design and sound. One room of the cottage is also occupied by a loom on which Mrs Aili Rattray carries on the tradition of hand-weaving taught to her by her mother, on the other side of the North Sea, in Sweden.

The south side of Spylaw Street is almost completely taken up by a long row of pantiled cottages with timber porches over the pavement. These cottages, originally owned by James Gillespie the snuffmaker, may well have been built for his own employees, and in recent years have been attractively renovated under the direction of the Merchant Company Endowments Trust, which grants them free of rent and rates to deserving pensioners. At the foot of the hill, Laurel Bank looks out onto what was the heart of the village beside the ford, the old bridge, the church, the school, and the mill. Part of the cemetery ground was once occupied by the sixteenth-century Kirkland Mill which was demolished in 1916 following a serious fire. A few yards downstream was Hole Mill, demolished in 1870.

On the far side of the bridge the old road through the village winds its way up Spylaw Bank Road towards Lanark Road. This part of the village is now almost completely dominated by the grand houses built in the late nineteenth and early twentieth centuries. At No 52 the harled and red sandstone dwellings enclosing a central fountain are the Sir William Fraser Homes, established by a bequest of £25,000 from Sir William Fraser, K.C.B., LL.D. (1816-1898), a noted genealogist and Deputy Keeper of the Records of Scotland. The homes were opened on 2nd March 1901 and the architect was Arthur Balfour Paul, a son of Sir James Balfour Paul, Lord Lyon King of Arms. These homes for the elderly are now administered by the Merchant Company Endowments Trust with the Fraser Trustees retaining the right to nominate a proportion of the residents. To the west of the Fraser Homes the narrow lane running north to Lanark Road is known as The Turlies, which is believed to take its name from a tirl or part of a mill wheel.

From Pentland Avenue access through a narrow lane and a flight of steps known as The Shoot leads back to the Colinton viaduct below

The seventeenth-century Dreghorn Castle, built by Sir William Murray, Master of Works to King Charles II, demolished April 1955. From *Views of Juniper Green and District*.

which was Colinton Railway Station on a spur line from Slateford to Balerno. Although the railway was at one time the main commuter link with Edinburgh, nothing remains of the track, sidings or station buildings, save a commemorative cairn with a 'station' sign erected when the ground area was being landscaped:

COLINTON STATION
OPENED BY
COUNCILLOR D MACLENNAN JP
31ST OCTOBER 1981

Under the arches of the viaduct, beside the ground display of mill wheels, a flight of steps leads to Spylaw Public Park and Spylaw House, now subdivided into private flats. Spylaw House was built in 1773 for James Gillespie beside a much earlier house of about 1650 in which the snuff factory was established. James and his brother John remained bachelors all their days. John looked after the retail shop in the High Street in Edinburgh while James lived at Spylaw House superintending the snuff mill. Frugal and industrious by nature, but not miserly, James acquired great wealth from the business, though he never ceased to live on close and amicable terms with his employees, his tenants and his animals. Kay relates the tale that Gillespie's horse frequently indulged in a little restive curvetting with its master, especially when he was about to get into the saddle. Addressing the animal in his usual quiet way Gillespie would say, 'Come, come, hae dune noo, for ye'll no like if I come across your lugs wi' the stick'. In fact he was never known to strike the animal or anyone else for that matter. To his young apprentice, Andrew, who returned one day with one shilling collected from overdue rents, Gillespie said, 'Weel,weel, it's aye better than naething; but it's weel seen they're the lairds and no me'. Gillespie had many of the trappings of wealth, although he did not always use them, including a carriage with the initials JG on the side. It was the Hon. Henry Erskine who suggested, rather facetiously, that the carriage should bear the motto:

> Wha wad hae thocht it,
> That noses had bocht it.

It is said by Kay that Gillespie never resorted to legal measures: on the other hand the Scottish Record Office possesses an interesting plan dated 26th July 1771, apparently produced in conjunction with legal process between James Gillespie and John Granger, on which there are some interesting spellings of place names—Collingtoun, Spoillaw and Water of Lieth.

When Gillespie died on 8th April 1797 he left a vast fortune for the endowment of a Hospital for aged men and women and a free School for poor boys. Gillespie's Hospital was erected in 1802 in Gillespie Crescent on the site of the old mansion of Wrychtishousis near Bruntsfield.

At the village end of the viaduct, the steps known locally as the Twirlies go up to Woodhall Road which leads back to the head of Bridge Road. Until recently the old school building was occupied as the doctor's surgery but was transferred on 1st November 1986 to a new building near the Telephone Exchange on Colinton Road. The villa called Fairhaven at the foot of Dreghorn Loan occupies the site of the infant school, demolished when the Thorburn Road school was built.

Dreghorn Castle

Dreghorn Castle was one of Colinton's grandest houses, probably built originally by Sir William Murray, Master of Works to King Charles II

The Covenanters' Monument in Redford Road, constructed by R.A.
Macfie out of columns from the old Royal Infirmary, which was demo-
lised c 1884.
Photograph by Phyllis Margaret Cant.

(1630-1685). It lay amid extensive wooded policies entirely hidden
from view between what is now Redford Loan and the City Bypass. Of
the castle nothing remains, but two lodge houses are still extant: one
lies beside the bridge across the Braid Burn south of Dreghorn Loan;
the other is about to begin a new lease of life as part of a modern villa
being built in Oxgangs Road North a few yards north of Hunters
Tryst. A third, beside the old bridge in Redford Road, has recently
been demolished.

The castle was home to a long list of influential people over the
centuries. Towards the end of the seventeenth century it belonged to
David Pitcairn who is buried in the now dilapidated tomb in Colinton

churchyard. After the death of David Pitcairn in 1709 his son sold the property in 1717 to George Home of Kello W.S., Town Clerk of Edinburgh during the time that his father was Lord Provost from 1698 to 1700. During the remainder of the eighteenth century there were four owners, two of whom remained for only a few years: 1735-1754 Robert Dalrymple W.S; 1754-1760 Dr Andrew St. Clair, Professor of Medicine at Edinburgh University; 1760-1764 George Dempster of Dunnichen and Skibo; 1764-1796 John Maclaurin (Lord Dreghorn), author of several books including a valuable *Essay on Copyright*. In a caustic review of Lord Dreghorn's poetical efforts, Dr Thomas Murray commented that Volume 1 of the *Works of Lord Dreghorn* consisted of his poems 'or rather verses that rhyme'. In 1797 Dreghorn Castle was bought by Alexander Trotter, paymaster to the Royal Navy, and remained in the possession of the Trotters for three generations. During this era, but probably nearer to 1820, large-scale alterations gave the castle its distinctive castellated appearance. The Trotters' involvement with Dreghorn came to an end when Mr Coutts Trotter, grandson of Alexander Trotter, disposed of the estate around 1871. The new owner was R.A. Macfie of the famous sugar refining family whose father John Macfie came from Greenock in 1804 to expand the business and to establish new premises in Elbe Street, Leith. In 1810 John Macfie married Alison Thorburn, daughter of William Thorburn merchant in Leith, and R.A. Macfie was born in 1811. After schooling in Leith and Edinburgh he attended Edinburgh University and then spent two years in a Leith merchant's office. Later he joined his father's sugar refinery business in Leith and also spent several years in Glasgow and Liverpool. After a long business career, combined with a close association with the Liberals under Gladstone, R.A. Macfie retired to Dreghorn where he became a prominent member of the Colinton community. As a member of the Colinton School Board he was closely involved in 1891 in the building of the new Colinton School in Thorburn Road, the street being named after his mother. He died on 16th February 1893 and was buried in South Leith Churchyard in the family grave.

During the early part of the twentieth century, Dreghorn Castle was used as a private school, after which it was acquired by the War Department. Access to the grounds by the public was effectively discouraged by several signs, strategically placed, bearing the portentous message: DANGER: SOLDIERS USE BOMBS HERE WHICH CAN KILL YOU: DON'T TOUCH ANYTHING: IT MAY EX-

Merchiston Castle School, Colinton Road, designed by Norman A. Dick and W.J. Walker Todd.
Courtesy of Merchiston Castle School. Photograph by Andrew Gorman.

PLODE. Explode it did, but not accidentally. In the early 1950s the War Department found that the castle was superfluous to their requirements and that a prohibitive sum of money would be required to remedy the effects of poor maintenance, vandalism and dry rot. Reluctantly a decision was taken to demolish the old building, after salvaging the lead and three ancient stone plaques bearing coats of arms. In April 1955, the 300 Parachute Squadron Royal Engineers T.A. moved in and with the use of flame throwers reduced the building to a desolate shell. On Sunday 1st May 1955 they returned with explosives and razed the castle to the ground—three centuries of history gone in a matter of seconds. The three armorial stones have not been traced. No part of the structure remains, although a solitary baluster, perhaps with its own story to tell, adorns the front garden of a bungalow in Redford Loan.

Redford House

Although Redford House dates from about the same period as Dreghorn Castle (mid-seventeenth century), its more modest design has enabled it to adapt more easily to change. It lies in private grounds to the north of the new broad section of Redford Road, near the junction with Redford Loan.

The name Redford came to prominence in 1674 when the eldest son of Sir James Foulis (Lord Colinton), the Lord Justice Clerk, was raised to the bench and took the title Lord Reidford. By 1712 Redford was in the possession of George Haliburton, Lord Provost of Edinburgh from 1740 to 1742. He sold it in 1740 to John Young, a brewer in Edinburgh, whose daughter, Mrs Allen, succeeded to it on his death. Mrs Allen's grandson James Allen was born at Redford in 1771, and distinguished himself in medicine and literature. At the end of the eighteenth century the estate was acquired by Alexander Trotter of Dreghorn and later by R.A. Macfie.

Although R.A. Macfie was not perhaps the most distinguished owner of Redford, he was certainly the most imaginative, spending large sums of money in acquiring ornamental stonework from the Royal Infirmary in Edinburgh. The first Royal Infirmary, designed by William Adam, was built in 1738 on a site later occupied by South Bridge School in Infirmary Street. Although additional accommodation was provided in 1853 for surgical patients, the medical hospital continued in the original 1738 building. In 1866 a decision was taken to rehouse both the surgical and medical hospitals in a new building at Lauriston designed by David Bryce, and opened on 29th October 1879. The 1738 building lay unoccupied for several years after Lauriston was opened, but when it was demolished in 1884 R.A. Macfie of Dreghorn put in a successful bid for most of the ornamental stonework. He deployed the stonework in a number of interesting schemes, most of which are intact today.

Perhaps the most ambitious scheme was the removal of the central pediment above the main doorway, consisting of three bays, or windows, flanked by massive leafy scrolls, one depicting thistles and the other roses. This very heavy masonry was built into the south wall of the stable block at Redford House, and Ionic pilasters and a niche with the inscription GEORGIUS II REX were built into the west wall. The niche is empty, however, as the statue of George II was retained by the Infirmary and placed in the forecourt of the new building in Lauriston Place. In the mid-1960s the stable block at Redford was renovated to create living accommodation, without altering the old scrolls, which can still be seen through a high boundary fence on Redford Road.

Within a hundred yards of the scrolls, near the entrance to Dreg-

Colinton village from the Parish Church showing the old single-arch
bridge across the Water of Leith, with Spylaw cottages in the centre of the
picture, and villas in Woodhall Road in the background.
Courtesy of N.B. Traction Group Collection.

horn Barracks, another of Macfie's transplants from the Infirmary has
given new life to a group of four Ionic pillars taken from a colonnade in
front of the old medical building. These pillars were re-erected in their
present position in 1885, primarily to commemorate the Covenanters,
although other historical references appear high up on the square
entablature: ROMANS; CROMWELL 1650; COVENANTERS
1666; CHARLES 1745. On a rough-hewn stone nearby are several
stirring verses beginning:

> A people of whose line was Patrick born
> Whose record Wallace Knox and Watt adorn
> Whose patriots, heroes, martyrs true and bold
> On fairest page of history are enrolled.

The third link with the old Infirmary is temporarily in store. It
consists of a large ornamental plaque, with a lengthy inscription
commemorating General Gordon which was on the front wall of an
isolated house, Fordel Cottage. The cottage stood on the south side of
Redford Road a few yards west of the Dreghorn Link from the City
Bypass. In recent years the cottage was well kept with substantial
timber fencing enclosing a well-tended vegetable garden, but it
became unoccupied during construction of the Bypass. Its demolition
in 1985 removed the last link with the hamlet of Fordel described in
W.B. Robertson's *Pictures of Colinton in the early Twentieth Century*. Mr

51

Robertson illustrates three houses: Fordel Cottage, at one time the gamekeeper's cottage for Dreghorn estate; a cottage with a pantiled roof used as a military post office by the army during the First World War; and a smaller thatched cottage used by an estate gardener.

Fortunately, the Department of the Environment, Property Services Agency, has arranged for General Gordon's plaque to be incorporated within the new Dreghorn Barracks scheduled for re-building in the near future.

Colinton Castle; Colinton House

The ruins of the once famous Colinton Castle, home of the Foulis family of Colinton, stand on the north side of Colinton Road in the grounds of what is now Merchiston Castle School. According to Small's *Castles and Mansions of the Lothians*, Colinton Castle dates from c1450, although the Royal Commission on the Ancient Monuments of Scotland, in its 10th Report, dates the castle not earlier than the sixteenth century. Whatever the exact age of the castle, there is no doubt that the Foulis family had a significant presence in Colinton in the early sixteenth century when they acquired the smaller baronies of Dreghorn, Baads [around Fordel Cottage], and Oxgangs.

Several members of the Foulis family were distinguished members of the Scottish judiciary. Sir James Foulis, King's Advocate in 1527, was appointed a member of the College of Justice at its institution in 1532. A later member of the family, also Sir James, became a Senator of the College of Justice in 1661 as Lord Colinton, followed by his son, who was raised to the bench in 1674 as Lord Reidford or Redford. Despite holding high office the family was not without its problems. Following the occupation of the castle by Cromwell's troops in 1650 the Foulis family sustained crippling financial losses. Damage to houses, barns, byres, corn and stock, particularly at the Mains of Colinton, was so great that large sections of the estate, Dreghorn, Craiglockhart and Comiston, had to be sold to recoup the losses. Towards the end of the eighteenth century part of the estate of Colinton, and the castle, were sold by the Foulis's to the famous banker William Forbes of Pitsligo.

At the present day Colinton Castle is an ivy-covered ruin bereft of almost all its original features. The oldest part of the castle, probably three storeys in height, was rectangular in shape, measuring 74 by 26 feet, with its long walls running east to west. The original staircase was in the south wall, but when the new wing was added to the north in the seventeenth century, the opportunity was taken to incorporate a new staircase in the angle between the old and new buildings. The external walls were of rubble with dressings of light-coloured freestone, incorporating a heavy corbelled cornice which was probably intended to carry a parapet or other projection on the south wall. The basement contained several vaulted passages and cellars, but rather surprisingly, the only known defence was a single gunloop in the stair turret on the north side.

When Sir William Forbes took over the estate in 1800 his first idea, after discussion with John Fraser, mason and architect in Colinton, was to repair and extend Colinton Castle. Plans were produced, but another team of architects, headed by Thomas Harrison, was busy preparing plans for a completely new house which was started in 1801 and completed in 1806. The new Colinton House was in stark contrast to the old castle. Craigleith ashlar was used extensively in the broad five-bay frontage, reached through a central porch of coupled Ionic columns. Fortunately the style and texture of the new stone was so different to the castle that it escaped at least the worst excesses of plunder. Unfortunately in 1804 the roof of the castle was deliberately removed in a 'well-intentioned' bid to create a picturesque ruin. Sir William died in 1806 as the house was nearing completion but before he had taken formal possession of it. It was an untimely end for a man who, by his own efforts, had risen from being a poor orphan to become the principal of the banking company Forbes Hunter & Co. of Edinburgh. One of his sons later disposed of the estate to the first Lord Dunfermline, Speaker of the House of Commons from 1835 to 1839, who spent his retirement at Colinton House until his death in 1858 at the age of eighty. Thereafter the estate passed to his son Sir Ralph Abercromby K.C.B. (the second Lord Dunfermline), whose only child, a daughter, married Major John Moubray Trotter.

Since 1930 Colinton Castle and Colinton House have formed part of the policies of Merchiston Castle School, the origin of which can be found more than a century earlier in central Edinburgh.

Merchiston Castle School

In 1828 Charles Chalmers, brother of Dr Thomas Chalmers, the famous leader of the Disruption of 1843, lived at Park Place near

Bristo, the site of which is now occupied by the McEwan Hall. He moved there to obtain more space for his university student boarders to whom he taught mathematics and science, but within a short time he was again in need of larger premises. He obtained a lease of the old Merchiston Tower on the Borough Muir (at one time the home of John Napier, inventor of logarithms) and moved there in 1833 with about thirty boys to establish Merchiston Castle Academy. The curriculum included the traditional subjects, French, English and the Classics, but there was also special emphasis on science and mathematics. Chalmers remained headmaster and owner of the school until 1850, when he was followed by John Gibson from 1850 to 1856 and then by Thomas Harvey from 1856 to 1863. By then the school had been established for thirty years but greater continuity was achieved on the appointment of John Johnston Rogerson who remained as headmaster for thirty-five years. Under Rogerson, or 'the Chief' as he became known, Merchiston 'advanced in number and renown', particularly as the City of Edinburgh extended from Tollcross. Academic and athletic achievement were the rewards of a most exhausting daily timetable: 7.30 a.m. prayers; 8.00 breakfast; 9.00 to 12.00 lessons; 12.00–2.00 p.m. games; 2.00–3.00 late dinner; 3.00–6.00 lessons; 6.00–7.00 tea; 7.00–9.00 prep. Towards the end of his term of office, Rogerson ensured the continuity of the school by making it a private company in 1896.

At the end of the First World War, Merchiston entered a decade of hectic activity, precipitated by the simple but laudable aim of providing a memorial to the 176 boys and masters who had been killed in action. By 1922 the architect N.A. Dick had completed plans for a Memorial Hall, but although the plans were approved by the Dean of Guild Court, it refused permission to build. Colinton Road was very narrow and a Memorial Hall abutting the roadway would prevent any road-widening scheme in the foreseeable future. Suddenly the Directors were faced with a greater problem than building the War Memorial. The school was hemmed in on all sides by residential development; there was no possibility of expansion; and their playing fields in Colinton Road were also under threat. Fortunately Colinton House came on the market and was acquired in October 1924, with financial assistance from the sale of Merchiston Tower to the Merchant Company of Edinburgh, along with the playing fields set aside for the new George Watson's College building. W.J. Walker Todd was employed as the architect for the new Merchiston Castle School in the grounds of Colinton House, and the boys were employed to clear hundreds of tons of stones to create new playing fields. In this way the name Merchiston, and a long tradition of sound education, came to Colinton.

Compared to Merchiston Tower the Colinton House policies provided unbelievable opportunities for expansion. Revised plans were drawn to accommodate two hundred and fifty boarders and in 1928 the first turf was cut by Mrs J.W. Dowden, wife of the Chairman of the Board. The first building erected was the groundsman's cottage on the corner of Paties Road and Colinton Road, to enable the clerk of works to live on the site. The main school was designed round a central Memorial Hall with classrooms to the south and ancillary accommodation to the north. Separate boarding houses flanked the main building on the east and the west, and Colinton House (renamed Gibson House) was converted to laboratories, the library, and art rooms. The opportunity was also taken to change the constitution of the school's Board of Governors, six of whom were to be elected from the Merchistonian Club and one from each of the following bodies: the University Court of the University of Edinburgh; the University Court of the University of Glasgow; the Faculty of Advocates; the Society of Writers to His Majesty's Signet; and the Royal College of Surgeons, Edinburgh. Although pupils were received at Colinton from 1930, no formal opening was arranged in view of the proximity of the school centenary. A special commemorative service was held in the Memorial Hall on Sunday 24th June 1933, and the following day the school was visited by the Duke and Duchess of York (later to be King George VI and Queen Elizabeth).

The modern history of Merchiston Castle School has been one of further expansion: in 1960 a swimming pool was added; in 1967 the sanatorium was converted into a junior house; and 1974 saw the construction of a new arts centre with a music school following in 1978. The 1980s have seen a major modernisation programme of the teaching, boarding and recreational facilities of the school, including individual study bedrooms for senior boys.

The 150th anniversary of Merchiston was celebrated in 1983, an occasion graced by a visit by Her Majesty The Queen, who toured the school, seeing studies and activities. An appeal launched at the time came to fruition in 1986 with the opening, by the Secretary of State for Scotland, of a large new complex comprising classrooms for computing and electronics, a theatre, a careers centre, a sports hall, and a shooting range and fencing area.

The Merchiston Castle roll has grown to some 350 boys, coming from all over Scotland, with one in five being the son of an expatriate. The school prides itself on high academic standards, with an emphasis too on modern technology and awareness of the contemporary world of industry and commerce, and so it continues the tradition established by its founder Dr Chalmers.

The aims of the school are, above all, to give each boy in his way the capacity and self-confidence to live in an uncertain world and to make that life as rich as possible; more specifically, to encourage him to work hard and to take a pride in achievement, to think independently, to face up to challenges, to accept responsibility, to show concern for others, and to develop wider skills and interests.

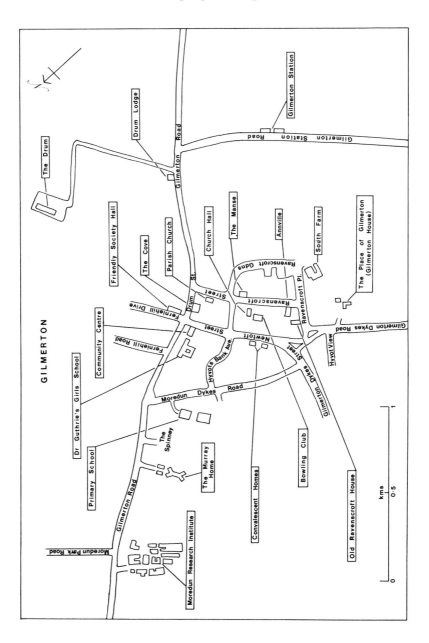

CHAPTER 3

Gilmerton

Gilmerton stands on a ridge of high ground to the south-east of the city, commanding excellent views of Craigmillar Castle, Edinburgh Castle and the Forth. Dating from at least the sixteenth century, its early history was undoubtedly associated with coalmining and limestone quarries, which were worked by successive generations until fairly recent times. A close-knit economy, and insistence on independence from outside sources, meant that much of the working population was engaged in carting coal, lime and sand to various outlets in Edinburgh. Those who were not engaged underground worked on one of the many farms, or on the estates of Drum and Gilmerton. Although Gilmerton House and its estate have long since disappeared, that of Drum, to the east of Gilmerton, retains all its history and many of its traditions. The basic lay-out of the old village has survived despite fairly widespread commercial and domestic development in the first half of the twentieth century. The most obvious development at the present day is the emergence of small groups of private housing on land previously used for farming.

The Drum (formerly Somerville House)

The Drum has a long and eventful history recorded from at least the fourteenth century when the lands of Drum were in the possession of Sir John Herring. Around the year 1320, however, an event occurred which completely changed the fortunes of this great landowning family. Motivated by the desire to see his elder daughter properly settled, Sir John made an arrangement which went dramatically wrong, and resulted, instead, in the death of his daughter, and the loss of half of his estate.

Sir John had two daughters, Margaret and Giles. It was his intention to marry the elder daughter, Margaret, to his brother's son, Patrick, thus making Margaret and Patrick heirs to the greater part of his estate. Margaret was an attractive young lady, but of a melancholy and devout disposition who observed all the ceremonies of the church. It was her practice to frequent Newbattle Abbey where she 'made the acquaintance of a young monk who under a pretext of holiness insinuated himself into her confidence and then took advantage of the ascendancy he gained over her, to ensnare and betray her'. Their secret meetings in a small cottage at Burndale near Gilmerton were made all the easier by the fact that the owner, a young widow, was also carrying on an intrigue with another monk. Alerted to the involvement of his daughter in these habitual practices, Sir John stormed out of the Drum one evening in the company of two of his servants, determined to discover the truth. On arriving at the cottage, but not receiving any reply, he took a flaming torch from one of his servants and set fire to the house. In the ensuing inferno his daughter perished along with the widow and two men of the cloth. Clearly guilty of arson, murder and sacrilege, Sir John fled the country, and his estates were forfeited to the King. Hunted, penniless and homeless, Sir John later went with his other daughter, Giles, to live with an old friend, Sir Walter Somerville of Carnwath, who campaigned for the pardon of Sir John on account of the scandalous conduct of the monks, even before the involvement of Margaret. This apparently welcome intervention was not without its price. When Sir Walter eventually secured a pardon for Sir John, the terms of the agreement were that Sir Walter would have young Giles for his bride and half the estate for all his bother. Sir John died shortly thereafter and left the other half of his estate to his nephew Patrick Herring, the groom intended for Margaret.

George Good, in *Liberton in Ancient and Modern Times*, devotes several pages to tracing the fortunes and misfortunes of the various members of the Somerville family, who owned the Drum until the beginning of the nineteenth century. Subsequent owners were Robert Cathcart W.S. whose trustees sold the property to Gilbert Innes of Stow, who was succeeded by his sister on whose death the Drum passed to Alexander Mitchell. It was purchased in 1860 by the More Nisbett family who are still in occupation.

There has been a mansionhouse on or near the present site of Drum House for at least six hundred years. Even as far back as 1584, Hugh, the seventh Lord Somerville, had a new house built at Drum by John Mylne. It was badly damaged by fire on more than one occasion and lay ruinous for many years before being pulled down by James, the thirteenth Lord Somerville, who commissioned William Adam to design the present house. The house of William Adam, built between

The Drum, designed by William Adam for Lord Somerville, was built between 1726 and 1734, the west pavilion incorporating part of the sixteenth-century house by John Mylne.
From Grant's *Old and New Edinburgh.*

1726 and 1734, incorporates part of the structure built by John Mylne in 1584. At the Gilmerton, or west, side it is reached by a long tree-lined driveway opening off the road from Gilmerton to Dalkeith. The main part of the house, by Adam, is flanked on the west by a three-storey pavilion, but an intended matching pavilion to the east was never built. The central facade is Palladian in style, with two main storeys and a basement. The front doorway and supporting windows form a projecting centrepiece, and there are similar pediments over the upper windows. Internally most of the ground-floor plasterwork is by Samuel Calderwood.

The extensive wooded policies around Drum House contain numerous features associated with its early history. Set into the garden wall to the west is a heraldic stone inscribed:

Arms of Hugh 6th Lord Somerville
1524 Brought from Cowthally
Castle to Drum 1694

To the south lies the stable block dating from 1806, but perhaps the most interesting feature is the shaft and cross of 1892 with the inscription:

> In memory of the old
> Mercat Cross of Edinburgh
> which stood at the Drum
> from 1756 to 1866 this
> monument was erected

The explanation is quite involved. The Mercat Cross of Edinburgh is mentioned in writing for the first time in 1365, when it was on the south side of the High Street about forty-five feet east of the present east side of St. Giles Cathedral. In 1558 the Cross had become unsafe, and although it was proposed to take it down and re-erect it on the same site, nothing was done. It was eventually taken down and re-erected further east in 1617 to reduce congestion of traffic. In 1756 it was again dismantled, and damaged in the process. The larger part of the pillar was removed and re-erected with its capital at Drum House, where it remained for the next century. There are conflicting reports as to when it left Drum House, but by about 1866 it was erected within a railing near the north door of St. Giles Cathedral. Finally in 1885 the Rt. Hon. William Ewart Gladstone restored the Cross and had it erected in its present position at the east end of St. Giles Cathedral.

The Place of Gilmerton

Gilmerton's second mansion was the Place of Gilmerton or Gilmerton House which lay to the south of Gilmerton Dykes Road, until it was finally demolished in the 1970s. Today the site of the old mansion is occupied by the rear garden ground of an attractive two-storey house built in 1951 and extended in 1985. The entrance to this modern villa is the eastmost gateway of the original entrance to the Place of Gilmerton, but the iron gates and some of the stonework have been lost or damaged. Sufficient original stonework remains, however, to indicate its former grandeur. The twin gateways are set back from the roadway with a dwarf wall curving in on the east and west sides. The eastmost gateway is in use but has lost much of the stonework of the original square gate piers and chamfered cap stones. The westmost gateway is much more complete, which may be due to the fact that for many years it has been filled in by a low wall of random stonework.

Baillie William Dow commands the attention of most of the crowd at the unveiling of the First World War Memorial in the grounds of Gilmerton Parish Church.
Courtesy of Miss E. Waldie.

The Place of Gilmerton is of great antiquity, dating from at least the middle of the sixteenth century, and has been described at various intervals by several writers. One of the earliest accounts, in 1792, by the Rev. Thomas Whyte obviously describes the property at the height of its grandeur:

> The mansion house has a most excellent site and is favoured with a most charming and delightful prospect on all hands. The like is hardly to be seen anywhere. What is called the long walk on the south side of the house is peculiarly pleasant. At the east end of it there is a large arch and above it a balcony in order to enlarge and improve the view.

Grant, in *Old and New Edinburgh*, devotes much of his description to the early families who owned the property, principally the Kinlochs, who later built Gilmerton House near Athelstaneford in the 1750s. George Good, writing in 1893 in *Liberton in Ancient and Modern Times*, states that the proprietor of the lands of Gilmerton was Sir David Baird of Newbyth but that the Baird family (in common with other owners) never occupied the mansion as their home. By the end of the nineteenth century, Speedy observed, in *Craigmillar and its Environs*, that the old house had been subdivided and tenanted to miners working in the pits near Gilmerton, and was 'rapidly losing its ancient character'. In 1926 John Geddie wrote in *The Fringes of Edinburgh* that Gilmerton House was roofless and nettlegrown and had become an 'abomination of desolation'.

There are several interesting features in the extensive grounds around the Place. The large arch and balcony noted by the Rev. Thomas Whyte in 1792 and believed to be an early eighteenth-century gazebo are still in reasonable condition within a private garden at the west end of the village. There were also several yew trees planted in a very distinctive style around a circular building known as the 'Bath', which was about eight feet in diameter and had a single door. Although the screening effect of the high trees has supported the notion that the building was a bath-house, no more definite evidence is available in support of that supposition.

Another interesting feature is the ice-house. It was examined in great detail and measured accurately in recent years by A. Niven Robertson, who set out his findings in an article under the title 'Ice Houses of the Eighteenth and Nineteenth Centuries' which appeared in the *Book of the Old Edinburgh Club* in 1953. Mr Robertson found that the Gilmerton ice-house was a vaulted stone chamber forming the basement of a two-storey farm building situated to the north of the old ruined mansionhouse. The construction was rubble sandstone roughly eighteen feet from east to west and fifteen feet from north to south, with walls forty-one inches thick. The entrance in the east wall was forty-two inches wide and six feet high and there was a square hole in the ceiling of the arched vault. In addition to the ice-house Mr Robertson was able to locate a much larger vaulted chamber known as 'the dungeon', which may well have formed part of an even earlier fortified keep or castle.

Much of the area previously belonging to the Place of Gilmerton is about to be developed for private housing. The farm buildings referred to by Mr Robertson have been demolished, although presumably some part of the ice-house and dungeon lie beneath the ground. A

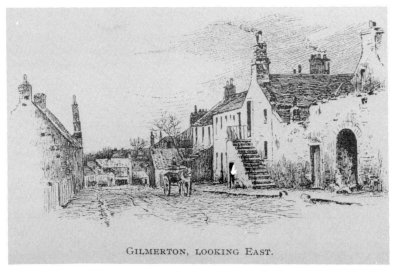

GILMERTON, LOOKING EAST.

Houses of every description, some with outside stairs, huddled together in Main Street, Gilmerton.
From Speedy's *Craigmillar and its Environs*.

heap of stones is all that remains of old Gilmerton House. To the east of the modern villa the circular remains of the bath-house stand in an open area of scrub, once known as Gilmerton Gardens. The trees which surrounded it have been reduced to decayed stumps, but the position of the 'long walk' referred to by the Rev. Thomas Whyte in 1792 is clearly visible between slightly raised embankments on each side.

Gilmerton Cove

One of Gilmerton's most intriguing stories lies within a few yards of the main road traffic, at the corner of Drum Street and Newtoft Street, yet is surprisingly unknown to many Edinburgh residents. Hacked out of solid stone at a depth of about ten feet below the surface is Gilmerton Cove, one-time dwelling, forge and workshop of the local blacksmith, George Paterson. That Paterson lived and worked in the Cove for many years is beyond doubt, but there is much less agreement over some of the other information recorded by the Rev. Thomas Whyte of Liberton as early as 1792. His account is in *Transactions of the Society of Antiquaries of Scotland*:

Here is a famous cave dug out of rock by one George Paterson, a smith. It was finished in 1724 after five years hard labour as appears from the inscription on one of the chimney-heads. In this cave are several apartments, several beds, a spacious table with a large punch-bowl all cut out of the rock in the nicest manner. Here there was a forge with a well and washing-house. Here there were several windows which communicated light from above. The author of this extraordinary piece of workmanship after he had finished it, lived in it for a long time with his wife and family and prosecuted his business as a smith. He died in it about the year 1735. He was a feuar or feodary and consequently the cave he formed and embellished so much and the garden above it was his own property, and his posterity enjoyed it for some time after his decease. His cave for many years was deemed as a great curiosity and visited by all the people of fashion.

Examination of the Cove reveals a labyrinth of very unusual rooms, passages and tunnels, all cut from the soft sandstone formation. A flight of stone steps leads down to a main passage about forty feet in length with rooms off on both sides. To the right-hand side of the passage there is a forge and a room measuring approximately fourteen feet six inches by seven feet, with headroom of about six feet. At one end of this room there is a stone mantlepiece and at the other end a stone table seven feet long with benches on each side. The arrangement of rooms on the left-hand side of the main passage is more elaborate. The first room is tucked in behind the stairway, and the next, measuring only eight feet by five feet, has all the available floor space taken up with a narrow stone table and benches on each side. The third room, on the left, is the famous drinking parlour, fifteen feet long with a ten-foot long table into which has been hollowed a stone basin. The ceiling in this room is supported by a roughly cut pillar. The parlour leads into a subsidiary passage running at approximately right angles to the main passage, and beyond the subsidiary passage there is another room. At its furthest point from the entrance steps the main passage curves slightly to the right into the last room, from which there appears to be the start of a tunnel. There is no definite evidence as to the purpose of the tunnel, but there has been no shortage of ingenious suggestions, including an escape route from Craigmillar Castle some two miles to the north-east.

The existence of the Cove has been well documented in various publications since the account in 1792 by the Rev. Thomas Whyte, but, generally, these references have merely repeated what Whyte says. In November 1897 a much more scientific approach was adopted by F.R. Coles, Assistant Keeper of the National Museum of Antiqui-

John Kerr chats to George Pendreigh as he drives past Wallace's Cottage
near Broken Brigs, 1926.
Courtesy of Mary McLean.

ties of Scotland, who visited the Cove in company with J. Balfour Paul
and George Good, F.S.A. Their findings were set out in the *Proceedings
of the Society of Antiquaries of Scotland*, and represent a major challenge to
the theory that the Cove was constructed by George Paterson.
According to Coles, the Cove could not have been hewn out in five
years by one man, and the nature of the tool-work on the stone
suggested a date much earlier than the eighteenth century. Indeed all
Cole's evidence suggests that Paterson merely used the Cove in the
mid-eighteenth century, but was certainly not its architect. Many
questions remain unanswered, the most pertinent of which is whether
Paterson is buried in the Cove, as suggested by the words of the early
eighteenth-century poet Alexander Pennycuik:

> Upon the earth thrives villainy and woe,
> But happiness and I do dwell below,
> My hands hewed out this rock into a cell
> Wherein from din of life I safely dwell.
> On Jacob's pillow nightly lies my head,
> My house when living *and my grave when dead*
> Inscribe upon it when I'm dead and gone
> I lived and died within my mother's womb.

Coles was never able to confirm any trace of the above inscription, which was said to be cut into the stonework above the fireplace.

Gilmerton Parish Church

1775 is one of the earliest dates associated with the development of the church in Gilmerton when the Rev. John Campbell set up a preaching station and held evening services in the old village. Although little is known of this early pioneering work, it eventually bore fruit in 1838 when the Parish of Gilmerton was erected as a Chapel of Ease associated with Liberton Parish Church. The first minister was the Rev. Walter Fairlie, whose allegiance to the Established Church, like that of so many of his contemporaries, was lost to the principles of the Disruption in 1843. In that year he left Gilmerton Parish Church and set up Liberton Free Church in Stenhouse Road (renamed Ellen's Glen Road in 1966 to avoid confusion with the Stenhouse district of Edinburgh, near Gorgie).

Perhaps the Rev. Walter Fairlie was more fortunate than some of his fellow Disruptionists in that he owned the manse personally, which was not, therefore, liable to forfeiture. For several years after 1843, Gilmerton did not have a permanent minister. The work of the church was continued by several Licentiates, the last one being Thomas Fleming who was inducted to the full Charge in 1860, serving until 1862. Over the next two decades the church prospered under the Rev. Peter Stewart (1862-73) and the Rev. Thomas Walker (1873-81), to the point where, by 1882, it needed to be greatly enlarged. The original church was built in 1837 on the north side of Main Street (now Ravenscroft Street) with a shallow-pitch gabled nave supported by buttresses and topped by a conical-shaped bellcote over the front entrance. The 1882 plans were drawn by John G. Adams to include an east and west transept, an entrance porch, and a vestry. The opportunity was also taken to renovate the whole interior, the entire work costing £1,500, of which £500 was contributed by the Baird Trust, £100 by the Home Mission committee and the remainder by voluntary subscription. On completion, the oak pulpit was gifted by William Ford of Fernieside who was also instrumental in carrying out much of the work of renovation.

Of the Communion cups, one is pewter with the inscription *Gilmerton 1861*, and the other is silver with the inscription *New, Canongate 1813* presented to Gilmerton in 1875.

Gilmerton Play Day in full swing as the band makes its way up Drum Street just before the junction with Main Street.
Courtesy of Mary McLean.

Gilmerton Manse and Church Hall are also situated in Ravenscroft Street. As the first manse belonged personally to the Rev. Walter Fairlie, it was not until 1861 that a suitable property was acquired as a manse on the north side of Main Street. At the end of the Second World War the manse was moved to a handsome detached property on the south side of the road, now 43 Ravenscroft Street. By an interesting coincidence, it is believed that the present manse (at No 43) is the same building, or on the site of the same building, as was occupied by the Rev. Walter Fairlie at the time of the Disruption. The present minister, the Rev. Donald Skinner, believes it to be the same building, whereas the authors of *The Buildings of Scotland—Edinburgh* suggest that the manse building dates only from c. 1890. Gilmerton is also fortunate through the generosity of Charles E. Green of Gracemount in having acquired the old school house on the north side of Ravenscroft Street as a hall in 1915. In 1956, during the ministry of the Rev. Alexander Keith, the building was completely renovated at a cost of over £12,000, much of which was met by the Home Board.

For several years now Gilmerton Parish Church has established a wide reputation for its involvement in the practical training of

youngsters who leave school looking for a worthwhile trade or voca-
tion. The work was first pioneered by the Rev. Donald Skinner in 1965
and has been continued under his direction with the assistance of a
small team of dedicated supervisors. From the very earliest days the
idea was to reorientate young people by providing them with a useful
outlet for their energies and abilities, at the same time introducing
them, some for the first time, to the teaching of the Church. Voluntary
teachers and supervisors were recruited from within the parish and, in
a relatively short time, classes had been established for youngsters
between the ages of ten and twenty in a wide range of crafts including
pottery, photography and boatbuilding. In many ways the work was a
decade before its time, and received considerable impetus from the
introduction, in 1976, of the Government Job Creation Programme.
With the broader financial base created, in part by the Manpower
Services Commission, a training for industry project now operates
under the name 'Pioneer Tec'. There are four main sections, housed in
various buildings near the manse. Altogether about fifty youngsters
pass through the various stages of the project every year, over 90% of
them going on to full-time employment.

The engineering and smithcraft section is based in the large garage
attached to the manse. The use of power machinery and welding
equipment, under the watchful eye of a trained supervisor, has
resulted in a steady flow of decorative ironwork for furniture, railings
and gates. Two recent projects have taken Gilmerton skills far beyond
the confines of a purely local craft. A crest and sign were made to hang
outside the headquarters of the Royal Scottish Corporation in London, the sign displaying the St. Andrew's Cross in addition to the
name. The crest, sitting above the sign, consists of an ornate crown in
gold, flanked by a pair of Scottish thistles.

Pottery and ceramics occupy a very old building to the east of the
manse where a large selection of mugs, bowls and vases are turned out
in almost every conceivable design. The day class of seven teenagers
works under the able direction of Gillian Mackay, a graduate in design
at Edinburgh College of Art. In addition to work on the potter's wheel
young trainees learn to hand-paint ceramic tiles either as single pieces
or as groups of four or six. The class usually has a retail outlet in
Edinburgh at the time of the Festival, and also staged a very successful
exhibition in 1980 at St. John's Church, Castlehill.

The church hall provides accommodation for the section dealing
with woodwork and boatbuilding. A well-equipped workshop of

A proud day for Euphemia
Waldie, crowned Queen at the
Gilmerton Children's Gala
Day in June 1927.
Courtesy of Miss E. Waldie.

power tools and hand tools, many gifted privately, forms the nucleus of
the section. Trainees learn the basic crafts of boat repair and boatbuilding, several orders for single and double canoes being received
from various sports centres in and around Edinburgh. One of the
largest contracts secured recently was for the construction of a seventy-
foot jetty at the Craiglockhart Sports Centre.

The fourth section, also housed at the church hall, is mainly, but not
exclusively, patronised by the girls and deals with knitwear, textiles
and tapestries. Training on one of the four knitting machines is under
the direction of Mrs Roberts. Usually the course lasts for one year,
during which time the girls learn handknitting, machine knitting,
embroidery and tapestry. The work of the unit has now become well
enough known for a fairly constant volume of woollen products to be
made to order. The introduction of a computerised knitting machine
in 1982, costing over £1,200, has greatly increased the number of
completed garments by reducing substantially the long hours of
preparation on the more conventional punchcard system. The latest
machine is able to 'read' the pattern from a pencil sketch of the
intended design.

In and around the old Village

Much of the basic street layout of the old village of Gilmerton has survived as the focal point of a much bigger district, built principally after the Second World War. Alterations in street names, and a slight reorientation of the village by a new approach constructed from the west, have meant that the main street is no longer regarded as the principal thoroughfare.

At the turn of the twentieth century New Street (now Newtoft Street) was little more than a bridle path giving access to sporadic building on the north and the south sides. Innes Cottages at the southwest end were extended from a single cottage which stood on its own for many years surrounded by fields of corn. The principal buildings were the Convalescent Homes on the north side, both of which remain. The first Home (eastmost building) was the Ravenscroft Convalescent Home established in 1878 with the object of providing 'convalescent treatment for men and women of the working class whose means are exhausted owing to illness'. Admission for a stay of two or three weeks was free, but applicants had to be respectable, necessitous, free from infectious disease, and recommended by a clergyman or respectable householder known to one of the trustees. In 1889 the Home held a Grand Musical Conversazione in the Balfour Banquet Hall, Waverley Market on Friday 6th December with entertainment under the personal direction of H.H. Morell Mackenzie of London. The programme included several *tableaux vivants* depicting the lives of Queen Mary, John Knox, and Prince Charles Edward Stuart interspersed with music by the Band of the Grenadier Guards. The proceeds provided greatly needed funds for the upkeep of the Adults' Home as well as the Children's Convalescent Home first established in 1881. Children, admitted at the rate of about two hundred and fifty each year, were referred from the Sick Children's Hospital, the Royal Infirmary and Leith Hospital. A new children's home was opened by the Very Rev. Dean Montgomery on 18th December 1888 to accommodate twenty-two patients, including one special unit for a mother and child. Generally speaking the children were from poor families but were admitted free under various charitable trusts. A plaque on the west wall of the westmost building bears the entwined initials C.C.H. in the centre and the date 1888. The other initials are M.A. and A.D., the latter presumably the architect Alexander Duncan of Blairquhosh.

Gilmerton Bowling Club lies midway between Newtoft Street and

Gilmerton Community Centre, built as Gilmerton Public School in 1914 to replace the Anderson Female School on the same site.
Photograph by Phyllis Margaret Cant.

Ravenscroft Street in an elevated position but reasonably protected by the buildings around it. Although there has been recent controversy over the exact date of its inauguration, the better opinion appears to be 1895. The books and minutes of the Club, before 1926, have not survived, but sufficient information is available to establish that there were twenty-nine founder members, many of whom were businessmen in and around Gilmerton. The green measured forty yards by thirty-seven yards and was built six feet above the natural ground level by using rubble from a nearby quarry. The Club was admitted as a member of the Midlothian Bowling Association in 1897 and the Scottish Bowling Club in 1948.

Several cups and trophies have been presented over the years: in 1915 Charles E. Green of Gracemount, Honorary President of the Club, presented the Championship Cup; John More Nisbett of the Drum presented the Club Handicap Cup; and in 1960 Alec Erskine presented the Hugh Erskine Cup in memory of his late father, Hugh Erskine, founder member and President 1938-1939.

In more recent years increased membership has resulted in expanded social activities, requiring an extension to the Club premises. This was first accomplished in 1971 and was followed by a further extension in 1977 to provide a function hall for three hundred persons, costing £27,000. The present membership is over three hundred. The Club badge depicts a drum, two bowls and a jack, surrounded by a figure eight for the number of players in a rink. Although the badge is intended to symbolise the Drum Estate, in fact the estate takes its name from the word *drum* meaning a hill or ridge.

The main street of Gilmerton was renamed Ravenscroft Street in 1968. It runs westward from Drum Street in a long irregular line, constructed at various stages in the development of the village. What the street may lack in cohesion is made up for in the variety of architectural styles. Many of the houses have been modernised: most have been sympathetically designed on the inside but some less so on the outside.

At its lower or east end, Ravenscroft Street begins on the south side with a rather grand building constructed around 1840, with a projecting centrepiece, and flanked by older properties in poorer condition. On the north side of the road one of the typical single-storey cottages of the old village has been modernised and extended to include attic dormers. Immediately to the west is the War Memorial within the boundary railings of Gilmerton Parish Church. Beyond the church there is further evidence of the widely differing styles of buildings. The north side is dominated by a neat row of terraced cottages set back from the pavement, with small front gardens and gabled entrances serving adjacent houses. To the west is a large tract of ground given over to commerce, and then the red stone block of Hawthorn Place. On the other side of the road a small modern housing development sits cheek-by-jowl with the old mission hall, now used as the post office.

The next group of buildings is closely associated with the church and the activities of 'Pioneer Tec'. The two-storey, barge-boarded manse sits on the high ground to the south, completely dwarfing one of the oldest surviving buildings on the main street, presently occupied by the pottery section of 'Pioneer Tec'. This building has very thick masonry walls, a pantiled roof and dormers which pierce the front wallhead. Immediately opposite is the church hall greatly extended from its original use as the Montgomery School for Boys and Girls. The large detached house with the stone pilasters on each side of the entrance, and iron finials over the half dormers, belonged to Mr Montgomery, the headmaster.

The upper part of Ravenscroft Street, according to *The Buildings of Scotland—Edinburgh,* retains some of 'the ghosts of Georgian prosperity'. Annville, a two-storey detached property sitting back from the street, has a slightly projecting centrepiece and a Roman Doric

The pedimented portals of Dr Guthrie's Girls' Industrial School designed by McArthy and Watson in 1903, opened in 1904 and closed in 1986. Photograph by Phyllis Margaret Cant.

doorway. Occupied formerly as the manse of Gilmerton Parish Church, it is now subdivided and bereft of any garden or foliage to soften its solid lines. Behind, the open ground and solitary gate pillar in Ravenscroft Place are all that remains of Old Ravenscroft House, destroyed by fire in 1984. To the west the long low modern building of Kingdom Hall, meeting place of the Jehovah's Witnesses, faces Brucefield Place, a block of two-storeyed terraced houses with a date plaque 1889. Immediately adjacent are the farmhouse and steadings of South Farm, where the Adams carry on the family tradition of dairy farming in what must be one of Edinburgh's few remaining farms within the city boundary.

Beyond the junction with Ravenscroft Place, the short cul-de-sac is bounded on the north by the red sandstone Westland Cottages built in 1902. The south side offers an intriguing amalgam of dwellings and outhouses surrounded by extensive old walled gardens. The westmost house was built around 1870, probably to replace a much older property, evidence of which can be traced in the boundary walls to the west and north. The garden ground is bounded to the east by the remaining wall of what was probably the dower house of the Place of

Gilmerton, and in the garden the original village waterhouse has now been converted into a small dwelling house. By far the most interesting historical feature is, however, the early eighteenth-century gazebo platform built over a west-facing arched shelter. Extensive work has been carried out by the present owner, Mr Muir, to repair and renovate this most interesting link with the Place of Gilmerton.

From the parapet of the gazebo the district surrounding Gilmerton can be studied in some detail. To the south, the fields of South Farm stretch down to Gilmerton Station Road and the remains of Gilmerton Station on the Edinburgh, Loanhead and Roslin branch line of the London North Eastern Railway. In the days when the Brosie Pit was in full production much of the good-quality coal was transported by rail from the sidings at the pit-head. At its east end, Gilmerton Station Road meets the continuation of Drum Street which forms part of the road to Dalkeith.

Drum Street is now the busiest road through Gilmerton. At its south end the West Lodge for Drum House sits to the left of the long tree-lined avenue, leading up to the old mansion. A few hundred yards north, the white-painted part of the terraced block on the right was the home of Willie Reilly, hawker and tailor in old Gilmerton, who used the small orange pantiled building adjacent as a coachhouse. His easy payment system of one shilling per week brought comfort and warmth, if not sartorial elegance, within reach of much of the village population.

A filling station is built on the site of the saddle room used by Tam Innes who owned Bessieville, a large house approached through gates immediately south of the Gardeners' Arms. The solid tenements, Innes Buildings, on the west side of the street were built around 1880. The remnants of another Gilmerton farm—East Farm—lie on the east side of the roadway where modern housing has been built recently. The substantial two-storey house on the corner was Craig's Dairy; the low cottage abutting was thatched; and the long building to the rear was the milk house.

The section of Drum Street between Ravenscroft Street and Newtoft Street has several original pantiled cottages, but many have been converted into shops, and others are in poor condition. On the right, the Royal Bank of Scotland, built in 1935 with curly gables and bow windows, contrasts well with the Mechanic Arms on the opposite side of the street built at least a century earlier. Near the traffic lights on the

Dr Thomas Guthrie, preacher, philanthropist and writer, pioneered the
success of the Ragged Schools on the simple philosophy of Patience,
Prayer and Porridge.
From *Disruption Worthies*, 1876.

left is the entrance to Gilmerton Cove, and on the right the solid block
of the Hall of the Junior Friendly Society. The stone plaque above its
front door reads:

Junior
Friendly
Society
Instituted
1787
Hall
Built 1888

Gilmerton Junior Friendly Society and Play Day

One of Gilmerton's most interesting Societies was constituted in 1787 'for the purpose of relieving such of its Members who by sickness or lameness should occasionally be rendered unable to attend their usual employment, and for defraying the funeral expenses of such of them or their Wives, at death'.

Although the Society no longer exists, several documents and books of account were deposited some years ago with the Edinburgh Room of Edinburgh Central Library by Mr Grossart of Gilmerton. One of the earliest entries, dated 21st December 1808, under the heading 'Widows Annuities' records regular payments of 15/- (75p) to Widow Anderson, Widow Hoggarth and other deserving cases. Anyone admitted to the Society had to be of good moral character, between twelve and thirty years of age, and free from all constitutional or hereditary disease. Entry money, payable each quarter, was on a graded scale beginning at 2/6d from 12 to 15 years up to 12/6d from 26 to 30 years. By paragraph 7 of the Articles an Allowance to a Sick or Lame Member was 6/- per week for three months and 4/- per week for three months thereafter. The penalty for cheating was instant dismissal from the Society, and all benefit was lost:

> . . . if any member feign himself sick or lame or be convicted of bringing trouble on himself by any immoral behaviour or vicious and irregular conduct and refuse the instruction of a Physician he shall lose all right; and if his trouble should appear to be the venereal disorder; or the result of it; or to proceed from any excessive drinking; or from fighting; or any other irregularity he shall exclude himself from the Society.

In 1908 the membership stood at 184, including sixteen committee members.

For many years the Gilmerton Play Day was closely associated with the activities of the Junior Friendly Society. Indeed there is evidence that the Play Day, or its progenitor, was celebrated in some form as far back as the sixteenth century. Had the Rev. James Begg of Liberton Church only taken the Laird of Moredun's advice to 'draw the manse blinds' on this great annual event, the New Statistical Account of Scotland would have been robbed of one of its most interesting accounts of Gilmerton life in the 1840s, as observed through the manse window:

Ravenscroft Street, 1987, looking towards Drum Street with Gilmerton
Parish Church behind the cottages.
Photograph by Phyllis Margaret Cant.

The only peculiar games here are what are called 'carter's plays'. The
carters have friendly societies for the purpose of supporting each other in
old age or during ill-health and with the view partly of securing a day's
recreation, and partly of recruiting their numbers and funds, they have
an annual procession. Every man decorates his cart-horse with flowers
and ribbons and a regular procession is made accompanied by a band of
music through this and some of the neighbouring parishes. To crown all,
there is an uncouth uproarious race with cart-horses on the public road,
which draws forth a crowd of Edinburgh idlers and all ends in a dinner for
which a fixed sum is paid. Much rioting and profligacy often take place in
connection with these amusements and the whole scene is melancholy.
There are other societies in the parish which have also annual parades
with a similar result. These societies have undoubtedly been in some
respects useful but the 'plays' are fortunately rapidly declining; and it is to
be hoped that savings banks in which there is neither risk nor temptation
to drunkenness will soon become the universal depositories for the surplus
earnings of the people.

Despite the Rev. James Begg's wish that the Play Days be restricted,
they existed for almost another hundred years without the need for
rioting, profligacy or drunkenness. Although the Play Day appears to

have been in decline in the years immediately prior to the Second World War, many older Gilmerton residents still recall when the Play Day was the most celebrated day of the year. Preparations began on the Thursday for the main event which was held on the last Friday in July. A lorry, scrubbed and bedecked, would carry a full load of earthenware basins round to Jimmy Veitch, the baker, in Main Street, where the Play Haggis was already being prepared. Oatmeal, suet and onions combined to create a culinary delight, seldom repeated in such large quantities outside Gilmerton. The earthenware basins, heaped with haggis and topped with a leg of mutton, were collected at noon on Friday and taken to the Society Hall to be distributed to the members of the Junior Friendly Society. In the afternoon the village band led the company round the neighbouring streets, stopping outside members' houses to play a favourite jig or reel in exchange for a little refreshment. Once back at the Hall the flags were auctioned amidst great rivalry between Gilmerton families, the bidding enhanced by the euphoria of the day and the excitement of being custodian of one of the favourite flags: *The Stenhouse Best*; *The Gilmerton Best*; and *The Auld Hundred*.

Schools and Institutes on Gilmerton Road

Although the east side of Gilmerton Road consists of traditional bungalows built in the 1930s, the west side was developed at a much earlier date for various schools and other institutes. Included in this long ribbon development is Gilmerton School, Dr Guthrie's Girls' Industrial School, The Murray Home and the Moredun Research Institute, each of which has developed quite independently of the others.

The earliest available school log for the district is 1864. It refers to Liberton Free Church School in Stenhouse (now Ellen's Glen Road), which was probably opened shortly after the Disruption in 1843. Following a period of dwindling numbers on account of the fees charged, the school was closed on 10th August 1874, and the children were transferred to a new school being built at Gilmerton. Although the logs do not give the exact location of the new school, opened on 5th October 1874, it was almost certainly the school premises in Main Street, later named the Green Halls. By 1885 the school roll was augmented by a further fifty-three new pupils when Gilmerton

Original School, run by Mr More, was closed. There was also an evening school attended by about thirty adults studying a variety of subjects including arithmetic, history, geography and composition. On one evening when the numbers attending were seriously affected 'by entertainments of a theatrical kind' the master proceeded un-daunted, with a much reduced class, to discuss, firstly, Mary Queen of Scots and Lord Darnley's murder, following this with an ambulance class dealing with the arrest of bleeding by finger and tourniquet— expertly demonstrated but too late in the day to change the course of history!

In 1910 negotiations took place between the School Board and the Anderson Female School which occupied modest premises on the corner of what is now Newtoft Street and Gilmerton Road (Drum Street). As a result the two schools amalgamated and a new building, to designs by J. Inch Morrison, was erected on the site of the Anderson Female School. The school was opened at 3.30 p.m. on 11th September 1914 by Lady Susan Gilmour, wife of the Chairman of the School Board who was absent on war service. In deference to the original founders of the Anderson Female School, the new school laboured under the rather awkward name of Gilmerton, The Anderson Public School until September 1926 when the Scottish Education Depart-ment altered the name to Gilmerton Public School.

In the fifty years from 1864 to 1914 those responsible for education in Gilmerton were confronted with numerous changes, but it was not until after the Second World War that the school suffered its most acute administrative problems. In the school log for 27th August 1951 the headmaster recorded that the school contained thirty-two classes with a total roll of 1254 in five different locations made up of: 365 in Gilmerton Main Building; 71 in the Green Halls; 76 in Ravenscroft; 312 in Moredun Infant Annexe; and 434 in Moredun Primary Annexe. The position was helped by opening Fernieside Primary School in 1952, and by moving Gilmerton School on 30th May 1968 to new premises in Moredun Dykes Road.

When Gilmerton School moved out of their 1914 building at the east end of Newtoft Street, it was used for a while by St. John Vianney School. In 1984 it was refurbished and opened as Gilmerton Commu-nity Centre.

Immediately to the north of the old school building, now occupied as Gilmerton Community Centre, is Dr Guthrie's Girls' School, harled and with red sandstone dressings, designed by McArthy and Watson in 1903. The front entrance has a steeply pedimented door-piece with the name in gold—DR GUTHRIE'S GIRLS' INDUS-TRIAL SCHOOL 1904—and above, the initials I.S.B. for Industrial School Board.

Dr Thomas Guthrie, preacher, philanthropist and writer, was born in Brechin on 12th July 1803, and died at St. Leonards, Hastings on 24th February 1873, a fraction short of his allotted three score and ten years. His energetic lifestyle, however, produced a catalogue of achievement which by normal standards would have taken much longer than a lifetime. Born of parents already established in Christian beliefs, Thomas studied at Edinburgh University from 1815 and was licensed to preach in 1825. His first charge was at Arbirlot near Arbroath in 1830, having spent the intervening period studying science and medicine at Edinburgh and Paris. When news of his transfer, in 1837, to Old Greyfriars in Edinburgh, reached his parishioners at Arbirlot, it is said that 'they were a' greetin'', knowing full well that they were losing a man who would be almost impossible to replace. On his arrival in Edinburgh he spent three years at Old Greyfriars and then entered the new church of St. John's, formed from the Old Greyfriars parish. Having already spent many years campaigning against Patronage in the church, it was no surprise to see him among the leaders with Dr Chalmers in 1843. Not only was he committed to the principles of the Disruption but he led a massive campaign immediately thereafter and raised £116,000 under the Manse Scheme for homeless ministers.

In Edinburgh, however, Dr Guthrie will always be remembered primarily for his creation of, and dedication to, the Original Ragged Schools. His philosophy was simple, easily understood, and uncomfortably difficult to ignore: Patience, Prayer and Porridge; porridge first and the other two might follow. In 1847 Guthrie acquired rooms in Ramsay Lane in Castlehill, where he took in seven boys, and later thirteen girls, who would otherwise have received no education and little guidance. By the end of the first year he was providing food, clothing and education for almost four hundred and fifty children. The pattern was set. The Ragged School concept spread throughout Scotland and was given further impetus by the Education Act of 1872 which provided Government grants to augment money raised by public subscription. Dr Guthrie died on 24th February 1873, but his charismatic enthusiasm had been transmitted to others. After his death a school for boys was opened at Liberton in 1888 and for girls at Gilmerton in 1904. In 1932 the system of Approved Schools was implemented, and replaced in 1969 by List D Schools with a residential and occupational influence in liaison with Children's Panels. In 1986 the Girls' School at Gilmerton closed its doors for the last time, the remaining pupils being transferred to Wellington School near Penicuik.

Dr Thomas Guthrie is buried in Grange Cemetery. In Princes Street Gardens, opposite the junction with Castle Street, there is an imposing statue to this early Victorian philanthropist. The huge fatherly figure of Guthrie, skilfully cut by F.W. Pomeroy in 1911, towers above the much slighter figure of a wee lad from the Ragged School, yet to be enriched by the philosophy of the day—Patience, Prayer and Porridge.

To the north of the new housing development called The Spinney, a small modern lodge house marks the entrance to The Murray Home, built in 1929 on the site of Moredun House, dating from the fifteenth century. Moredun House, originally known as Goodtrees or Gutters, belonged successively to the families Herries and Somerville, landowners in and around Gilmerton. In the middle of the seventeenth century the House belonged to the McCulloch family, and in 1648, through the marriage of their only daughter and heiress to Sir James Stewart of Coltness, Goodtrees passed to the Stewarts, in whose hands it remained until 1775. Sir James, merchant and moneylender in the city, was made Lord Provost of Edinburgh in 1648, but by 1659 feelings were running high against him on account of his Covenanting sympathies. In 1660 he was arrested and sent to the Castle to face two very different charges: that he countenanced the execution of Montrose; and that he embezzled public funds whilst Receiver-General of the Army in Scotland. A pardon was negotiated and eventually Sir James was released from prison. He died in 1681 without having reentered public life.

Towards the end of the eighteenth century Goodtrees was acquired by David Stewart Moncrieff, one of the Barons of Exchequer who changed the name to Moredun, after the name of a hill on the Perthshire estate of the Moncrieffs. At the beginning of the nineteenth century Moredun was bought by Samuel Anderson and his son David, of Sir William Forbes & Co., Bankers in Edinburgh. In recognition of

David Anderson's work as a trustee of Sir William Fettes' estate, one of the residential houses attached to Fettes College was named Moredun. He was also founder of the Anderson Female School in Gilmerton. The last proprietor was John Welsh, who bought Moredun in 1888.

Moredun's modern history began in 1918 on the death of Miss Helen Murray, a citizen of Edinburgh who died at Melrose in January that year. She left the residue of her estate for the purpose of founding a home in or near Edinburgh to be called 'The George and Agnes Murray Home' in memory of her parents and brothers and sisters. Miss Murray's primary wish was to establish a convalescent house for wounded British soldiers and sailors; and in the event of the house being no longer required for that purpose it was to become a convalescent home for patients from the Royal Infirmary of Edinburgh. In 1923 the managers of the Royal Infirmary acquired the old mansion of Moredun for £4,500 from the estate of the late John Welsh. The original intention was for the old house to be remodelled and refurbished by the architect Thomas W. Turnbull, but closer examination of the structure revealed that it was too badly affected by rot and general decay. Reluctantly a decision was taken to demolish it and build a new convalescent home on the same site. This was done in 1929, and it consisted of a central two-storey block flanked by two Y-plan wings to provide maximum light and ventilation for each of the rooms. Two small Ionic columns from Moredun House were incorporated in the south front of the new building.

Originally the Home, although administered by the George and Agnes Murray Trustees, was supervised and managed by the Royal Infirmary. With the advent of the National Health Service there was no place for a private trust within the public body and the Trustees were therefore left to run the House by themselves. In 1978 the finances of the Home were such that it was necessary to allow it to be absorbed by the closely allied ex-Service charity, the Scottish Naval, Military and Air Force Veterans' Residence, who were then able to set about the necessary modernisation of the long-established home. In 1984 the parent charity abbreviated its title to Scottish Veterans' Residences, with the subtitle of Whitefoord House, Rosendale and The Murray Home, and thus the George and Agnes Murray Home became officially known as The Murray Home.·

During 1986, on the 75th anniversary of the first veterans entering Whitefoord House, an appeal was launched to raise the £300,000 necessary to complete the modernisation and expansion of The

Murray Home such that it could continue to meet the needs of the ex-Service veterans into the twenty-first century.

Moredun Research Institute lies immediately to the north of The Murray Home, on land which once formed part of the estate of Goodtrees, or Moredun. The Research Institute is furthest from Gilmerton and is almost adjacent to the old village of Stenhouse at Ellen's Glen Road.

Prior to 1920 insufficient veterinary research was being undertaken in Scotland, although a few scientists were carrying out limited research, sometimes at their own expense. This state of affairs could not be allowed to continue indefinitely, especially as continued losses in farm livestock became increasingly serious from an economic point of view. A group of Scottish farmers formed a committee, and, along with representatives from the Highland and Agricultural Society, the Scottish Chamber of Agriculture and the National Farmers' Union of Scotland, initiated the Animal Disease Research Association. The first President was Mr Colin Campbell of Jura who was elected on 17th July 1921. Shortly thereafter sufficient funds had been obtained to appoint two veterinary investigators, Professor Gaiger, at that time Principal of the Glasgow Veterinary College, and Mr Thomas Dalling, who, later as Professor Sir Thomas Dalling, became Chief of the Veterinary Department of the United Nations Food and Agricultural Organisation. In March 1924, as a result of subscriptions and donations received, the Association was able to buy thirty-five acres of land, part of the Moredun Estate. A grant was obtained from government funds which assisted with the cost of a laboratory and other buildings, designed by the architect A.K. Robertson. When the buildings were completed in 1926 the research work was transferred from Glasgow under the Association's new scientific director, W.A. Pool. The Institute was officially opened by Sir John Gilmour, Secretary of State for Scotland, on 4th November 1927, *The Scotsman* devoting several columns to this historic day in Scottish farming.

Since 1926 the Moredun Research Institute has been extended on various occasions, particularly in 1961 when major expansion led to the creation of several new departments. At the present day the staff of about one hundred and fifty includes about forty science and veterinary graduates, plus technical, administration and trades staff. Several research workers and postgraduate students visit the Institute every year.

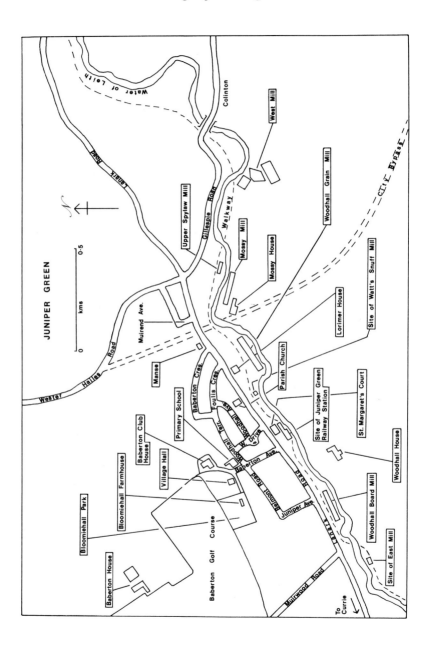

JUNIPER GREEN

CHAPTER 4

Juniper Green

Juniper Green, on the moor between Currie and Colinton, developed around the numerous industries which obtained power from the Water of Leith. The village formed a natural hinterland for the thriving mills which were frequently built in very restricted positions nearest to the best source of water power. Although it is known that mills were operating along the valley from the sixteenth century, Juniper Green did not develop as a distinct community until very much later. Adair's Map of 1735 shows the line of what is now Lanark Road passing through Curriemoor, but the only places of habitation shown are Baberton to the north and Woodhall to the South. The position had not altered very much by 1766 when Laurie drew up his map showing Baberton, Fairniflate, W. Hales and Curriemuirend. It was not until well into the nineteenth century that the village took on anything resembling its present-day layout. There was a sufficiently large population in 1843 to support the newly formed Free Church, and in 1874 Juniper Green railway station was opened by the Caledonian Railway Company. The railway greatly improved communications for passengers and for freight going to and from the mills along the track. Increased prosperity saw the construction of large detached houses along both sides of Lanark Road, many by eminent architects of the day. After Edinburgh was extended in 1920 to include Juniper Green, extensive bungalow development took place on the north side of the village. In recent years the most obvious change has been the numerous blocks of flats, many intended as sheltered housing for the elderly, built either on open sites or after demolition of older buildings.

The origin of the name Juniper Green is uncertain, although two main theories vie for acceptance. The editors of *The Streets of Edinburgh* suggest that the village is named from the juniper bushes which were at one time very common in the neighbourhood. The alternative contention is that the name is derived from the juniper which forms part of the coat of arms of John Murray of Polmais, whose daughter Mary married John Cunninghame of Woodhall in 1677. Circumstantial evidence tends to support the second theory. The name Juniper Green appears in Colinton church records for the first time in 1707 only a few years after the death, in 1702, of Mary Murray who was married firstly to John Cunninghame and later to Sir John Foulis of Woodhall.

The exact position of 'the Green' is also a matter of conjecture. Gillespie's Farm estate plan of 1771 shows a small bleachfield at Curriemuirend (near the present Tanners Pub) where a road came from Woodhall House, over the Water of Leith, and passed Denholm's Mill. In 1706 Denholm paid rent to Foulis for his mill and lands, including 'the little bank'. Whilst there is no definite proof, it has been suggested that this little bank might be the bleaching green which gave rise to the name of Juniper Green.

The Mills at Juniper Green

The mills at Juniper Green are more than a century older than the village, and therefore must be regarded as the original focus of population along the banks of the Water of Leith, between Colinton in the east, and Currie in the west. Although it is still possible to locate many of these mills, the topography of the area has greatly altered from the days when grain, flax, paper and snuff were produced. From at least the sixteenth century, mills were located on the north and south banks at strategic points, where a weir and lade could be built to give the maximum head of water to power the machinery. The pathway, or rudimentary roadway, linking these small settlements alternated between the north and south banks according to the spread of population, and the existence of fords where people and carts could cross. Access to the turnpike roads of the neighbourhood was generally up the steep embankment on the north side of the water of Leith.

In the late 1860s the Caledonian Railway Company surveyed the Water of Leith valley with a view to laying a spur, from the main track at Slateford, to Balerno. Authority to build the railway was obtained on 20th June 1870 and the line was opened to traffic on 1st August 1874 with stations at Colinton, Juniper Green and Currie. The steep-sided valley dictated that only a single track was laid, requiring several bridges and cuttings, as well as realignment of access roads, and the provision of level-crossing gates. Although the passenger service ceased on 30th October 1943, goods trains used the line until the early 1960s. Thereafter the track lay derelict for several years before being renovated as a public walkway. From this walkway it is possible, with patience and imagination, to reconstruct some of the flavour of the locality in

Seventeenth-century Upper Spylaw Mill in the valley of the Water of
Leith with the walkway on the left constructed on the old railway line to
Balerno.
Photograph by Graham C. Cant.

the days when Juniper Green's economy was firmly based on water-
powered mills.

One of the most convenient access points to the Juniper Green
section of the walkway is at West Mill, Colinton, which can be reached
either through Spylaw Park, or from the foot of West Mill Road. From
Spylaw Park a gap in the stone boundary wall on the north side of the
park leads onto the walkway, a few hundred yards short of the huge
five-storey West Mill. Alternatively, the same point can be reached by
turning right, at the foot of West Mill Road, into the short roadway
which gives vehicular access to the mill. This short roadway crosses
over the original mill lade which can be seen running eastwards into
the mill complex. To the west, the lade is lined in concrete for a short
distance and appears capable of holding water, especially after periods
of heavy rainfall. The present buildings at West Mill, occupied by the
Forth River Purification Board and Bonaly Farm Dairy, are of
modern appearance, but grain and flour mills, and waulk mills where
cloth was beaten or thrashed, operated here from at least the late
seventeenth century. In the eighteenth and nineteenth centuries the

main products were grain and paper, and well within living memory, the mill was used for the manufacture of Cerebos Salt and Scott's Porage Oats.

The walkway proceeds westwards from West Mill on what was a long straight section of single-track railway. The Water of Leith lies on the right at a much lower level, and on the left, the mill lade runs for several hundred yards between the walkway and the long gardens at the back of the mill cottages. As the walkway begins to curve to the left, the first bridge is immediately ahead, crossing to the opposite bank of the Water of Leith. The single-arch stone bridge was designed to carry the railway and is, therefore, of much stronger construction than is required for pedestrian use only. From its left-hand parapet the weir (or waterfall) for West Mill can be seen with the entrance sluice at the head of the lade. Very little of the sluice-gate mechanism remains, but some of the access masonry is in position on the left-hand side, looking upstream.

To the west of the bridge at the West Mill weir a paddock and range of stables on the left form part of the policies of Upper Spylaw Mill. This is one of the oldest and best-preserved mill buildings in the valley, the main entrance to which is protected by the original level-crossing gate. The narrow road up the steep slope on the right provides vehicular access from Gillespie Road. Upper Spylaw Mill is believed to date from 1681 when it formed an integral part of the papermaking industry in the valley. A century later it was producing snuff along with several other mills at Colinton and Juniper Green. Its transformation to a dairy around 1880 is recorded in the colourful language of John Geddie in 1898 when he says: 'The water wheel sulks in its dark chamber; but there are cream barrels and butter-milk pails where brown Taddy was ground for the noses of our great-grandfathers'. These cream barrels and milk pails were the everyday tools of trade of the Frail family who ran the dairy and piggery from 1880 to 1930 after which Upper Spylaw Mill was used as a riding school. In 1960, however, third-generation descendants of the Frails re-established the family connection, when Mr & Mrs Downie purchased the mill as a private dwelling. Fortunately, the Downies resisted professional advice to demolish the Mill, preferring instead to undertake an extensive programme of repair and renovation. This imaginative stand against the general trend of the 1960s has conserved the exterior stonework, almost intact, and much of the interior. Unfortunately nothing remains of the mill machinery although it is possible to detect

East Mill Snuff Mill on the right bank projecting over the Water of Leith beside Wyllie's Farm, with East Mill Bank Mill on the left.

the position of the lade and the point on the west wall at which it entered the mill to drive the wheel and machinery.

Immediately west of Upper Spylaw Mill the dilapidated buildings of the former Mossy Mill can be seen through the trees on the south bank. Several small businesses occupy this extensive brick-built complex but there is very little mill atmosphere remaining. The high square chimneys have long since gone and there is little evidence of the broad strip of river bank which gave access to the works and the small cottages occupied by the mill workers. Access to Mossy Mill (and back to Colinton on the north bank) is by the small pedestrian bridge reached from the deeply cut pathway, which turns under the walkway at the foot of the steps leading up to Juniper Green. According to John Tweedie in *A Water of Leith Walk* the original Mossy Mill dates from the sixteenth century when it was a waulk mill owned by the Brothers Mosie from whom the modern name is derived. In the early nineteenth century the mill was acquired by the McWhirter family who owned the bleachfields at Inglis Green near Slateford, and in 1838 it was converted to a paper mill. Although Mossy Mill closed in 1972 there are several remnants of the water-wheel age a few yards upstream. The weir which served the mill is in almost perfect condition, with the lade being taken off on the south bank. The entrance sluice, relief sluice, gate and winding gear are still extant, but the lade, well constructed for a few hundred yards, disappears completely as it enters the old mill

91

complex. Mossy House, a handsome stone-built residence of uncertain date, previously occupied by the mill owner, stands high on the bank in attractive wooded policies, within sight of the concrete viaduct carrying the City Bypass across the Water of Leith. The walkway passes beneath the Bypass, the concrete pillars of which are spoiled by drip marks below the superstructure and graffiti enthusiasts at ground level.

Beyond the Bypass, in the open landscape created at the time of the roadbuilding programme, Woodhall Grain Mill operates on the north bank under the name of Alexander Inglis & Son Ltd, Grain and Agricultural Merchants. This was the approximate site of Curriemuir Mill, previously named Denholm's Mill in the early eighteenth century, and once the home of Hunter's Famous Lothian Oatmeal in the late nineteenth century. The modern works owned by Inglis is one of the few working mills in the valley, which was also provided with a greatly improved access road when the Bypass was built. There is no evidence of the original water power within any of the buildings, but two hundred yards upstream, beside the white timber fencing on the left, some hewn stones mark the position of the weir. On the north bank, below a rocky promontory, the lade began its journey to Inglis Mill.

The next place of interest is probably the one which requires the greatest imagination to unravel its past, as there is so little remaining. It is at the point where the walkway is carried on a short stone bridge across a shallow gulley, in which there is an unusual arrangement of stone channels. This is the site of Watt's Snuff Mill, known to have been the last snuff manufacturer in the valley. John Mackay, writing in the *Evening News* in 1967, recalled when the snuff mill was a going concern in the 1930s. The Water of Leith drove a system of gear wheels to rotate the rollers for grinding, and to shake the sieve in the production of three main blends - Black, Brown and Imperial Snuff. Watt's mill, which ceased production around 1940, and another one for grain a few yards upstream (Wright's Mill), were also known as Woodhall Bank Mills, but nothing remains of them now. The stone channels below the bridge carried the lade water away from Watt's Snuff Mill and back into the Water of Leith. An illustration from John Tweedie's collection, with the caption 'Watt's Snuff Mill, Juniper Green c 1900', gives a clear idea of the layout. The two-storey mill sat on the north side of the railway track with the basement below the level of the railway line. The lade entered from the west along the north side

Juniper Green Parish Church, built as a Free Church in 1879 to replace the much smaller Colinton and Currie Free Church established in 1844.

of the track where there was a branch to a goods yard siding. A signal box was built north-east of the mill and a tall signal mast was erected on the south side of the track. The only remaining evidence of the railway is a small wooden platform which appears to have been used as an access point for the signal mast.

West of Watt's Snuff Mill site is a large brick-built warehouse owned by the G.P. Inveresk Corporation, part of which is built on the site of the former Juniper Green railway station and its sidings. Accommodation for passengers was quite modest, consisting of one long narrow building with a flat roof and scalloped eaves, on the north side of the track, behind which was a larger open shed built across the goods train siding. Access for pedestrians and vehicles was by the steep Station Brae from Lanark Road.

Immediately west of the station site, where the walkway forks, little remains of the once spectacular curved weir which served Watt's Snuff Mill and Wright's Grain Mill via a long lade which ran at the back of the railway goods yard. The blocked up culvert can still be seen below the level of the fork in the walkway. The left-hand path leads to the site of Woodhall Board Mill, once one of the largest mill complexes in the valley. The huge site between the walkway and the Water of Leith has recently been levelled, except for one or two rudimentary buildings along the north side. At the apex of this triangular site the weir and sluice gates are still in good condition although it is more likely that the water was used in recent years in industrial processes rather than to power machinery. Woodhall Board Mill began life as a lint mill in the early eighteenth century but, as the name suggests, it moved into the manufacture of paper and cardboard packaging.

After a gradual left-hand curve at the back of Veitch's Garden Centre, the walkway again crosses the Water of Leith by a rather curious bridge laid with lengths of timber on top of the normal walking surface. On the far side of the bridge the Water of Leith is seen on the right, passing very close to an old house, whose ground floor is protected by a substantial stone embankment on the north side. This is one of the old mill houses beside which is the ruin of East Mill Bank Mill owned by James Watt at the end of the eighteenth century. On the south bank, lying between the walkway and the Water of Leith, was East Mill Grain Mill and East Mill Snuff Mill. All the buildings except one private house have disappeared but there are remains of the weir and the lade outflow just west of the bridge. Photographs taken at the beginning of the twentieth century show the very distinctive construction of East Mill Snuff Mill built high on the south bank with part of its structure protruding precariously on timber supports towards the river. A small wooden pedestrian bridge linking East Mill Bank Mill and East Mill Snuff Mill has long disappeared. Also demolished are the steadings of Wyllie's Farm on the south bank, which provided ponies for local Gala days, and theatrical events in Edinburgh.

A few hundred yards west of the bridge at East Mill Bank Mill the massive buttresses of a much older bridge appear. This ancient structure, previously known as Mutter's Bridge, carries Blinkbonny Road over the Water of Leith, the East Mill lade and the walkway on a series of arches of various sizes. On the outside of each parapet within an oval-shaped recess is the inscription:

BUILT BY
GENERAL
THOMAS SCOTT
OF MALLENY
1831

Beyond, the walkway straightens out to pass Kinleith Industrial Estate and so to Currie and Balerno.

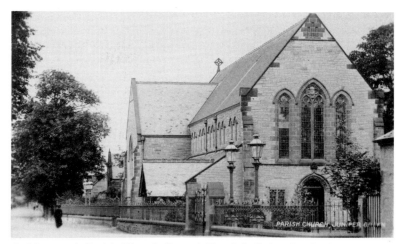

St.Margaret's Parish Church, Lanark Road, built in 1895 by Messrs. Turner of Juniper Green, demolished for the construction of St.Margaret's Court in 1979.

Juniper Green Church

Although Juniper Green's churches cannot claim great antiquity, nevertheless the circumstances in which the first congregation was established are interesting in relation to the religious thinking of the day. Prior to 1843 the inhabitants of Juniper Green travelled either to Colinton or Currie for Sunday worship. At the famous Disruption in 1843, however, neither the minister at Colinton nor the minister at Currie 'came out' in support of Dr Chalmers and his supporters. It followed, therefore, that although Free Churches were springing up all over Edinburgh and throughout Scotland, there was no focal point for Disruptionists in the area from Colinton to Currie. This was remedied by protesters holding services in Society Hall at Currie and the Old Ballroom in Colinton. In 1844 the Rev. Harry Anderson was ordained as minister of Currie and Colinton Free Church, and in the following year a feu charter was obtained from Sir William Liston Foulis, Bart., for a piece of land on which to build a permanent church. The feu charter, signed by Sir William on 30th July 1845, describes the intended site as 'All and Whole that piece of ground at Juniper Green, part of my lands and Barony of Woodhall consisting of Thirty Five Falls or thereby Scots measure and extending along the North side of the Turnpike Road leading from Edinburgh to Lanark . . . ' The feu duty was fixed at £3 per annum and there were the usual restrictions as to use in order to preserve the character of the area: all the buildings erected were to have slated roofs; no offensive trade or manufacture was to be carried on; and no dunghill or other nuisance was to be accumulated which would in any way be prejudicial or offensive to the vicinity. On the credit side, the new church trustees were relieved of the ground obligation to contribute to the minister's stipend, the schoolmaster's salary and other public and parochial burdens. On the list of trustees were several names associated with the thriving mill industries along the Water of Leith: John Hunter, Millmaster, Woodhall Mill, Colinton; James Miln, Wright, Malleny Mills, Balerno; James Cowan, Paper Maker, Kate's Mill, Colinton; James Allan, Paper Maker, Kate's Mill; and James Henderson, Malleny Mills near Balerno.

On completion of Colinton and Currie Free Church, the Rev. Harry Anderson continued as minister until 1868 when he was granted leave of absence on account of ill health. He died the following year and was succeeded by the Rev. Charles McNeil in 1870. During the next decade it became clear that the fairly modest church erected in 1845 was insufficient for the congregation's needs and in 1879 James Fairley, the architect, was employed to draw up plans for a much bigger church. The resulting building, still in use today, was erected in a raised position, with a central bellcote above the front entrance on the south-facing gable, and flanked by pairs of twin towers at different heights. Before this imposing structure was consecrated, it played host to one of the greatest orators of the day—Mr Gladstone—during the famous Midlothian Campaign of 1879-1880. On completion and consecration, the church was named Juniper Green Free Church.

The Rev. Norman C. Macfarlane was inducted at Juniper Green Free Church in 1893, and during his thirty-five years as minister saw considerable progress made in re-uniting different denominations of the church. In 1900 Juniper Green changed its name to Juniper Green United Free Church on the union between the Free Church of Scotland and the United Presbyterian Church of Scotland. Further progress was made towards a unified church in 1929 when the United Free Church joined with the Church of Scotland. At that time Juniper Green United Free Church became known as St Andrew's Juniper Green. The Rev. George Gunn was minister from 1926 to 1938, the Rev. George Reid from 1938 to 1949, followed by the Rev. John

Starched collars give a cutting edge to a class of forty-three at Juniper Green, 1906.
Courtesy of Alex Mackay.

Malcolm from 1949 to 1968, and the Rev. G.G. Cameron from 1968 to the present day.

Whilst Juniper Green had a Free Church almost from the time of the Disruption in 1843, it was not until about 1890 that members of the Church of Scotland in Juniper Green were successful in their bid to establish a local church. Prior to that, most people who were not members of the Free Church went to Colinton Parish Church which had almost twice as many people on the roll as it had seats in the church. With financial assistance and encouragement from the Home Mission Committee, an Iron Church, previously in use at Craiglockhart, was purchased and erected on ground on the north side of Lanark Road a few yards west of the junction with Woodhall Drive. Unfortunately this small prefabricated building was severely damaged by storm on 1st December 1891, but by 21st February 1892 it had been repaired and re-erected, and was opened for worship under the charge of the Rev. Charles M. Short, M.A. As soon as sufficient funds were available, a site occupied as a dairy on the south side of Lanark Road was obtained for the erection of a stone church. Drawings were prepared by the architect R.M. Cameron and the foundation stone was laid in 1895 for a red sandstone Gothic church by the local builders, Messrs. Turner of Juniper Green. When the new church, St.

Margaret's, was opened on 23rd January 1897, the Iron Church was retained as a hall until it was destroyed by fire in 1907, and replaced by a new hall in 1913 immediately to the east of the new church.

The Rev. Charles M. Short remained minister at St. Margaret's for thirty-four years until his death in 1925. It was a remarkable incumbency, almost as long as the following five ministries put together: 1926-1930 the Rev. William B.C. Buchanan; 1931-1943 the Rev. John Henderson; 1944-1950 the Rev. Denis M. Duncan; 1950-1955 the Rev. Charles B. Edie; 1955-1961 the Rev. H. Forbes Watt. The last minister at St. Margaret's was the Rev. Eric M. Davidson who came to Juniper Green in 1962 and remained there until 1974.

In 1974, following the policy of rationalisation of church buildings, and congregations, it became obvious that Juniper Green would be more conveniently served by one parish church. A decision was therefore taken to unite the congregations of St. Andrew's and St. Margaret's under the new name Juniper Green Parish Church. The Service of Union was conducted on 10th March 1974 in St. Andrew's Church building, and St. Margaret's Church building became surplus to requirements. Eventually the site was sold, the old church was demolished and a block of flats for the elderly was constructed in 1979. The flats, appropriately named St. Margaret's Court, are built on the site of the main church, the only part remaining being a stone cross from the roof which is incorporated as a feature near the new entrance doorway. The stone hall, built in 1913, has also been saved and forms the function hall to St. Margaret's Court.

At Juniper Green Parish Church photographs of the ministers of St. Andrew's and St. Margaret's hang in the Session Room beside an old painting of the original Free Church by the artist F. Johns. In a small hall to the rear, two grey marble slabs commemorate two young men of the parish:

In Grateful Memory	In Grateful Memory
of a True Hero	of
Alfred Charles Macdonald	Dr Ian MacFarlane
Aged 25	the distinguished son of our minister
A member of this church	worker in this church
Who nobly sacrificed his life	medical missionary at Nazareth
in saving others	Captain R.A.M.C. in the war
in the Bloemfontein Flood	Died at Kantara Egypt 18th July 1917
17th January 1904	Aged 29
	Erected by the Office Bearers

Hutton's shop at 558 Lanark Road with (left to right) Mrs I.Hutton, Mrs M.Hutton and Mrs M.Ireland.
Courtesy of R.S. Porteous.

In the vestibule there are three plaques facing the front entrance: the central copper plaque was brought from St Margaret's and confirms the date of dedication on 23rd January 1897; to the left there is a War Memorial also brought from St. Margaret's commemorating those of the parish who fell in the First World War; and to the right is the War Memorial of the former St. Andrew's Church commemorating those who fell in both World Wars.

Such is the history of the churches at Juniper Green. Ironically, the original pewter collection plate, which presumably helped to make it all possible, is no longer in use, its well-worn inscription read only by inquisitive strangers—Colinton and Currie Free Church opened 15th Sept. 1844.

East to West through the Village

At the east end of Juniper Green the elegant detached houses near Gillespie Crossroads were constructed around 1900, but traditionally the village does not start until Curriemuirend: The name is commemorated in Muirend Avenue on the north side of Lanark Road, and on the south side, in the centre of a row of terraced dwellings, is the Pentland Arms, recently renamed Tanners. Immediately west of Tanners, beside modern flatted property, the remaining frontage of an old two-storey house marks the position of the road which gave access to the mills before the construction of the City Bypass. The village landscape was completely altered at this point during the construction of the new road round the south of Edinburgh. This required the complete removal of Juniper Green Bowling Club on the north side of Lanark Road, and the shoring up of the garden ground of the manse belonging to Juniper Green Parish Church. On the south-west side of the Bypass the rural scene returns momentarily at Woodhall Nurseries whose south-facing glasshouses and cultivated land stretch down to the Water of Leith walkway. Already sections of this attractive area are being developed for further housing on plots of land very much smaller than the two older properties to the west. The first of these is Southernwood from which Dr Ross ran his practice for many years. The second was named Torduff, a large detached house of white harl and red tiles in magnificent grounds built in 1905 by Sir Robert Lorimer for a Miss Bruce. It has recently been acquired and renovated by Mr & Mrs Young for use as a nursing home, taking the name Lorimer House, after the architect.

Between Foulis Crescent and Woodhall Drive, the handsome Gothic lines of Juniper Green Parish Church share the north side with a variety of individually designed villas, one of which, Castle Bank, has a most interesting castellated frontage built in 1845 for its first owner, James Fortune. On the south side of the road several smaller houses have retained their original names, Pentland View, Broughton and many others. Also on the south side of Lanark Road, opposite Woodhall Drive, the new flats of St. Margaret's Court are built on the site of St. Margaret's Parish Church, demolished in 1975. Immediately west of St. Margaret's lies the heart of the old village bounded by Baberton Avenue, Belmont Road, Juniper Avenue (formerly Belmont Avenue) and Lanark Road.

Juniper Green School has been located in Baberton Avenue for a very long time, albeit in a variety of buildings. Halfway along on the east side the building with the long windows now occupied by the school janitor, was once the Female Subscription School. A new building was erected on the site of the Free Church School at the junction of Baberton Avenue and Woodhall Terrace, and in more

Silver Band leading 4/5th Royal Scots Volunteers c.1900, in Baberton Avenue.

recent times another building has been erected on the open ground to the north, near the clubhouse for Baberton Golf Club. One of the best known of the early headmasters was Peter Malloch who taught at Juniper Green from 1876 to 1899 and took a keen interest in the history of the village. Although he never published a formal history of the district his copious notes have been of great value to subsequent researchers. So great was the respect for Mr Malloch that as recently as 13th August 1955 a group of about seventy ex-pupils met at the old school to pay their respects to their late headmaster. Among those who attended was ninety-four year old Tom Napier, Sir David Henry of Auckland and Andrew B. Dea, Rector of Bo'ness Academy.

On the west side of the entrance to Baberton Golf Club the village hall is now used as a Community Centre with much the same aims as when it was first built. The hall was started in 1900 by the local Company of the Volunteers but in 1910 when the Volunteers were disbanded the hall was purchased on behalf of Trustees. For many years the organisation was undertaken by the Young Men's Club but membership dwindled and by 1957 the building was in need of substantial repairs. Juniper Green Village Association was formed to represent all the interests in the district, and funds were raised to put the hall and the caretaker's house in good order. The constitution of the Association drawn up on 9th July 1957 under the chairmanship of Alec Wallace laid out the main aims and objects, followed by general paragraphs on the hall, membership, management committee, meetings and finance.

To the west of the village hall one of the oldest buildings in Juniper Green stands close to the entrance to Bloomiehall Public Park. This long single-storey building was constructed originally as byres for Bloomiehall Farm, but is now a private dwelling. Adjacent is Bloomiehall Farmhouse, a neat two-storey house with unusual castellated stonework on its east side. Prior to 1974 it was used by the park keeper at Bloomiehall Park but when he retired there was local anxiety that the house might be demolished. Fortunately, it was bricked up and protected against vandalism until 1978 when it was put up for sale as a private residence. The *Evening News* report of 11th March 1978 proclaimed the house 'For Sale – this former Royal residence'—a reference to the belief that Bonnie Prince Charlie slept there on his way to Edinburgh with his troops before the Battle of Prestonpans in 1745.

The last section of Lanark Road west of Baberton Avenue has several houses of historic interest. At No. 547 the large L-plan dwelling on the south side was formerly the manse for St Margaret's Church and, before that, was the Dower House to Woodhall in the eighteenth century. Further west, at the city boundary, the neat cottage beside Veitch's Garden Centre takes the name Enterkin from Enterkins Yett, the north entrance to Woodhall House.

Although Juniper Green does not claim to have been the forum for events of national importance, nevertheless its local traditions and customs have steadily evolved through several generations. Some idea of the lifestyle of the ordinary people can be obtained from a variety of sources, particularly the *Statistical Accounts of Scotland*. Mr Malloch in his study of the village reviewed the employment prospects and living conditions in the neighbourhood when the entire economy was based on either farming or milling. Farms at Easter Hailes and Wester Hailes were providing crops of oats and wheat: cattle, sheep and pigs were reared; and cheese and pork formed an important part of the everyday diet. The state of the roads in the middle of the eighteenth century was so bad that loads of hay could not be transported to Edinburgh by a wheeled vehicle, and the journey by horseback was tedious and costly. Early in the nineteenth century several schemes were implemented to improve the state of the roads and to give employment to local people. Money to finance these ventures was advanced by the landowners, among whom were Sir Thomas Carmichael of Hailes and Mr Gibson

Baberton House, previously known as Kilbaberton, built in the early seventeenth century for James Murray, Master of the King's Works. Photograph by Phyllis Margaret Cant.

of Wester Hailes. A start was made at Thieves Road which ran north from about Gillespie Crossroads to Sighthill. This was followed by a spate of cash grants, modest yet well intentioned: £5 for labour to repair Woodhall Mill Road; three separate sums totalling £4:10s for Juniper Green Road; £1:10s for Wright's Mill Road; and a huge capital expenditure of £8 for labour and materials to build a small bridge over the Murray Burn on the way to Sighthill.

Vastly increased prosperity was evident by 1888 when the editors of the *Juniper Green Observer* brought out their first issue costing one penny. The advertisments provide an interesting insight into the services and commodities of the day:

> Henry Blyth Shirt Maker & Draper Earl Grey Street
> Every Gentleman should give these Shirts a trial
> No 1 Quality 2/3d each.

> The Dandie Dinmont Whisky
> The recognised Blend of the Parish
> When you ask for it see that you get it.

Gilbert Meikle, the farmer at Fernieflat, conscious of being within a mile of a lucrative market, wooed the residents of Juniper Green in swaggering style:

> The Tenant Farmer of Fernieflat
> begs to intimate that he is prepared
> to execute orders for the finest Milk
> and Cream as well as Hay, Straw and
> Potatoes the quality of which is not
> to be surpassed, if equalled, in Midlothian.

And from the same paddock, though perhaps directed towards a different clientèle:

> Two Cows for Sale to Calve
> (one time up) and the other on
> 1st August. Both young Cows
> and grand quality. Apply to
> Gilbert Meikle, Farmer, Fernieflat.

The greatest section of the second issue of the *Juniper Green Observer* was devoted to a report on the Grand Bazaar opened by Mr Erskine Scott of Woodhall and held in the Public School on 27th and 28th July 1888. The inner part of the school was given over to stalls presided over by Mrs Erskine Scott, Mrs Brown of Mount Pleasant, and Miss Wood of Claremont Cottage, and the outer part to Miss Corstorphine of Woodhall Mills, Miss Scott of Mossie Mill and Mrs Jameson of Spylaw Bank. And who better to display every refinement in farm produce in the open air than the wife of Gilbert Meikle?

In 1966 The Scottish Women's Rural Institute produced a *Village History Book* in which they included reference to many of the social activities and organisations associated with Juniper Green. Many of these were founded in the nineteenth century and continue to the present day. One of the oldest was the Literary Society which offered a full syllabus over the winter session. A clock made by Robert Watt of Watt's Snuff Mill on the Water of Leith was gifted by the Society to the village school and bore the inscription: 'Presented to the Free Church School by the Juniper Green Lecture Committee 4th April 1856'. As well as the Area Headquarters for the British Legion there are two Friendly Societies, the Ancient Order of Foresters established in 1875 and the Pentland Lodge of the Loyal Order of Ancient Shepherds established in 1892. Sports and carnival meetings at Bloomiehall Park were always a feature of the annual calendar, greatly enhanced by the presence of one of the Juniper Green bands. The Colinton and Currie Pipe Band gave frequent displays as well as the brass bands and bugle bands of the 59th Boys' Brigade Company, affiliated to the United Free Church and later amalgamated with the 53rd Company at Colinton.

Baberton Golf Clubhouse designed in 1902 by J.N. Scott and A. Lorne Campbell and erected at a cost of £1620.
From *Views of Juniper Green and District*.

The *Village History Book* contains an interesting article on Colinton and Currie Pipe Band by Isobel Campbell whose grandfather was one of the founder members in 1887. The band's first informal meetings took place in the open at a bench seat at the top of Wester Hailes Road, but when a committee was formed, meetings were held at Bennet's pub at Curriemuirend. As with any other emerging band, lack of money and equipment was a serious problem, the original inventory extending to one chanter only. With assistance from the community, pipes and drums were acquired and practice nights were held in a hut behind the Kinleith Arms. Under the watchful eye, and ear, of Pipe Major William Thomson, young pipers learned to birl, strike and 'throw the D', before graduating to *The Banks of Allan Water* and *The Barren Rocks of Aden*. The band performed at all local events but was disbanded during the two World Wars. After the Second World War it was reconstituted by Pipe Major Andrew Thomson, a dance team was formed, and girls were admitted to the band for the first time. Pipe Major Thomson retired in 1958 but continued to assist in training the younger members until shortly before his death in 1971. Other Pipe Majors who led the band in competitive playing were Alexander Campbell, Robert Peat, James Dawson and John McKernon. Juniper Green's contribution to piping will always be heard far beyond the boundaries of the village: at the World Championships the first prize in Grade IV is the John Neill Memorial Shield presented to the Scottish Pipe Band Association in 1962 by the widow of John Neill, one of the founder members of the Colinton and Currie Pipe Band.

The activities which drew the greatest crowds were, of course, the traditional village galas. A Gala Day was originally organised by Juniper Green Co-operative Society which was taken over in 1916 by St. Cuthbert's Co-operative Association. The other great summer event was the Infirmary Pageant which began each year with prize judging opposite Juniper Green School. The Currie and Colinton Pipe Band led the procession by Belmont Road, Belmont Avenue (now Juniper Avenue) and Lanark Road to Currie and back to the village to regroup before marching to the Sixpenny Tree at Colinton. One of the leading attractions was Mr Wyllie's ponies from East Mill which took pride of place in the long line of bands, carts and marchers.

Baberton House; Baberton Golf Club

Baberton House lies in extensive wooded policies, flanked on two sides by Baberton Golf Course. Access from the south is by a long tree-lined avenue at the north end of Baberton Avenue. Well into the twentieth century this entrance was marked by high railings and gates adjoining a lodge house on the east side of the driveway. Baberton House can also be reached from the north side by a much shorter driveway, leading off the road between Baberton Mains and Whitelaw.

Baberton House, previously known as Kilbaberton, dates from at least 1622, although there is evidence that the vaulted ground-floor rooms may be of earlier date. It was built for James Murray, Master of the King's Works, on land granted to him by James VI. The 1622 double-L plan of three storeys created a south-facing courtyard with stair turrets built into the two angles. Although the basic structure was harled rubble, there were many fine architectural features incorporated on the windows, door and chinmeys. The most significant alteration to the house was in 1765 when the courtyard was filled in by a semi-octagonal bay, projecting to the south.

The 1765 bay appears on a map of uncertain date produced in connection with a legal dispute over a small area of ground on the south side of the estate. As the map bears the title 'Baberton Plans taken from the plan drawn by Mr Mather in 1755', it seems likely that

Woodhall House to the south of Juniper Green, built around 1630 for Lord Woodhall, and at one time the home of the Bannatyne Manuscript of medieval Scottish poetry.

the information needed for the legal dispute has merely been superimposed on Mr Mather's map of 1755. Nevertheless, the topographical information is interesting. No trees are shown on the north or south driveway, although there are numerous trees shown, forming the boundary with Mr Carmichael's ground to the east. On the west side of the estate, going north, is 'Road to Hermiston on the Glasgow Road', and, going south, 'Road to Currie o ı the Sclatefoord Road'. On the east side of the estate is a road following approximately the line of the old Wester Hailes Road past Fernieflat. It is described, going north, as 'Road to Edinburgh' and, going south, as 'Road to Coalington by the Sclatefoord Road'. The long narrow piece of land in dispute, wedged between the east boundary of Baberton and the west boundary of Mr Carmichael's land, is rather quaintly described as 'Gushet in Dispute'.

Although the outcome of the dispute is not recorded, there is little doubt about the purpose of the survey undertaken on the north side of the estate in 1847, by George Buchanan, Civil Engineer. He was employed by the Caledonian Railway Company to draw plans and sections for proposed alterations to the 'Parish Road and Approach to

Baberton House' by the crossing of the Caledonian Railway. The Parish Road ran straight from north-east to south-west, and the proposed railway line was also to run in the same direction, but nearer to a west-east axis. To facilitate the crossover, the roadway was excavated to a depth where it could turn under the new railway bridge in an awkward S-bend. On completion, the railway completely dissected the Baberton estate, separating the farm buildings of Baberton Mains on the north side of the Parish Road from Baberton House on the south side.

To this day the awkward S-bend must be negotiated in approaching Baberton House from the north. The north entrance is less impressive now but leads up the tarmac drive to imposing double gates set into a walled courtyard adjacent to the caretaker's house. Baberton House, the headquarters of Cruden Investments Ltd since 1980, is maintained in excellent condition in well-tended policies of several acres. Despite its three centuries of use many of the original features can be observed without difficulty. On the south-facing walls of the original house, a window pediment on the east flank bears the date 1622 and the initials I.M. for James Murray. A similar window on the west flank bears the initials K.W. for Katherine Weir, wife of James Murray. The north facade contains three interesting half-dormer windows: the centre one has the date 1623; the eastmost bears the initials IM; and the westmost appears to be blank. The elegant semi-octagonal bay to the south contains some of the principal rooms of the house, dating from 1765. This date appears above the doorway and below an octagonal-shaped crest, divided diagonally by a serrated cross with a five-point star in each of the segments.

At the close of the nineteenth century Baberton Estate was owned by Sir James Gibson Craig, Bart., who leased part of the land in 1893 for the construction of Baberton Golf Course. The original nine-hole course was designed by Willie Park, but within a very short time it was extended to eighteen holes. Membership was initially restricted to residents of the parishes of Colinton and Currie, but when the course was extended, the opportunity was taken to admit a limited number of non-resident members. The non-resident membership rapidly increased to three hundred, far outnumbering the local membership, which remained fairly constant at around a hundred. In recognition of their increased numbers, non-resident members were given representation on the Committee. Baberton can claim to be the birthplace of the

The changing face of transport at Juniper Green, as buses queue outside the Railway Inn, 1987.
Photograph by Phyllis Margaret Cant.

steel-shafted golf club, a patent application being taken out on 1st May 1894 by Thomas Horsburgh who was later captain of the club from 1914 to 1917 and again from 1929 to 1931.

The original clubhouse, designed in 1902 by J.N. Scott and A. Lorne Campbell, was erected at a cost of £1,620 and has been enlarged on numerous occasions. The Jubilee celebrations, scheduled to take place in 1943, were postponed until 8th June 1946 when plaques were unveiled in memory of the members who had fallen in the Second World War, and to commemorate the Jubilee. Shortly after the Jubilee the club suffered severely from an extensive fire on 22nd March 1948 which destroyed the dining room and the ladies' room.

In the post-war years Baberton has steadily built up its membership and has improved the playing surface out of all recognition from the first nine-hole course, hemmed in by menacing rough and formidable hazards. At a height of four hundred feet above sea level, and commanding interesting views of the Forth and Arthur's Seat, Baberton Golf Club maintains great sporting traditions, albeit somewhat more refined than in the days when Baberton was used as a hunting estate for James VI and his entourage.

Woodhall House

Woodhall House, on the south side of Juniper Green, was built around 1630 and is almost as old as its counterpart, Baberton House, on the north side. It was built for Adam Cunninghame, Lord Woodhall, whose family retained ownership until the early eighteenth century when John Cunninghame of Enterkin sold the estate to the Foulis family of Colinton. The original house was greatly enhanced around 1820 by the addition of decorative stonework over the windows, and a new buttressed central tower containing a rib-vaulted porch. A later Georgian wing was added on the north side, and in 1960 a large stone-fronted addition, containing a chapel, was erected on the east side by the Society of Jesus. After the Jesuits sold the property, it was developed as individual flats, retaining the exterior stonework and some of the interior.

At the present day, Woodhall House is approached from Woodhall Road, Colinton, under the Bypass which crosses the Water of Leith. Many years ago Woodhall's association with Juniper Green was very much stronger than with Colinton, when the principal entrance was down the steep slope at Enterkin's Yett on Lanark Road. Woodhall Dower House, built in the eighteenth century, was also on Lanark Road and was used at one time as St. Margaret's Manse. The Dower House is now in private occupation at 547 Lanark Road.

Woodhall was once the home of the famous Bannatyne Manuscript, a unique two-volume collection of medieval Scottish poems now in the National Library of Scotland. The Manuscript was written in 1568 by George Bannatyne, a young Edinburgh merchant. When the business community in Edinburgh came to a standstill that year following an outbreak of plague, Bannatyne occupied himself by bringing together examples of Scottish poetry of all kinds—religious, moral, love and fables. The collection of about four hundred poems by about forty authors represents a major source of fifteenth and sixteenth-century Scottish verse. Nine poems by William Dunbar are found nowhere else, and for a further twenty-seven poems the Manuscript provides the best text. There are six short poems by Robert Henryson and an important text of ten of the fables.

The Manuscript passed to Bannatyne's daughter Janet and her husband George Foulis of Woodhall and Ravelston. Their great-grandson, William Foulis, gave it to William Carmichael of Skirling in 1712, and his son the fourth Earl of Hyndford presented it in 1772 to the Advocates' Library, predecessors of the National Library of Scotland. It was used extensively in the eighteenth century by Allan Ramsay, Lord Hailes and others who revived interest in the older poetry, and the name Bannatyne was adopted by the Club founded by Sir Walter Scott to reissue Scottish literature and history. The Manuscript has been published by the Scottish Text Society in four volumes, 1928 to 1934, edited by W. Tod Ritchie, and a facsimile of it was produced by the Scolar Press in 1980 edited by Denton Fox and W.A. Ringler.

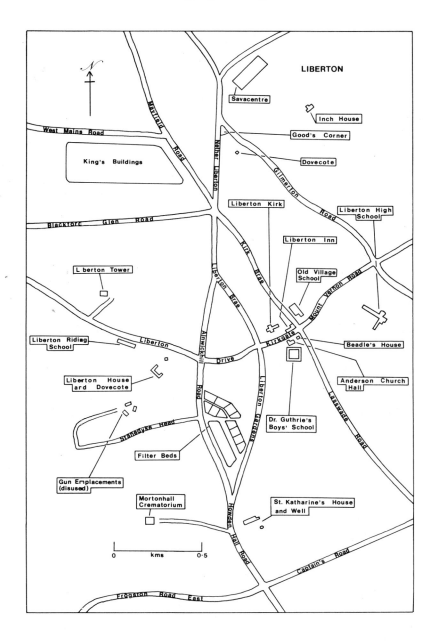

N

LIBERTON

Savacentre

Inch House

West Mains Road

Good's Corner

King's Buildings

Mayfield Road

Nether Liberton

Dovecote

Gilmerton Road

Liberton Kirk

Liberton High School

Blackford Glen Road

Liberton Inn

Kirk Brae

Liberton Tower

Old Village School

Liberton Brae

Mount Vernon Road

Liberton Riding School

Liberton Drive

Alnwickhill Road

Kirkgate

Beadle's House

Liberton House and Dovecote

Anderson Church Hall

Stanedyke Head

Filter Beds

Liberton Gardens

Dr. Guthrie's Boys' School

Lasswade Road

Gun Emplacements (disused)

Mortonhall Crematorium

St. Katharine's House and Well

Howden Hall Road

0   kms   0·5

Captain's Road

Frogston Road East

CHAPTER 5

Liberton

Liberton is perhaps one of the most elusive villages on the south side of Edinburgh in that it is possible, even today, to identify four separate communities with Liberton as part of the name. The most important, by position and reputation, is Kirk Liberton, which grew up around the old church at the head of Kirk Brae. Half a mile to the west, Over Liberton or Upper Liberton came into prominence through the Littles of Liberton who resided, firstly, in the defensive Liberton Tower, and later in the much more elegant Liberton House. Two other communities to the north complete the group: Liberton Dams nestles at the foot of Liberton Brae, and Nether Liberton is clustered around the junction of Gilmerton Road and Craigmillar Park. All four, although distinct within themselves, came within the parish of Liberton and have in many ways developed along similar lines. The way that development has taken place is what makes Liberton historically interesting.

The origin of the name Liberton is beset with problems. The most prevalent theory, supported by several eminent writers, is that it is a corruption of Leperton or Lepertown, from a hospital for lepers which is said to have stood in the district. Support for the theory comes from the name Spittleton which was applied to part of the parish in the seventeenth century. *The Concise Scots Dictionary* defines spital as a charity hospital or hospice or shelter for travellers. Two factors contradict the theory. The first objection is that no trace has ever been found of a hospital in the district which admitted people suffering from leprosy. The second objection is perhaps even more convincing: the name Liberton or Libberton, as a surname, existed in the district of Liberton more than a hundred years before known outbreaks of the disease in Edinburgh. It has to be admitted that the etymology of the name is uncertain, although the Rev. Campbell Ferenbach, in *Annals of Liberton*, gives a comprehensive review of six separate possibilities.

Kirk Liberton

Kirk Liberton, as the name suggests, is that part of the parish of Liberton situated around the old church. In this small area all the

113

main elements of village life were located. Even today it is the focal point of the greatly enlarged suburb of Liberton.

The old approach to the village was by Kirk Brae to the crossroads at the junction of Lasswade Road, Mount Vernon Road and Kirkgate. The school and schoolhouse were in the building now owned by the Liberton Inn; the church and manse occupied a large area of ground to the north-west; and the village smiddy was on the north-east corner of Kirk Brae and Mount Vernon Road. Altogether it was a very compact community with most of the outlying district under cultivation. Although the layout of the village suggests a rural scene, the inhabitants were not ignorant of the benefits of commerce and education. Two early nineteenth-century reports make interesting reading.

The first was a Report of the Committee of the Heritors of the Parish of Liberton dated 16th March 1815 'to consider the establishment of a Bank for the savings of labourers, mechanics, servants etc, in the parish'. Andrew Wauchope of Niddry was appointed Governor, Henry Trotter of Mortonhall was the Deputy, and there were nine honorary directors and twelve ordinary directors appointed from the landowners and professional people of the district. The nearest office, at Gilmerton, was open in the summer months every Saturday from 7 p.m. to 8 p.m. and in the winter months every Saturday from 3 p.m. to 4 p.m. Interest was at the rate of four per cent, no deposits of less than one shilling were permitted and the money retained by the bank was deposited in an account with Sir William Forbes & Co. As local banks were almost unheard of in certain parts of the parish, the Committee felt obliged to give an explanation to the public of the anticipated advantages. The prospectus stated that a father could provide for his son entering into an apprenticeship or for the marriage of his daughter; a husband could provide for his widow; or a cottager could in time purchase a cow, a horse or a cart. To show the effects of accumulation, and to encourage depositors, it was pointed out that two shillings paid into the bank every week for twenty years amounted to £158 principal and interest.

The second report was an Address by the Members of the Libberton Library to the Working Classes of the Parish of Libberton in September 1833. Libberton library was formed on 15th February 1828 from a small sum paid by each of the founder members and donations from gentlemen in the neighbourhood. Its stock of three hundred volumes of approved works only in Divinity, History and Miscellaneous Literature could be lent out at the rate of six pence per book per

On 1st June 1929 car 349 ran out of control down Liberton Brae and
came to rest in the garden of number 40. Immediately after, two ladies,
completely uninjured, were seen to leave the tramcar remarking that that
was not their usual stop.
Courtesy of N.B. Traction Group Collection.

quarter. Books were located in the parish schoolhouse and were given
out every Friday from 7 p.m. to 8 p.m. The President, Robert
Denholme, and the Secretary, Andrew Kerr, put their signatures to
the final words of encouragement: 'as the winter season is commencing
you will have a great deal of leisure time which you cannot better
employ than in storing your minds with useful information'.

At the time of the *New Statistical Account*, written in 1839, the picture
painted by the Rev. James Begg was still one of a rural parish with
thirty-four farms varying in size from 40 to 268 acres, many of them
adopting a five-year crop rotation of potatoes, wheat, barley, grass and
oats. The Rev. Begg observed that most of the living accommodation
was abysmal with cottages on some farms in worse condition than the
stables. The latest invention was the steam threshing mill powered by a
six horse-power engine made by Douglas of Edinburgh. It was capable
of dealing with sixty bushels of grain per hour but needed back-up
labour of nine women, six men, and two horses and carts to keep it fed,
and to clear away the grain and straw. Despite the condition of the

housing Begg was able to say that there had been a vast improvement in the state of the parish since the Rev. Whyte's account of 1792. That improvement obviously gathered momentum, enabling Grant in 1880 to quote: 'the parish itself has a thousand attractions, and is dressed out in neatness of enclosures, profusion of garden grounds, opulence of cultivation, elegance or tidiness of mansion, village and cottage, and busy stir and enterprise, which indicate full consciousness of the immediate vicinity of the proudest metropolis in Europe'. This consciousness of the metropolis was interpreted rather differently by Whyte nearly a century earlier when he said of Edinburgh's influence on Liberton that 'large cities never fail to corrupt and debauch the generality of the surrounding inhabitants'.

In the early part of the twentieth century the transformation of rural Liberton into a busy suburb was quite gradual up to the end of the Second World War. Prior to that, new building was largely confined to ribbon development on Liberton Brae, Alnwickhill Road, Lasswade Road and Kirk Brae. After 1945, however, the population grew rapidly when Edinburgh Corporation built large housing estates at the Inch, Gracemount and other localities.

Liberton Parish Church

The most recent authoritative account of Liberton Kirk is contained in *Annals of Liberton* by the Rev. Campbell Ferenbach, minister of the parish from 1942 to 1970. Ferenbach reviews the scant evidence of the church's early history, which can be traced back to the Great Charter of Holyrood in 1143 during the reign of David I. The inclusion of Liberton in the Charter suggests that there must have been a significant Christian presence in the area prior to 1143. This contention is supported, firstly, by the existence of two Celtic stone crosses found in the district, and secondly by Our Lady's Well, located until recently a few hundred yards to the east of the church. The Celtic crosses were removed to the Royal Museum of Scotland, in Queen Street, but the well was demolished, despite efforts to renovate it in 1948. Although the exact age of old Liberton Church is not known, there have been several useful descriptions of it over the years. The Rev. Thomas Whyte, writing in 1792, said:

The distinctive pinnacled tower of Liberton Parish Church, designed by James Gillespie Graham, and built in 1815 on the site of an earlier church.
Photograph by Phyllis Margaret Cant.

> The main entry to the church is on the south under a porch. The steeple at the west end makes a decent and venerable appearance. The spire or cupola was formerly of wood; in August 1744 it was struck by lightening (sic); it is now of stone. The bell here, as the inscription bears, was made by Henderson and Ormiston 1747. It is far superior to any in the neighbouring country parishes; but not at all like the former. The former was heard at Soutra-hill no less than sixteen miles distant.

George Good reproduces in *Liberton in Ancient and Modern Times* the results of research and sketches by the architect Andrew Kerr and others. From the sketches it is possible to establish the layout of the interior of the church with its numerous additions and alterations made by the great landowning families of the district. The whole interior was taken up by a series of aisles and galleries arranged around the main body of the church. The north wall contained three sections: ground-floor seats for Thomas Rigg of Morton and a gallery above for Lord Somerville of Drum; seats and a family burying-place for the Craigmillars but no gallery; and a ground-floor family burying place for Baird of Newbyth with seats for tenants in front and family seats and a retiring room in the gallery above. The south wall contained two sections only: ground-floor seats for Stainhouse with a gallery for the Gilmerton colliers; and a burying place for Gavin Nisbet of Muirhouse. The east and west walls contained the Niddry gallery and the Mortonhall gallery respectively, with the pulpit placed in the centre of the south wall between Stainhouse and Nisbet. This interesting old building reached the end of its useful lifetime in 1814 when it was demolished owing to damage by fire and the effects of old age.

The new church was built in 1815 exactly on the site of the old one. It has been described, rather unkindly, as a rectangular semi-Gothic box, a description which hardly does justice to the work of its eminent architect, James Gillespie Graham. The very distinctive west tower with its corbelled parapet and four slender pinnacles is a prominent landmark seen from several viewpoints. The main body of the church is rectangular but its symmetrical walls are interrupted by gracious windows and several doorways.

The foundation stone of the church was laid on 27th January 1815 in the presence of the minister, the Rev. James Grant, the heritors and many of the parishioners. Coins of George III, a newspaper and the *Scots Almanack* for 1815 were deposited in a special urn laid beside the foundation stone on the south-east corner of the site. Alex Peacock, a resident of the parish and Proxy-Master to the Grand Lodge from Cambuslang Royal Arch, laid the stone, testing its position for accuracy with a square, plumb line and level. When he was satisfied that the stone was correctly positioned he gave it three distinct knocks with a mallet, stood up on top of it and addressed the crowd at great length. The Rev. Campbell Ferenbach rightly observes that although the ceremony for laying the foundation stone was given great publicity, no equivalent notice was taken of the opening and dedication of the new church. Despite research over the years by various members of the parish, no report has been traced confirming the official opening date.

Although the exterior of the church remains unaltered from Gillespie Graham's original work, the interior has been rearranged on more than one occasion. In 1882 the original plan for 1480 sittings was considered to be much more than was required. The opportunity was therefore taken to reduce the size of the gallery which extended round three sides of the church and spoiled its appearance. George Good was not entirely happy with the result but he thought it was better than the old gallery which he said 'projected too far, and was besides, flat, dark, and too near the roof, which gave it an uncomfortable appearance,

The village school built in 1873 by Liberton School Board and given a second storey in 1898. As Liberton Primary School it closed on 2nd July 1965 but is now used as a nursery school by Lothian Regional Council. Photograph by Phyllis Margaret Cant.

and prevented the people from seeing and hearing with advantage'. On completion of the 1882 works, the church had sittings for one thousand which was reduced to nine hundred in 1958, when more space was created in front of the communion table for baptisms and marriages. The pulpit has been retained on the south wall. Two very different memorials honour previous ministers: on the west wall an ornate group in stone commemorates the Rev. William Purdie whose 'short but eminently useful ministry' was from 26th January 1832 until his death on 16th November 1834; and on the east wall a small bronze plaque commemorates the Rev. John Spence Ewen D.D., minister of Liberton Kirk from 1928 to 1941. The Baird Vault on the north-east corner is accessible and contains several ornate marble stones to various members of the Baird family. The grandest stone has a lengthy inscription in Latin, beside which is a smaller stone to Sir David Inglis Bart., of Newbyth, who died on 7th January 1852.

When Liberton Church was built, pipe organs were unheard of. It was not until 1884 that the idea of a harmonium was mooted, but following various objections it was not installed until more than a year later, and even then only to be used at the evening services. It was not until 9th January 1890 that full agreement was reached to use the harmonium at all services. Seventeen years later, on 11th March 1907, the same problem arose again when it was suggested that a pipe organ be installed. Opposition delayed the 'yes' vote until April 1914, by which time the First World War put an end to any such expenditure. Eventually an Ingram two-manual pedal organ was installed in 1930 and operated for more than forty years before being replaced in 1972 by a digital Allan organ.

Liberton is fortunate that the church halls, beadle's house and manse are all within a short distance of the church. On the south side of Kirkgate the Anderson Church Hall, with an imposing wheel window to the north, was erected in 1888 partly by public subscription and partly from a grant made by the Trustees of the late Miss Anderson of Moredun. An additional small hall was built in 1929 and a further hall was built in 1954 in response to the increased population in the district. The present beadle's house (previously the schoolmaster's house after the Mount Vernon Road School was built) on the south-west corner of Kirkgate and Lasswade Road was acquired in 1956 and named Kirk House. The original manse dates from before 1701 but shortly after the new Liberton Parish Church was built another manse was erected in 1821. This was a handsome square Georgian house situated in three and a half acres of ground to the north of the church. It was sold in 1960 for redevelopment along with most of the garden ground, and a new manse was built on the remaining piece of ground.

The old kirkyard which surrounds Liberton Parish Church has many examples of interesting old stones. On the outside of the south wall of the church is a Gothic memorial erected by the parishioners to the Rev. James Grant, minister of the parish from 1789 to 1831. It is enclosed by a small railing in front of which is a seat in memory of Eddie, Dorothy and Aileen Moir, 1978.

On the left-hand side of the path which leads from the kirkyard entrance to the bell tower two contrasting stones have only the family name in common. The first is a tiny plain stone with the epitaph 'A man is best known when he is dead', on one side, and 'Jas. Taylor' chiselled across the rounded top. Within a few yards of this modest gravestone is a ten-feet-high ornate pedimented stone to James Baxter Taylor of Gilmerton who died on 6th June 1737. A central family

The pipe band at Dr Guthrie's Boys' School in Lasswade Road, opened in 1888 and closed just short of its centenary.
From Speedy's *Craigmillar and its Environs*.

inscription is flanked by Corinthian pillars sitting on pedestals which incorporate a scythe, skull and hour glass. The pedimented top contains a monogram in the tympanum, flanked by angels.

The west wall also contains some interesting stones set into the boundary masonry. One has angels along the top side and a deeply recessed stone beneath, now devoid of any inscription, to the north of which is a wall stone with a finialled mantleshelf to Robert Bryden, Portioner in Greenend 1.4.1819. On the same wall a tall pedimented and pillared tomb marks the grave of John Nicol who died on 17.3.1765, and his wife Helen. The mason has made a neat job of cutting a pointed hand at the top of the inscription but has transposed the letter 'N' in the name Helen despite using the more orthodox style on numerous other parts of the stone. Perhaps the most interesting tomb lies midway between the west boundary wall and the west door to the bell tower. It is a table tomb to William Stratton of Tower Farm 1754, whose effigy reposes beneath the tablestone. Elaborate detail includes a panel on the west side depicting ploughing, raking and sowing.

Between the north wall of the church and the manse there are some smaller and more recent stones. A small dark stone was erected by

Gilbert Elliot, servant to Mr Hume of St. Katherine's, to the memory of his children, beside which is a larger white stone in memory of James Priestly, gamekeeper for fourteen years on Craigmillar Estate, died 18th April 1868. On the east wall the arrangement of stones is similar to the west wall. No one here could fail to see KELLY in large bold lettering on a white slab for Thomas Johnstone Kelly, schoolmaster of Liberton, who died on 9th December 1876. Nearby lies Robert Stevenson, Surgeon, of Gilmerton, the Founder and President of Gilmerton Library, 21.5.1815.

Schools

One of the earliest references to education in the village is contained in the Rev. Thomas Whyte's account of Liberton in 1792. The schoolmaster's salary was two hundred merks ($\pounds$11.11p), with forty merks extra for being session clerk and twenty-five merks from the lands of Moredun. In addition to his salary, the schoolmaster had the benefit of a free house but he was also obliged to teach, *gratis*, the poor children of the district. Although Whyte does not describe the actual school, it is known to have been the building on the corner of Kirk Brae and Kirkgate presently occupied by the Liberton Inn, the annexe of which is named after Reuben Butler, the schoolmaster in Scott's *Heart of Midlothian*.

Log books from 1873 for Liberton Public School provide a detailed account of the administration of the school under the control of Liberton School Board. At the beginning of term on 26th September 1873 forty-eight pupils enrolled at a single-storey school building in Mount Vernon Road, which contained one schoolroom and two classrooms. There was ample accommodation when the school first opened but it was necessary to build a new infant room in 1879 and another classroom in 1886. Although school log book entries should not be read in isolation, they do illustrate the problems and attitudes of the day as seen through the eyes of the headmaster: 'in 1873 two boys have begun the study of Latin but I am afraid neither of them will ever make much of it; 22nd January 1874 tomorrow being the marriage day of the Duke of Edinburgh and as we are all loyal subjects we are to have a holiday in honour of the happy event; in 1884 a disease called 'Crystal-pox' (Chicken-pox) has broken out among the infants; in 1892 seven pupils died this year of scarlet fever'. Towards the close of the nineteenth century the accommodation problem was again acute with

The tall grey fortress of Liberton
Tower to the north of Liberton
Drive, probably built in the
fifteenth century, later the home of
the Littles of Liberton.
From Grant's *Old and New
Edinburgh*.

enrolment reaching two hundred and forty in 1896. Two years later
plans were drawn up to provide two additional classrooms by adding a
second storey to the existing building. With the minimum of administrative delay the school closed early for the summer holidays on 30th
June 1898 and nine weeks later the pupils returned to a two-storey
village school. The logs also provide interesting comment on the
domestic effects of national crises. With almost two years of the First
World War still to run the headmaster noted with obvious emotion
that Miss Tait was to be married to Captain McHardy as he was about
to proceed to the Front: and with less tolerance he observed the other
side of human nature: 'this heavy absence [of pupils] is due to the
indolence, indifference and selfishness of parents and chiefly the
mothers to whom the spirit of sacrifice and duty does not yet appeal,
even in these days of stress'. In 1926, in the year of the General Strike,
nine children each received a pair of boots from St. Cuthbert's Co-
operative Association and two received boots from the School Fund.
The school operated throughout the Second World War without
serious mishap but on 22nd August 1960 no new infants were enrolled
as Liberton Primary School 'now begins to die out preparatory to a
final closing of this old village school'. By April 1961 the roll was down
to one hundred and fifty and on 28th May 1965 there was a Reunion of
Former Pupils. The log and the school closed on 2nd July 1965 with

the entry 'Today Liberton Primary School ceases to exist as such. It has always been a happy place with a family spirit and it is hoped that one day children's voices will once again be heard within its walls'.

At the present day, the old village school is used as a children's nursery under the control of Lothian Regional Council.

By contrast with the village school, Liberton Secondary School is but in its infancy, having been built in 1959 to designs by Rowand Anderson Kininmonth & Paul. It was opened by Her Royal Highness the Duchess of Kent at 11.15 a.m. on Thursday 14th May 1959. In the special opening ceremony brochure it is recorded by the first head-master, John A. Jack, that in 1947 the only schools in the area were the primary schools at Liberton and Gilmerton with fewer than four hundred pupils between them, whereas in 1959 there were eight schools and five thousand pupils. Liberton Secondary School, in-tended for one thousand pupils, was built with two long wings at right angles to each other, intersecting in the assembly and administrative areas. The north-west wing of four floors was designed for the practical classrooms, and the south-west wing of three floors contained eighteen ordinary classrooms.

Almost exactly ten years after the opening of the school, Liberton had the good fortune to receive a visit from Her Majesty The Queen. The Royal Visit took place on 28th May 1969 when the Queen was received at Liberton School by the Lord Provost. It was a day in which all aspects of the school curriculum were displayed to advantage by pupils of all ages. Naturally some disciplines lent themselves more easily to visual display than others: static displays of outdoor activities included orienteering and ski-ing; the Technical Department exhibit-ed its newly built Hovercraft; the Homecraft Department prepared a three-course meal for display but not consumption; and the Science Department took timing as their theme using oscilloscopes to record heart beats and auxanometers to record plant growth rates. The History Department, not wishing to be outmanoeuvred through apparent lack of action, announced that on the day of a Royal Visit they were not *doing* history, they were *making* history. After a display of singing, dancing and fencing by various classes, the Queen left to the strains of *Will Ye No Come Back Again*.

In the mid-1970s Liberton's roll reached 1600 but has gradually decreased to around 1000, and is estimated to fall to the optimum level of 750 by 1990. The staff at one time totalled one hundred and ten but

Horses and riders gather at Tower Farm Riding Stables in Liberton Drive.
Courtesy of Mrs Judy Forrest.

has been reduced to around seventy on account of the declining number of pupils. Over the years Liberton Secondary School has built up a strong reputation in each of the main disciplines, taking pupils from the feeder schools of Inch, Gilmerton, Moredun, Fernieside and Glenvarloch.

Dr Guthrie's Boys' School was also at Liberton on the west side of Lasswade Road. The plain Gothic building in pink and red sandstone was designed in 1885 by Sydney Mitchell and opened in 1888, fifteen years after the death of its founder. Biographical notes on Dr Guthrie appear in the chapter on Gilmerton where the corresponding Girls' School was opened in 1904. Dr Guthrie was born in Brechin in 1803 but it was not until after the Disruption of 1843 that he set himself the task of improving the education and living standards of hundreds of children in and around the Cowgate in Edinburgh. His vision is usually traced to an event which occurred one day when he was strolling with a friend in Holyrood Park near St. Anthony's Well. The habit had grown up of young boys and girls congregating at the well where they offered to supply to any passer-by a cup of cool refreshing

spring water for a ha'penny. In conversation with the children Dr
Guthrie asked if they would go to school if they were also fed, to which
one young boy answered: 'Ay will I sir, and bring the haill land, too',
meaning of course the whole stair or tenement. Eventually a soup
kitchen was started in a basement room of Dr Guthrie's church of Free
St. John's, but it was necessary to make a specific plea to the public
before the idea gained ground. In the *First Plea for the Ragged Schools* Dr
Guthrie acknowledged the assistance of his contemporaries Dr Alison
and Dr Chalmers: 'They meet in our school room. Dr Alison comes in
with his bread—Dr Chalmers with his Bible: here is food for the
body—there for the soul'. The *Second Plea* contained statistical information in support of the original ideals: in 1851 the Ragged Schools
claimed over two hundred successes and a marked reduction in the
number of children in prison or openly begging in the streets.

The movement was given impetus by the Education Act of 1872 and
developed through the system of Approved Schools, replaced in 1969
by List D Schools.

Over Liberton

George Good, in *Liberton in Ancient and Modern Times*, describes the
barony of Upper or Over Liberton as extending 'from the Braid Burn
on the north to the boundary of the Mortonhall estate on the south,
and from the Braids on the west to a point beyond Liberton Church,
including what is called Lesley Park and that piece of ground which
belongs to the poor of the parish, on the east'. The old hamlet of Over
Liberton, as distinct from the barony, was never more than a handful
of houses and farm steadings, huddled around two principal buildings:
to the west stood the ancient, high-walled fortress of Liberton Tower;
and to the east, at the end of a long tree-lined avenue, lay Liberton
House.

Although several writers at the end of the nineteenth century
include references to the district of Liberton, it is Tom Speedy and
George Good who provide the most comprehensive genealogy. According to these sources, the lands of Over Liberton were gifted by
David II (1324-71) to John Wigham, who later granted a charter in
favour of David Libertoun. In 1453 John Dalmahoy secured a charter
of part of the lands of Upper Liberton, but in the sixteenth century the
barony was gradually acquired by the Little family. In 1528 the
Dalmahoys granted a merk of land to Clement Little, burgess of

Corinthian columns support four female figures, emblems of Justice, Mercy, Peace and Love, erected in 1683 over the grave of William Little of Over Libertoun in Greyfriars Churchyard.
From *Epitaphs and Monumental Inscriptions in Greyfriars Churchyard.*

Edinburgh, and his wife Elizabeth Fisher, and in 1587 Alexander Dalmahoy sold another part of the land to William Little, whose descendants eventually acquired the whole barony.

The Littles were a strong and influential family who remained in possession of Upper Liberton for several centuries. Clement Little, who acquired the first interest in 1528, had two sons, Clement Little, the advocate, and William Little, merchant and later Lord Provost of Edinburgh. Clement, the advocate, was a man of considerable intellect, who gifted several hundred books to the Town to form the nucleus of a library for Edinburgh University. He died on 1st April 1580 and was buried in Greyfriars Churchyard. Less well known was his younger brother William Little, Lord Provost of Edinburgh from 1585 to 1587, and again in 1591. William died in 1601 and was buried beside his brother in Greyfriars. The family tomb may well have remained in relative obscurity but for the efforts of William Little's great grandson, who erected an imposing monument over the site of the grave in 1683 in memory of his great grandfather WILLIAM LITTLE OF OVER LIBERTOUN. This huge structure on the south wall of Greyfriars Churchyard, resembling a four-poster bed in stone, consists of ten Corinthian columns on chamfered pedestals, supporting a massive roof, on each corner of which is an elegant female figure looking out over the graveyard. Within the pillars, a serene recumbent effigy faces the churchyard exit, with not a hint of the seditious rumours which compelled James Brown to include a special note in the Appendix to *The Epitaphs and Monumental Inscriptions in Greyfriars Churchyard*:

> Little's Tomb, on the South Wall—An impression has got hold of the popular mind that the four female figures on the top of this tomb represent four daughters who poisoned their father, who is supposed to be the reclining figure in the centre of the tomb. We need scarcely add that this is pure fiction, without the least semblance of truth in it. The figures are emblems of Justice, Mercy, Peace and Love.

Margaret Warrender observed in 1895 that the barony of Upper Liberton was in the possession of a direct descendant of the Littles, namely Captain Gordon Gilmour of Craigmillar. During their long ownership the Littles resided, firstly, in the defensive Liberton Tower and, later, in the much grander Liberton House.

Liberton Tower

The tall grey fortress of Liberton Tower stands, surrounded by farm buildings of considerable antiquity, a few hundred yards north of Liberton Drive, almost opposite the private road leading to Meadowhead Farm. The Tower was probably built in the fifteenth century, but by whom, and in what year, is not known. Suffice it to say that one of the earliest families to reside there were the Dalmahoys, who eventually sold out to the Littles. Although the Tower is not open to the public an understanding of its construction and layout can be obtained from the excellent description given in the Edinburgh volume of *The Buildings of Scotland*.

The basic plan is a four-storey rectangular block thirty-five feet long, twenty-five feet wide, and rising forty-five feet to a pitched roof of stone slabs surrounded by a parapet walk. The construction is rubble with dressed stone confined to the windows, doors and corners. The Tower's horizontal division was into four floors but the wooden joists for two of these floors have now disappeared. For the purpose of this description, however, they are deemed to exist.

The basement (at ground level) has a restricted headroom of about six feet and is reached by a central doorway on the south wall, at some time enlarged so that its construction breaks through the line of the corbels which supported the first floor above. The use of the basement was probably confined to sheltering cattle. The first floor, constructed

Bringing in the harvest at Little Road with Liberton Gardens in the background, 1949.
Courtesy of Mr & Mrs Philp.

of timber resting on corbels, was probably also used for storage, and has a hatch cut in the ceiling to the main hall above. A stairway in the north-west corner, built into the thickness of the wall, leads past the barrel-vaulted roof to the main hall.

The residential accommodation is above the level of this barrel-vaulted roof. The main hall, the floor of which is at least fifteen feet above ground level, contains the main entrance on the east wall reached at one time by a temporary external stairway. The corbel, against which the staircase was built, is still in position. The hall has a long fireplace on the south wall, a garderobe in the north-east corner, and two staircases giving access to the top floor. The top floor was also used residentially and appears to have been divided into two compartments, as it has two fireplaces and two access staircases. Within the east staircase is a spy-hole giving a clear view of the main hall and the staircase coming up from the lower floor. The top floor is completed by a pointed tunnel vault which supports the heavy slabbed roof. The wallheads are quite plain, except for spout holes to carry rain water off the walkway, and rise flush with the walls without corbels or machicolations of any kind.

George Good surmised that there was probably a moat or ditch round the Tower and that the ground has been made up since. He records that two cannon balls were found when drains were being cut, and that when a well was being sunk, traces of a road were discovered eight feet below the surface.

Tower Farm Riding Stables lie on the south side of Liberton Drive within a few hundred yards of the bridle paths on the lower slopes of the Braid Hills. The buildings were originally a dairy, then a piggery, before being bought by Mrs Slessor in 1963, and converted to riding stables in 1971. The present proprietors, Mr & Mrs Forrest, members of the British Horse Society and the Association of British Riding Schools, have developed the business from fairly modest beginnings. A great deal of work was required on drainage, plumbing and the installation of electricity, resulting in well-equipped stables for about fifty animals. To the rear of the private accommodation there are two separate yards, one for ponies and horses belonging to the riding school, and the other for livery horses on behalf of clients in and around Edinburgh. This range of buildings also contains the tack room and a small shop.

Adjacent to Liberton Drive, an all-weather ménage has been constructed to provide facilities for a wide range of experience in the saddle. The most recent construction is a large covered building to the south, which provides excellent indoor facilities for teaching and exhibition purposes.

Liberton House

Liberton House lies at the end of an avenue of elm trees, a few hundred yards south of Liberton Drive. The entrance is marked by twin gate pillars, unusually close together, supporting tall ornamental iron gates bearing the letters LH in gold. The driveway leads past a seventeenth-century dovecot on the west side, and closes in a courtyard formed by two aspects of the main house and a two-storey addition built slightly later as the servants' quarters.

The exact age of Liberton House is uncertain although the best informed opinion places it in the late sixteenth century. It was built for the Littles of Liberton who were previously resident in the much plainer Liberton Tower. During its four centuries the house has been altered on numerous occasions, so that its layout is now rather confusing. Its L-plan has three storeys in the main block and four storeys on the wing, with a round stair tower formed within the angle,

The lintel stone with the date 1563 on the Balm Well of St Katherine in Howden Hall Road.
From *Fothergill's Stones and Curiosities of Edinburgh and Neighbourhood*.

and corbelled out to become square-shaped at the second floor. The numerous windows are generally small and there are gun loops overlooking the principal entrance although this was enclosed by a stone porch about 1840. Extensive restoration work was done around 1890 by the tenant Godfrey Cunninghame, Advocate, and in 1936 Rowand Anderson, Paul and Partners restored the wallhead with late seventeenth-century style dormers after removing a Georgian top floor.

Like many similar dwellings, Liberton House has several date stones which enhance its appearance but confound the historian. On the south-east corner there is an angle dial, round the top of which is the motto: AS.THE.SVNE.RVNS. SO.DEATH.COMES. Above the dial is a carved scroll containing the arms of the Littles, the initials WL for William Little, and the date 1683, this being the year when the commemorative tomb was erected in Greyfriars Churchyard. The most intriguing stone, however, is older than the house itself and has been re-sited over a doorway in the two-storey west extension. This lintel stone, bearing the inscription WILLIAME—1570—LITIL, prompted the authors of the Edinburgh volume of *Buildings of Scotland* to question where the stone had come from. As the lintel stone is positioned immediately below a much larger square, moulded stone with the initials WL, the answer may well be contained in an interesting account given by Wilson in *Memorials of Edinburgh in the Olden Times*. At page 220 of Volume 1 Wilson says: 'On the east side of an open court, immediately beyond the Roman Eagle Hall (in the Cowgate) stood the ancient mansion of the Littles of Craigmillar, bearing on a large moulded and deeply recessed stone panel the name of one of the old city worthies: WILLIAME—1570—LITIL'.

The dovecot at Liberton House is rectangular with a lean-to roof of slate, walls of stone covered with harling, and crowstepped gables. It measures approximately twenty-two feet by twenty feet and is entered by a door in the centre of the south wall above which is a circular light. The birds enter by two rows of ten holes in a shallow dormer window in the slated roof. The interior, which is still in excellent condition, has twenty-four tiers on the high north wall, and a reducing number on the sloping east and west walls, providing more than a thousand nesting places. Despite active encouragement from the present owner, however, the birds will not nest: indeed it is said that for some unknown reason no living creature has adopted this warm dry south-facing habitat.

No respectable Scottish house of comparable antiquity is without its ghost, and Liberton House is no exception. An apparition is said to have appeared on numerous occasions over the years in a variety of forms, one of which was reproduced in *The Scotsman* on 17th June 1936 along with a letter from David Hunter Blair who possessed the original photograph taken at Liberton House in which 'a large and extraordinarily sinister human face appeared with handsome features and a smile as enigmatic as that of Mona Lisa'. The original has not been traced but the newspaper reproduction, with its consequent reduction in quality, is disappointing. Tradition has it that the ghost has appeared in at least three different guises: Pierre, a French nobleman, with a propensity to startle the occupants by whistling when least expected, especially near the dovecot; a female member of the Little family who was imprisoned in Edinburgh for assisting the Covenanters; and a Cavalier in costume and headgear of the seventeenth century, believed to be the one whose photograph appeared in *The Scotsman*.

On the opposite side of the driveway from the dovecot, enjoying a warm southerly aspect, there is a bee wall not unlike that which existed until recently at Ferrybank in Corstorphine. The rubble wall has four or five recesses (now built up) in which the hives were situated.

Good's Corner at the junction of Nether Liberton and Gilmerton Road,
for long occupied as a sawmill and joiner's shop by the Good family.
From Speedy's *Craigmillar and its Environs*.

Alnwickhill

On the west side of Alnwickhill Road, at its highest point, a modern
two-storey building is the Headquarters of 230 Squadron, Royal
Corps of Transport. The more dominant stone building to the north at
Stanedykehead was the Edinburgh Industrial Home for Fallen Wo-
men, built in 1891 on the site of an earlier asylum for the mentally ill.
Some years ago the building was divided into flats for residential use.

To the east, several acres of land bounded by Alnwickhill Road,
Liberton Gardens and Liberton Drive house the filter beds for the
public supply of water to the east side of Edinburgh. This extensive
arrangement of reservoirs and filter beds operates on a simple gravity
system without the need for electrically driven pumps. Water reaches
the main reservoir of twenty million gallons from the Tala, Crawley
and Moorfoot pipes and then falls by gravity to each of the twelve slow
sand filter beds, before entering the two clearwater storage tanks of five
million gallons each. There is also an additional outflow on the main
reservoir which can be used as an overflow, or to empty the reservoir in
the event of its becoming contaminated accidentally. In typically
Victorian style the various dates and the names of the people involved
in the construction of the scheme are listed on two ornate plaques on
each side of the front door of the Clear Water Tank House, built of
good quality stone in the style of a small classical temple with a stone
flagged roof:

EDINBURGH
AND DISTRICT
WATER WORKS

SCHEME PROJECTED	1873	JAMES GOWAN
ACT OBTAINED	1874	LORD PROVOST
WORKS COMMENCED	1875	NOV 1872 TO MARCH 1874
WORKS OPENED	1879	SIR JAMES FALSHAW BART.
SCHEME COMPLETED	1885	LORD PROVOST
J & A LESLIE		MARCH 1874 TO NOV 1877
ENGINEERS		SIR THOMAS J. BOYD KT.
		LORD PROVOST
		NOV 1877 TO NOV 1881
		W H CAMERON
		TREASURER

Within a few hundred yards of the filter beds a much more ancient source of water, believed to have had medicinal properties, can be found at the Balm Well of St. Katherine. In relation to modern street names the well is within the garden ground of St. Katherine's on the east side of Howden Hall Road almost opposite the entrance to Mortonhall Crematorium.

The age of the well is uncertain but according to tradition it was established by St. Catherine of Alexandria who brought the precious oil from Mount Sinai to Scotland, some of which now floats on the surface of the water. The better opinion is that the black tarry substance on the water is produced from the bituminous shale beds found at Burdiehouse and Straiton. Whatever its origin, it has been commented upon by several eminent writers over the years and has benefited from Royal patronage on more than one occasion. In 1504 James IV made an offering to 'Sanct Katrine's of the oly well' and in 1617 James VI ordered 'that it should be built with stones from the bottom to the top and that a door and a pair of steps be made for it that men might have the more easy access to the bottom to get the balm'. Unfortunately, the King's refurbishment was completely destroyed by Cromwell's troops in 1650. The Rev. Thomas Whyte remarked in 1792 that 'it was much frequented in ancient times, and considered as a sovereign remedy for several cutaneous distempers'. Perhaps the most comprehensive account of the well is contained in *Stones and Curiosities of Edinburgh and Neighbourhood* by Dr George A. Fothergill. The author's medical background compels him to point out 'that the corpulent, overfed hunting man, whose body may be subject to

The old iron mill wheel at Nether Liberton was in operation in the nineteenth century when the mill was owned by Andrew Dick. Photograph by Graham C. Cant.

eczema, is recommended by his physician to eat less and hunt more', rather than surrender his malady to the powers of the oily water:

> Some went to St. Katherine's Well
> That magical, wonderful well,
> To be rid of their bigness—
> Preternatural bigness—
> Their burden of beef—
> In the full belief
> They'd be quit of their sickness
> And return as sound as a bell.

After his humorous start Dr Fothergill goes on to review in depth the early references and to describe the lintel stone which bears the date 1563 and the initials A and P on either side of an unknown coat of arms. It has been suggested that the initials are of Preston of Craigmillar or Alexander de Pardouin of Newbattle.

At the present day the well is accessible but has lost much of its old-world charm. It is situated in the centre of an extensive lawn without protection and has been badly vandalised. Fortunately pieces of the ornamental masonry broken from the top of the well have been retained and are to be repaired and re-set. The interior of the well is protected by a wire grille, and although the famous lintel stone is becoming very worn, the inscription 15 A.P. 63 can still be read. Several people visit the well every year: some come on account of its historical significance and others for spiritual and medicinal reasons.

The Balm Well is in the garden ground of St. Katherine's which is also vandalised and appears to face an uncertain future. It was designed by John Simpson for his own use and built by David Bell in 1806, but has been altered on several occasions since. The castellated north front probably belongs to the original plan with the south-facing rooms and new entrance hall added shortly thereafter. Towards the end of the nineteenth century the entrance was again moved, this time to a large single-storey extension at the west side. In 1914 a plain three-bay block was added on the east side.

Nether Liberton; Liberton Dams

George Good traces the origins of Nether Liberton to at least the year 1143. Although direct references are not numerous, *Charters and Documents relating to the City of Edinburgh 1143-1540* refers to an Indenture dated 29th November 1387 'between Adam Forester, Laird of Nether Liberton, and the Provost and the Community of Edinburgh on the one part and certain masons on the other in regard to building five chapels on the south side of the parish church of Edinburgh'. The population probably reached its peak in the late eighteenth century when there was a community of about three hundred persons. There was a village cross, a weekly market, a school, a schoolhouse, and a schoolmaster. The two main occupations were brewing and milling, both of which relied heavily upon the water of the Braid Burn. The *Edinburgh Advertiser* for 1789 includes an interesting advertisement for the lease of the brewery: 'To let immediately that Brewery at Nether Liberton, Malt Barns etc, containing every requisite for carrying on the business of Brewing and Distilling, having an easy and complete supply of running Water which comes in above the Work: the present Utensils, which are in good repair, may be had by agreement'. The mill building, which is still extant with an iron wheel on its south wall, was operated in the nineteenth century by Andrew Dick. Perhaps the part of Nether Liberton best known to travellers going out of Edinburgh is Good's Corner at the junction of Gilmerton Road and the road to Liberton Dams. For many years the old buildings were used as a sawmill and joiner's shop by the Good family.

The Nether Liberton doocot, dating from the fifteenth or sixteenth century, is believed to be the largest in Edinburgh with more than two thousand nesting boxes.
Photograph by Phyllis Margaret Cant.

On Gilmerton Road, a few hundred yards south of Good's Corner, is Nether Liberton dovecot dating from the fifteenth or sixteenth century. It was probably built by the proprietors of Inch House now on the east side of the main road. The dovecot is believed to be the largest in Edinburgh, measuring 36′ 9″ long and 19′ 6″ wide. It is built on the lean-to, or lectern, principle, with two main chambers, each with its own heavily protected doorway. There is a single string course about ten feet above ground level, crow-stepped gables, and a square recess in the front wall which may at one time have contained a family coat of arms. The roof is slightly unusual in that it is built in two stages separated by a row of thirty-six pigeon holes. In addition to the roof holes the birds are able to enter by five holes in each chamber located below the eaves. All the internal walls have nesting boxes totalling two thousand and seventy-two.

Inch House, now a Community Centre, lies to the east of Gilmerton Road. As the name suggests, it may at one time have been surrounded by water and reached by a drawbridge. History records several

Pedestrians and cyclists take the most direct route up Liberton Brae, apparently in comparative safety, c.1908.
Courtesy of N.B. Traction Group Collection.

occasions when deep flooding surrounded the old house, notably in 1760 and 1870.

The earliest date on the house is 1617 when the property belonged to James Winram whose descendant George Winram became a Lord of Session in 1649, taking the title Lord Liberton. Originally the house was L-shaped in plan, three storeys and attic in height with a square five-storey stair turret in the angle. James Winram added a two-storey extension to the north in 1634, and in 1660 the house was acquired by the Gilmours of Craigmillar. Although the Gilmours owned the property from 1660, they do not appear to have taken up residence there until the late eighteenth century when they added a west wing. Extensive external and internal renovations were done in 1891 under the supervision of the architects MacGibbon & Ross. At that time a sundial dated 1660 brought from Craigmillar was also restored.

Laurie's Map of 1766 shows Liberton Dams between Mayfield Road and Kirk Brae on the main route out of Edinburgh from Causewayside to Liberton. Liberton Brae and Craigmillar Park were not constructed until the road improvements of 1815, referred to on a stone built into a bridge across the Braid Burn adjacent to the garden of 17 Gordon Terrace. The inscription contains some unusual spelling:

138

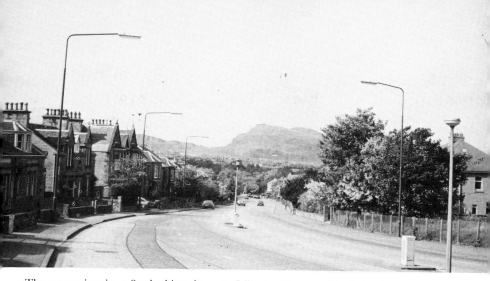

The same view in 1987, looking down to Liberton Dams, with Arthur's Seat in the background.
Photograph by Phyllis Margaret Cant.

> This improved access to
> the City of Edinburgh
> extending from Libberton
> Daams to Newington was
> executed by the trustees of
> the Laswade district
> Anno 1815

The Dams was the smallest of the four Liberton communities but was still large enough to have a school and mission hall up until 1890. There was also a large dairy owned by the Laidlaw family on the triangular piece of ground on the corner of Mayfield Road and Craigmillar Park. The deep hollow at the foot of Liberton Brae was bridged by an artificial embankment to carry the Crawley water pipes laid in 1822. Prior to that, in 1788, raising water at Liberton Dams required the very latest machinery. The *Edinburgh Advertiser* stated that 'An engine to raise water from Braid's Burn to the city pipes was employed, and has been most successful. Eighteen or twenty men have been constantly engaged, and the engine raises every day upwards of a hundred Scots pints or four hundred English pints per minute. This has given great relief to the inhabitants since it was adopted'. A photograph reproduced in *The Print of His Shoe* by James Goodfellow, the missionary, shows Liberton Dams in the early 1900s. There are no

139

villas built at the south end of Mayfield Road but among the old houses on the west side, opposite Laidlaw's Dairy, is a small general shop reached by a tiny stone bridge across the mill lade returning to the Braid Burn.

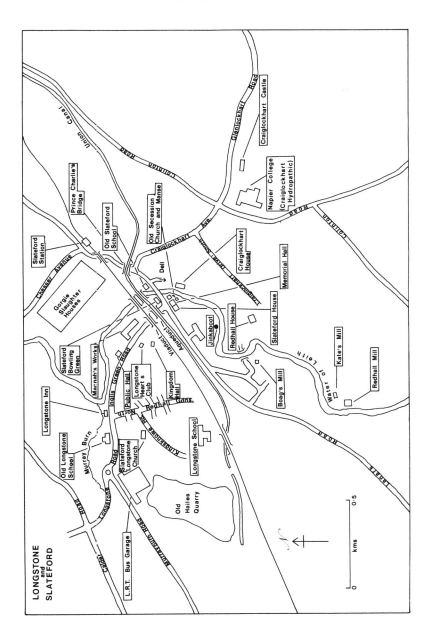

LONGSTONE and SLATEFORD

CHAPTER 6

Longstone; Slateford

Longstone and Slateford lie within a few hundred yards of one another in the shallow-sided valley of the Water of Leith. The two villages grew up at different times for economic and topographical reasons which do not now have the same impact on the community. Whilst pockets of independence may yet exist, for the most part the villages remain separate in name only. For several years now the school and the church have drawn their numbers from both areas, without detriment to either. Perhaps the greatest influence in breaking down any remaining barrier has been the influx of population in the peripheral housing estates, the inhabitants of which have not generally felt the need for specific affinity to one village or the other. The result is a community spirit based on a way of life far removed from the origins of either Slateford or Longstone, yet conscious of the long history of both.

Slateford, as the name implies, grew up around the ford slightly upstream from the bridge which now carries Lanark Road over the Water of Leith. In the upper valley, several mills thrived on the good supply of water used for milling paper, corn, barley, snuff and spices, as early as the sixteenth century. Other mills were located on the lower reaches of the Water of Leith near the Murray Burn tributary at Longstone. It is said that Longstone derives its name from a long stone which was once used as a bridge for crossing the Water of Leith, but there is doubt about its exact identity. Another suggestion is that the long stone refers to a large section of stone cut in one piece from Hailes Quarry, which is known to have been operating at least as early as the eighteenth century.

Over the years, road, rail and water transport has converged on Longstone and Slateford as the most convenient point at which to cross the Water of Leith. In 1818 the Union Canal was carried across the valley on a series of elegant stone arches, and in 1847 the railway followed the same line, but at a slightly lower level. The main road through Slateford has also been widened on several occasions in the past, the last of which almost completely destroyed what remained of the old village street.

The Union Canal

Towards the end of the eighteenth century several speculative reports had been compiled on the possibility of linking Edinburgh and Glasgow by a ship canal suitable for freight and passenger services. At a meeting of interested parties in Edinburgh in January 1793, John Ainslie and Robert Whitworth were appointed to make the necessary survey. Four separate routes were suggested to which John Rennie, the bridge engineer, added a fifth, to the north of the others. Some years later, amid growing speculation as to the commercial viability of the scheme, Hugh Baird was commissioned to draw up another report with the assistance of Francis Hall, the surveyor. The result was a lengthy *Report on the Proposed Edinburgh and Glasgow Union Canal* dated 20th September 1813 in which Baird explained the line of the canal, the technical difficulties, the anticipated objections and, most importantly, the estimated costs and expected revenues.

Baird proposed a contour canal, without locks, from Lothian Road in Edinburgh to join the Forth and Clyde Canal at Falkirk, a distance of twenty-eight miles, being only four miles more than the turnpike road. To accommodate boats up to thirty tons the canal required to be five feet deep, twenty feet wide at the bottom, and thirty-five feet wide at the surface of the water. The problem of providing that amount of water constantly was more difficult than the layman might imagine. Canals leak. They also lose millions of gallons of water by absorption, evaporation and the effects of the wind. Baird also faced a daily loss of water through the lock system linking the Union Canal with the existing Forth and Clyde Canal. He calculated that on the basis of ten boats passing up, and ten boats passing down each day (i.e. twenty lockfulls lost daily) the canal would require to be replenished to the extent of seventy-two million cubic feet of water each year. That figure was required for only four months of the year as it was anticipated that for the greater part of the year the canal could be topped up by the numerous rivers and burns along its route. Substantial reservoirs were, however, proposed, to deal with the summer months, and the anticipated complaints from the millers on the Avon and the Almond who were also dependent upon a good supply of water for their machinery. The total cost of the canal, basins, aqueducts and reservoirs was estimated at £235,167.

Baird then outlined the economic reasons for building the canal. One of his main arguments was that great savings had been made by

The Slateford aqueduct, constructed in 1818, carries the Union Canal in an iron-lined bed across the valley of the Water of Leith on a series of eight stone arches.
Photograph by Graham C. Cant

utilising the Forth and Clyde Canal instead of taking a direct route to Glasgow. He also produced compelling figures on the uneconomic cost of road transport between the two main cities in Scotland. A sum of £30,000 a year was paid for coach passengers and parcels, with an additional £40,000 paid for the carriage of heavier goods. Edinburgh paid one third more for its coal than Glasgow, and three times as much as was paid in localities along the route of the proposed canal. The carriage of freestone from Hailes quarry alone required forty horses and carts going twice a day to Edinburgh with an average load of sixty tons, and other areas were producing limestone, ironstone and farm produce. Special emphasis was placed on the transport of valuable consignments of sugar, tea, coffee and rum, which by road were liable to pillage, but by canal 'in a close boat with her hatches locked down, goods are not liable to such thefts'. The special prospectus of revenue produced some interesting comments: Edinburgh has 20,000 families each burning between seven and eight tons of coal per annum; coach passengers between Edinburgh and Glasgow amount annually to 20,000 insides and 20,000 outsides 'nearly the whole of whom have business, otherwise they would not submit to the expense and fatigue of the journey', at a fare of twenty shillings inside and fourteen shillings outside.

Baird's report was considered at a General Meeting of Subscribers at the Town House of Linlithgow on 8th October 1813, but the following year the Magistrates of Edinburgh objected to the plans and appointed Robert Stevenson (grandfather of Robert Louis Stevenson) to advise on a different route to connect with Leith Docks. Bitter controversy followed, with allegations that Baird's plan favoured his own coalmining interests to the west of Edinburgh. By 1817, however, the Union Canal Act was passed and Baird was instructed to begin work. On Tuesday 3rd March 1818, after the adjournment of a General Meeting, the Committee of Management proceeded to the west end of Fountainbridge 'attended by a vast number of people to witness the commencement of so grand an improvement to the Metropolis'. A prayer was said by the Rev. David Dickson, and Mr Downie of Appin, Chairman of the Committee of Management, dug the first spadeful, proclaiming that the entire venture would bring much-needed employment to the city. After the speeches, ten guineas were given to the Rev. Dickson for the benefit of the poor of St. Cuthbert's parish and five guineas to the contractor to enable the workmen present to drink success to the undertaking. By 1822 the first passenger boats, *Flora MacIvor* and *Di Vernon*, were in operation and the canal was officially opened in May 1823. Its depth at five feet and breadth at thirty-seven feet on the surface followed Baird's original report of 1813 and accommodated boats sixty-nine feet long and twelve and a half feet wide. The length of the canal was increased from twenty-eight and a half miles to thirty-one miles and the cost was increased from £235,167 in 1813 to £461,760 on completion.

An undertaking of that magnitude is seldom accomplished without difficulties and alterations to the original plan. One such alteration at the Edinburgh end of the works is of particular interest. Baird proposed that a branch of the canal be built at Gilmore Place to enter the Meadows through Mr Haig's Lochrin Distillery at the junction of present-day Home Street and Gilmore Place. As the canal would have crossed 'the Linton Road', a drawbridge with a house and keeper was proposed. After passing by the north end of Drumdryen House the canal entered the Meadows, crossed the Middle Meadow Walk about fifty yards below the North Walk and passed the Archers' Butts to a basin at the east end of the Meadows. Where the canal ran through the Meadows it was to be faced in stone on the north side for taking up and

Colinton Sunday School leave Stoneyport on the Union Canal (near Lanark Road) for their annual picnic at Ratho.
Courtesy of Miss E.D. Robertson.

landing passengers. The total cost of £8203:10s was considered to be too costly and Baird was instructed by the Subscribers to abandon that section of the works.

One of Baird's other problems was crossing the valley of the Water of Leith at Slateford. His original idea for a four-arch aqueduct was not implemented as per the 1813 report:

> leaving Dumbryden, without interfering with any house or garden, the line passes close to the south side of the famous quarry of Hails; here the line keeps in solid ground, passing close by the north side of the farm steading of Kingsknows, from thence it goes in rather uneven ground till it reaches the quarry and farm road, which lying in a hollow will require to be passed by a small Aqueduct and embankment. This takes the line to the bank of the Water of Leith; the width of the valley at the Canal water level is 300 yards, and the bank sloping gently narrows it at bottom. This I propose crossing by an Aqueduct of 4 arches of 50 feet each, the height being 43 feet; as the grounds on both banks consist of a kind of pleasure ground it will be necessary to have this Bridge neatly finished and the lands properly fenced. A little deep cutting in the east side on Dr Munro's grounds will serve to embank the ends, and the excavation, if neatly faced up, and a handsome foot Bridge put over it, the place will not be hurt by the Canal passing through it, or to avoid any objections it may be built up and arched over for 150 yards at little expense, as the ground admits of it, and the surface may be restored to nearly its present state.

Item 17 Slateford Aqueduct

45' high 4 arches of 50'	£8196
Embanking the ends, puddling etc	2028
Land	1088
Fencing	240
	£11,552

Instead of the four-arch aqueduct the final work was an aqueduct six hundred feet long and sixty feet high supported by eight arches each fifty feet in length. The bed of the canal was lined with iron, and iron balustrades were erected on each side. Altogether it was a magnificent feat of engineering described by Telford as 'superior perhaps to any aqueduct in the kingdom'.

Dark days lay ahead. Ten years were spent planning and building the Union Canal. Almost exactly twenty years after *Flora MacIvor* sailed out of Port Hopetoun (later occupied by Lothian House in Lothian Road) with a cargo of excited passengers, the Edinburgh and Glasgow Railway Company opened a line from Edinburgh to Glasgow. Passengers travelling by boat ceased immediately and in 1849 the Railway Company bought the canal for £209,000—less than half the cost of its construction. Subsequently ownership passed to the British Transport Commission and later the British Waterways Board. Despite the early decline of passenger traffic, freight was carried on the Union Canal up until the mid-1930s. In 1937 the old single-arch stone aqueduct at the foot of Craiglockhart Avenue was replaced by a single-arch concrete bridge. The date of construction is shown on the outside of the west parapet, and below the north side of the arch a small bronze plaque commemorates a much earlier event:

> Prince Charlie Bridge
> Near this spot at Gray's Mill
> Prince Charlie's Army Halted
> in 1745 prior to the occupation
> of Edinburgh

Today the Union Canal enjoys a partial revival of interest as a place of leisure and recreation rather than its original function as a commercial waterway. Its tunnels, aqueducts and embankments remain as important examples of industrial archaeology. Several boating and rowing clubs are established along its route, including the St. Andrew's Rowing Club, the Honourable Society of Edinburgh Boaters, and the University of Edinburgh Rowing Club. The largest

Prince Charlie's Bridge, constructed in 1937 to carry the Union Canal over the main road through Slateford at the foot of Craiglockhart Avenue. Photograph by Phyllis Margaret Cant.

blockage in Edinburgh is at Wester Hailes where the canal is piped for more than one mile, seriously curtailing expansion of water sports on the Edinburgh side of the break. Nevertheless the 1985 brochure of the British Waterways Board states that the Union Canal 'offers the visitor dramatic contrasts, with peaceful countryside and secluded woods, interwoven with the fine aqueducts, tunnel and splendid canalside buildings recalling the throb of industries the Canal was built to serve'. There are also ambitious proposals for commercial and residential redevelopment on several acres of ground to the west of Port Hopetoun, where it is hoped to recreate the Canal basin and waterside atmosphere.

Some Old and New Industries

In many ways Slateford's early industrial history developed along similar lines to that on the Water of Leith between Colinton and Currie. Unfortunately much less remains of the weirs, lades and mills around Slateford than at Juniper Green. Nevertheless, a brief study of the old mills provides an interesting insight into the development of later industry.

Coming down the Water of Leith from Colinton towards Slateford, the first point of interest is at Redhall Mill. A broad weir feeds a well-constructed lade on the east bank reached by crossing the rustic bridge built on a series of stone piers. On the east bank the pathway hugs the lade for a few hundred yards before crossing it by a small pedestrian bridge onto higher ground. Below, the lade can be seen going towards the mill but most of the water is discharged by a relief sluice back to the Water of Leith. The dry part of the lade enters Redhall Mill, on the south wall of which a well-worn plaque commemorates its acquisition and reconstruction by Admiral John Inglis in 1803. Prior to Inglis' ownership Redhall Mill was producing paper in 1718 and barley in 1742. Nearby is Redhall Mill Cottage, with a few smaller buildings between the mill and the water's edge.

Proceeding downstream, the next locality, also on the east bank, is Kate's Mill which takes its name from Kate Cant of Thurston, wife of John Balfour the mill manager. Kate's Mill dates from 1718 when it was a waulk mill, but it was burned down in 1890 after producing paper from around 1783. Although nothing remains of the actual mill, Kate's Mill Cottage nearby is an attractive whitewashed dwelling house.

Much further downstream, on the west bank, is the site of Vernour's Mill or Boag's Mill dating from 1598 when it was a waulk mill. Its colourful history is described by John Geddie in equally colourful language:

> The mossy bridge and white-washed group of houses at Boag's Mill occupy one of the prettiest and most secluded of the riverside nooks. The mill, one of the oldest on the Water, has shown marvellous power of adaptibility (sic). It has ground grain, and made paper and snuff. It turned out the first bank notes manufactured in Scotland, a picquet of soldiers mounting guard in the cottage on the bank above; and in the first decades of the century, when the Balfours were its tenants, the hospitable cellars of Boag's Mill entertained county magnates and bank directors. At present the dust-begrimed windows announce it to be still in part dedicated to meal and barley milling. But there comes wafted from the doors also a breath as from the spicy East. For along with the more commonplace output of peasemeal and pot barley—besides grinding chemicals, breaking sugar, and turning millwrights' machinery—the wheels of Boag's Mill liberate upon the air of the Water the pungent flavour of pepper, curry, and ginger, and the sweet odours of cinnamon, mace, and cassia.

Although the original aqueduct eventually created a serious traffic ob-
struction, its massive stone supports provided ample space for the advertisements of the day: Chivers Jellies; Raleigh Bicycles; Scott's Porage Oats;
and Zebo: 'so clean, so quick, so bright'.
Courtesy of Edinburgh City Libraries.

After being in continuous use for more than three centuries it was
burned to the ground in 1924. Its position is now occupied by a modern
house a few yards from the handsome stone bridge which carried the
private road from Lanark Road across the Water of Leith to Redhall
House high above the dell on the east side.

The last mill before reaching Slateford, also on the west bank, is
Lumsdaine's Mill which went under the intriguing name of Jinkaboot.
It is believed to have been operating as a corn mill in 1506, a paper mill
in 1714, and a barley mill from 1735 to 1755 before being demolished
and replaced by a walled kitchen garden for Redhall House. At the
present day, the garden is still in good condition with a range of
glasshouses along its north wall. Nearby on the east bank a stone
grotto, with unusually shaped windows, overlooks a small tributary of
the Water of Leith.

Beyond Jinkaboot the dell suddenly opens out at the Dell Inn above
the new bridge which carries Lanark Road across the Water of Leith..
The weir can be seen clearly from the bridge parapet, but the lade;

taken off on the west bank, is now blocked up. Previously it ran in its own culvert under Lanark Road to emerge along the side of Slateford Bowling Green and then into the Inglis Green complex of Gray's Mill and Slateford Mill (now Pritchard House) before re-entering the Water of Leith a few hundred yards before Longstone Inn.

Another of the early industries was at Inglis Green, midway between the old villages of Slateford and Longstone. In 1773 George Inglis of Redhall leased an area of ground to Joseph Reid to be used as a bleachfield. The lease included Gray's Mill and the Haughs below Slateford on which Reid erected a bleaching house and mill. Unfortunately Reid became bankrupt in 1778 and the business was acquired by his creditors. A series of advertisements in the *Edinburgh Courant* between 1777 and 1780 suggests that the ailing business was gradually acquired by Hugh McWhirter of Traiflat, near Dumfries. He offered to bleach all plain linen at prices from 2½d per yard; tweelings and satinettes 4d; damasks 5d; lawns 3d; all subject to a final cautionary note: 'all those who choose to have their cloth only half bleached will please to mark "Half White" on the end of their web'. Hugh McWhirter was succeeded by his son George who continued the business by acquiring another lease, in 1828, of Inglis Green and the Waulk Mill of Redhall and Gray's Mill. The McWhirter family was succeeded in 1849 by the Macnab brothers whose name became synonymous with Inglis Green for more than a century. Alexander and John Macnab were sons of a calico (cotton) printer who had traded as Macnab and Boyd at Milton-of-Campsie, near Glasgow. For almost thirty years the Macnab brothers ran the business, with Alex controlling administration and John controlling production. After Alex died the business was sold to their sister and her husband Alex Stevenson, the Edinburgh draper, who kept the name A. & J. Macnab. In 1899 the trustees of Alex Stevenson formed a new limited company A. & J. Macnab Ltd with the sons Murray, Charles and Herbert as Managing Directors.

In *A Company History* published privately in 1960 for A. & J. Macnab Ltd many of the early processes and business dealings are described. The main entrance to the works was from Inglis Green Road through a clock tower which housed a large bell for sounding the start and finish of the day's work. Small sheds under the arches of the railway viaduct were used for hand looms and a 'beetle house' where cotton and linen were given a beetled finish by flattening down the weave. In the cotton

The stone arches of the canal aqueduct tower above Slateford Bowling Club with the Railway viaduct beyond.

piece trade, cloth was sent to Macnabs for processing from the North British Rubber Company and other similar companies. The cloth was then scoured, bleached and dyed for use as the cotton base of rubber boots, and for raincoats, waterproofs and hose pipes. The retail drycleaning and dyeing business developed through the Stevensons' drapery shops and was treated as a separate business from 1910. Inglis Green Laundry, also under the control of the Stevensons, was developed into an extensive network from humble beginnings in 1820 when it occupied a two-storey building on the mill lade.

It has been suggested that the earliest quarries in the neighbourhood of Hailes and Redhall were started for the production of millstones for use in the various industries along the banks of the Water of Leith. Whilst this may well be true, it is unlikely that trade based solely on the production of millstones would have any great future, even in the middle of the eighteenth century. In fact it is known that Hailes Quarry was producing fairly large quantities of stone around 1750, and that the workings grew to support a substantial industry, before going into decline at the end of the nineteenth century. A plan of Hailes Quarry, in the Scottish Record Office, shows the progression of workings in 1820, 1825 and 1832. Hailes Quarry is shown as a large oblong, lying roughly south-west to north-east, with its southern boundary adjacent to the Union Canal. Smaller workings are shown going under the Union Canal and emerging on the south side of what is now Lanark Road. The administrative offices were located at the northern boundary, furthest away from farm steadings and houses not associated with the quarry. Substantial buildings were erected for the quarry clerk's house and offices, to the east of which lay the engine house and smithy. Mrs Anderson's feu was between the east face and a service road lined by quarrymen's cottages. The farm steadings of Kingsknowe Farm and Dumbryden House are also shown.

In 1892 George Craig made an interesting study of the sources of building stone used in Edinburgh. He describes Hailes as having been quarried to a depth of over a hundred feet in beds 'remarkable for the regularity of the laminae'. Three distinct colours of stone were produced: the lower levels produced a dark grey stone; the upper levels produced a red stone; and in various beds a blue tint was located. The hard, close-grained nature of the stone made it useful where great strength was required, notably in the construction of foundations. Its excellent resistance to weathering also made it a popular choice for many public and private buildings in Edinburgh: grey stone was used for Dalry School in 1876, Lochend Road School in 1886 and Sciennes School in 1891; blue stone was used for Plewlands Villa, Morningside, in 1878; and red stone for Red House, Cluny Gardens, in 1880.

Craig's report of 1892 also contains comments about the nature of stone available from Redhall Quarry nearby. Redhall stone was considered to be softer than Craigleith stone, but, being more easily worked, was frequently used, especially when demand for Craigleith stone diminished. Redhall produced two colours: the better stone was red, containing a high percentage of iron; and the less attractive stone was white which had a tendency to become discoloured when exposed to the atmosphere. Its weathering capabilities were good, proof of which remains in the many public buildings in Edinburgh constructed of stone from Redhall Quarry. These include: St. Paul's Church, York Place, 1816-1818; St. John's Church, Princes Street, 1817; Lothian Road United Presbyterian Church, 1831 (now the Film House); St. Ninian's Free Church, Leith, 1839; Synod Hall, 1871 (demolished in the 1960s for Edinburgh's proposed Opera House); Fountainbridge School, 1874; and Gorgie School, 1876.

When Hailes Quarry was eventually abandoned in the opening

Slateford village before the various road improvements, with Back Row
leading off to the left, the old stone bridge in the centre, and on the right
the Cross Keys Inn and Slateford House.
From *Picturesque Views of Colinton and District.*

years of the twentieth century it was one hundred and twenty feet deep
and extended over nearly thirty acres. Without the benefit of pumping
gear it began to fill with spring water. When a survey was undertaken
in 1949 it was estimated that the quarry contained four hundred
million gallons of water which could be pumped into the Murray Burn
at the rate of two million gallons per day. Two 45-horsepower electric
motors, capable of lifting 2500 gallons per minute, were installed on a
former Merchant Navy life raft and extraction began. Allowing for the
rate of extraction to fall as the level went down, it was anticipated that
the quarry would take six months to empty—and twenty years to fill
with tons of screened rubbish. By 1961 one million tons had been
deposited and the once great Hailes Quarry was only thirty feet deep.
Following a further period of infilling and consolidation the area was
eventually laid out as a public park for the benefit of the residents of
Slateford, Longstone and the new district of Wester Hailes.

Public slaughterhouses were first established in Edinburgh by the
Edinburgh Slaughterhouses Act of 1850. The purpose of the Act was to
protect the public by regulating the standards of hygiene required in
slaughtering animals for public consumption. The slaughter of cattle

anywhere else in the City was prohibited and dues were levied on cattle taken to the slaughterhouse and on carcases brought into the City from elsewhere. Up until the beginning of the twentieth century slaughterhouses and markets were located in several densely populated areas of the town, notably at Fountainbridge and Lauriston Place. Following a number of studies in 1902, the Town Council, as Governors of Trinity Hospital, feued twenty-five acres of ground at Gorgie to establish new markets and slaughterhouses in one complex. Plans for the new buildings were drawn by James A. Williamson, under the direction of Councillor Chesser, the Convener of the Market Committee. It was a costly and ambitious scheme to accommodate slaughterhouses, cattle markets, corn markets, St. Cuthbert's Co-operative Association, a restaurant, auction marts and room for expansion. In addition to the building costing £100,000, a sum of £7,000 was estimated for the construction of Chesser Avenue and bridges, and a further sum of £20,000 to construct a private railway from Gorgie. Sidings and cattle docks were constructed to the east of the markets under the direction of Messrs Blyth and Westland, Civil Engineers, to provide a frontage of 3600 feet to take two hundred waggons at a time.

The largest area of the complex was given over to the slaughterhouses capable of dealing annually with 28,000 cattle, 8,000 swine, 4,500 calves and 178,000 sheep. Each part of the building had its own special function including the killing and cooling halls, the slaughter halls, tripery, dung house, fat searching house, boiler house and condemned meat plant. Hygiene was of the utmost importance, the dadoes being built of salt-glazed bricks with rounded bricks in the angles for ease of cleanliness. The stomachs of the animals were removed from the slaughterhouse to the dung house where the contents were discharged by means of chutes into iron dung waggons at a lower level. By this means it was claimed that the slaughterhouse was kept cleaner than was usual.

The cattle and sheep market extended over four and a half acres with pennage for eight hundred head of cattle and six thousand sheep. Special arrangements were made for ventilation and steam heating to control the temperature in the milch-cow byres. There was also a sale ring staged for buyers and fitted with a rostrum for auctioneers who sold 100,000 sheep and 28,000 cattle annually.

The opportunity was also taken to locate the corn market at Gorgie in a grand stone building with Doric columns on the front. The main arena was the exchange hall with stalls for merchants along each of the

On the extreme left the bellcote of the old Secession church, beside which is the Chalmers Memorial Hall designed by James Jerdan, and on the right Slateford House dating from c.1770.
Courtesy of Royal Society for the Prevention of Accidents.

walls, adjacent to which was a large settling and business room. A special feature of the construction was the asphalt floors sealed to exclude vermin.

The 1902 complex was updated on numerous occasions in response to new technology and legislation, but in 1981 a new slaughterhouse was constructed at a cost of almost nine million pounds. The new Gorgie complex, opened by Princess Anne on Friday 27th November 1981, was designed to deal with the requirements of Edinburgh, Lothian, Fife and the Borders well into the next century. Its capacity of two hundred and fifty lambs, one hundred pigs and fifty cattle per hour was planned and researched in accordance with the provisions of the latest legislation. The line permits immediate removal of any contaminated material from edible meat and prevents any back-tracking of material which could lead to contamination. The stunning area is blocked from the view of incoming animals in an effort to minimise animal stress. As soon as the meat comes out of the slaughter-house it is moved to one of the fifteen chills. A slaughterhouse of this complexity can have a varied list of by-products including bone meal, meat meal, blood meal, tallow, cleaned and washed sheep and cattle stomachs, beef threads for surgical sutures, hides, manure, and specimens for teaching and research. Great emphasis is placed on meat inspection. Unloading of animals is supervised by a meat inspector, and if any animal is injured or suspected of being diseased it is placed in the isolation pens for further inspection by a veterinary surgeon. Careful identification of the carcases and their products is also maintained so that if any infection is found on the line, the other parts can be traced quickly and disposed of.

There is also a lecture theatre to seat fifty in which a comprehensive educational programme is maintained for a variety of audiences including veterinary students, catering students, meat inspectors, Meat and Livestock Commission employees, and others.

Schools

Records for Slateford School are available from 1864, although it is clear that a school existed prior to that date on the same piece of ground between Lanark Road and the canal aqueduct. The 1860s were a trying time for the headmaster both on account of the wide-ranging curriculum and the standard of discipline required to ensure the safety of the children. A logbook entry for 13th November 1866 refers to a warning given to the pupils against going to the Hallow Fair (an agricultural gathering held from time immemorial throughout Scotland), which was held in a field close to the school. Unfortunately a similar warning against going on the ice in winter was not heeded, with tragic consequences. Peter Maxwell and James Cockburn, both aged about nine, 'having incautiously gone upon the ice on the canal nearly opposite the Railway Station—during the play hour from 12 til 1 o'clock—were drowned'. The headmaster dismissed the rest of the pupils in the afternoon and repeated his earlier caution about going on the canal or the Water of Leith. Three days later his patience turned to punishment when thirteen boys ventured on the curling pond, 'their reason being that it was not specially named'.

By all accounts the standard of the examinations was high, as can be seen from the list of subjects for 1867:

Redhall House, designed by James Robertson for George Inglis of Auchendinny in 1758, braces itself for an uncertain future. Photograph by Graham C. Cant.

Religious Knowledge—	Exodus and Numbers; Betrayal and Death of Christ; Whole of Shorter Catechism with proofs of questions 1 to 38
Reading	Spelling Dictation and Recitation
History	Outlines of Scottish History; Roman and Saxon Periods and the Succession of the English Sovereigns
Geography	Scotland and North America
Grammar	Grammar generally and Parsing
Etymology	English Word Book; Saxon and Latin Prefixes
Arithmetic	Simple Rules to Simple Interest
Latin	Rudiments and Woodford's Caesar (Ch. 1–30)

These subjects were taken to a greater or lesser extent by the total roll of 135 pupils, ranging from five to over fourteen:

Number of children on the Enrolment
Register on the last day of 1867

	Boys	Girls	Total
Aged under 4	–	–	–
" 4 to 5	–	–	–
" 5 to 6	9	–	9
" 6 to 7	8	5	13
" 7 to 8	11	12	23
" 8 to 9	6	15	21
" 9 to 10	7	11	18
" 10 to 11	10	9	19
" 11 to 12	6	7	13
" 12 to 13	3	5	8
" 13 to 14	2	2	4
" over 14	6	1	7
	68	67	135

On prizegiving day the successful candidates received their certificates from the Rev. Lockhart, Mr Macnab of Inglis Green and Mr Hobkirk of Craiglockhart House. During the 1870s Slateford School went through a very difficult time. The School Board Inspector's Report for 1875 stated that the school was not in a satisfactory state and that the logbook was not kept properly, having omitted many of the unfavourable remarks made in the previous inspector's report. Although the infant school was considered to be reasonable, the mixed school was said to be so bad in 1879 that 'some of the pupils who are leaving now have had their whole school life wasted'. From 1882 the work of the school steadily improved to acceptable standards, but later reports suggest that the earlier problems might not all have been the fault of the staff or the pupils. A series of logbook entries from 1885 to 1900 makes interesting reading: 1885, the premises have been improved by the addition of a door but the pressing want of a lavatory pointed out last year has not yet been supplied; 1891, promise of satisfactory accommodation and building operations have begun; 1898, plans for new school buildings; 1899, senior department teaching carried on in a temporary iron building in the playground while extensive alterations are being made; 1900, building work complete. In the early years of the twentieth century the school received very favourable reports on the senior department and the infant department, which included several children from Craiglockhart Poorhouse. By 1921, however, the roll in the infant department had fallen to

Craiglockhart House in Craiglockhart Dell Road was built in 1823 for Dr Alexander Monro, Professor of Anatomy at Edinburgh University.

thirty-three, and on 18th July 1924 the school was closed and the remaining children were transferred to Longstone.

After the school was closed in 1924 it was used from time to time for classes from Longstone School when the roll increased. On 5th March 1945 Slateford School was used for the education of thirty handicapped children, between the ages of eight and fifteen, transferred from St. Nicholas Special School in Gorgie. The teaching staff consisted of Marion MacLean and Margaret King, assisted by a janitress, dinner attendant and bus attendant. Great emphasis was placed on vocational subjects including woodwork, basketwork, cobbling, cooking, sewing, art and leatherwork. Following administrative reorganisation the school closed on 4th July 1952 with the remaining pupils being transferred to Balfour Place School and St. Nicholas School.

After 1980 the Slateford School building faced an uncertain future. At present it is used as offices for the Architectural Services of Lothian Regional Council.

The known history of Longstone School dates from 16th February 1877. On that day Longstone Female School was opened at twelve noon with a service of praise and prayer attended by various members of the School Board. The average attendance in the first year was 57.9, which included boys up to the age of seven. The original building, with the date 1877 on the gable, has obviously been extended on numerous occasions, as the first school record gives details of only one classroom, measuring forty feet long, eighteen feet wide, and fourteen feet in height. The Inspector's Report for the first year was rather grudging in its praise: 'for a first inspection this school, composed of a rather neglected class, makes a creditable appearance'. Two early comments by the headmaster give an interesting insight into the everyday life of Longstone a century ago: 26.7.1878, the workmen in Hailes Quarry have their annual trip today—a great many of the children have gone with their parents and only 25 scholars are present at the school; 23.6.1882, a farmer (Mr Shaw of Old Saughton) has been employing a number of school children to weed his fields this week—reported matter to School Board Officer.

Within ten years of opening, Longstone found itself with accommodation problems almost as severe as at Slateford. An additional classroom was planned but as it had not yet been built, it was suggested that both schools should be reorganised with the infant department and Standards 1 and 2 remaining at Longstone, and the higher Standards going to Slateford. This scheme does not appear to have been implemented, but by 1903 Longstone had four classrooms with classes of 41, 38, 56 and 35 respectively. In 1912 an extension was built for woodwork, cookery and laundry.

Between 1914 and 1919 the school logs have numerous entries illustrating the involvement of staff and pupils in the Great War:

23.10.1914	Today the children brought to the school large quantities of flowers. These have been packed and sent by van to Edinburgh and are to be for sale in the streets tomorrow, the proceeds to go towards the Belgian Relief Fund.
28.5.1915	Pupils have contributed the following to the War Funds this week—10½ dozens of eggs for wounded soldiers, 18/10d to the Empire Day Fund, and 8/4d to the French Red Cross.
28.3.1918	Today the children were asked to give up their Easter eggs to the wounded soldiers at Kingsknowe Hospital.

The children's reward came on 16th July 1919 when they were taken to Spylaw Park for a celebration of peace, and the following day the school closed for a specially extended summer vacation.

In 1921 control of the school was transferred to Edinburgh Education Authority when the suburbs of Longstone and Slateford were amalgamated with the city. As a result of rationalisation of school accommodation Slateford was closed and forty-one pupils were transferred to Longstone on 5th September 1924. At the start of the session in 1930 children from the Stenhouse area, who had been attending Longstone, were transferred to the new Stenhouse Primary School designed by John A. Carfrae in 1929.

After the Second World War an increased roll at Longstone again brought acute problems with accommodation. In January 1950 Mr Reith, then Deputy Director of Education, visited the new aluminium classrooms in Longstone Street which had been delayed owing to difficulty with the supply of materials. Temporary accommodation was also taken at Slateford Public Hall and in 1953 classes were held at the main Longstone School, the Annexe, Slateford School and Juniper Green. In 1954 the headmaster recorded with muted exasperation that he had visited classes at Juniper Green, Slateford, Longstone and North Merchiston—all in the one day. Relief came in 1956, by which time Longstone had eighteen primary classes. A new school in Redhall Grove designed by the architects Reid and Forbes of Edinburgh was in use by November 1956, and was formally opened on 21st February 1957 by Lady Banks, the Lady Provost. The new building was designed as a two-stream primary school with classroom accommodation for 650 pupils on a site of about eleven acres. The building consisted of four wings or groups of buildings partly two-storeyed and partly single-storeyed. The Infant Department was allocated four classrooms and the Junior Department was given twelve classrooms. These two departments were linked by the administrative department of the school which was built around the main entrance hall.

In the session 1986/87 Longstone has a total roll of about three hundred children, a proportion of whom are from service families stationed at Redford Barracks and at various other places. The children are organised into ten primary classes, three of which are composites containing children of two different age groups. There is also a morning nursery class of thirty children and an afternoon class of twenty children. The nursery class moved from the Annexe in November 1986 and is now housed in a renovated transportable unit in the main school playground. This transportable unit once served as classroom accommodation when the school roll was higher. Rooms in the main school building which are no longer needed as classrooms are now used by visiting specialists, by staff involved in learning support teaching, and by classes watching television and engaging in drama. Other uses include the housing of library facilities and the storage of teaching equipment. On March 3rd 1987 the new Community Education Centre was officially opened by Councillor Brian Fallon. The Community Education Centre, the Longstone Playgroup and a school Parents' Room are all housed in renovated transportable units in the playground next to the nursery class.

Longstone School in Redhall Grove now looks forward to a future in which the school and the community will forge new links and work together towards many common aims. Old Longstone School in Longstone Road is occupied by the Longstone Training Centre of Lothian Regional Council's Department of Social Work.

From Slateford to Longstone

Traditionally, Slateford begins at the junction of Chesser Avenue and Slateford Road on the old route out of Edinburgh to Juniper Green, Currie, Balerno and Lanark. The junction was a convenient focal point for earlier transport systems. For several years Slateford Railway Station (recently reopened) was used by many local commuters and employees at Gorgie Slaughterhouse and A. & J. Macnab Ltd. In the days of Edinburgh Corporation's tramway system the No. 4 electric tram terminus was at the head of Chesser Avenue, beside the stance for horse-drawn coaches, which took visitors from the station up to Craiglockhart Hydropathic in Colinton Road.

A few hundred yards to the west of Chesser Avenue the first of Slateford's many bridges carries the main line railway across Slateford Road, which curves rather awkwardly between the supporting stone buttresses. Beyond, the roadway opens out with the bungalows of Allan Park and Craiglockhart on the left, and on the right a block of shop units with houses above. Beyond the shops, all that remains of a large railway goods yard is a few cottages abutting the pavement, before the entrance to the snooker and squash centre, constructed in 1979 on land previously owned by British Rail. There are two glass-backed championship squash courts with spectator seating, two additional conventional squash courts, and twenty-seven top-class matchplay snooker tables, also with spectator areas. In addition there is provision for professional tuition, leagues and tournaments.

At the foot of Craiglockhart Avenue, the Union Canal is carried over Slateford Road in a single-arch concrete aqueduct constructed in 1937 to replace the narrow and congested arch of the original Prince Charlie Bridge. Between this bridge and Inglis Green Road lies the heart of the old village of Slateford, although much of it has disappeared in various road improvement schemes. It is convenient to look, firstly, at what remains of the north side, and then look separately at the south side, which borders Craiglockhart Dell and the former policies of Craiglockhart House. Strange as it may seem, Slateford Road stops at Prince Charlie's Bridge, and the main road through Slateford village is named Lanark Road.

Opposite Craiglockhart Avenue a small lane gives access to several industrial properties, one of which was formerly a dairy. The first house on Lanark Road to the west of this lane was the village police station which had living accommodation on the upper floor, and cells built to the rear. A few original village houses remain between the former police station and the school, the playground of which has been severely restricted by road widening. The traditional nineteenth-century school architecture masks the much smaller and older building to the rear. To the west of the school, Lanark Road is carried across the Water of Leith on a wide double-span reinforced concrete bridge, which replaced, in 1967, a narrow three-arch stone bridge, supported by buttressed cutwaters and a separate culvert for the mill lade. The area of ground between the Water of Leith and Inglis Green Road has altered greatly within the last few decades. Slateford Bowling Club, with much improved facilities, still nestles below the canal aqueduct but the lade, which ran between the clubhouse and a row of old cottages, has long since been cut and filled in. A narrow street, previously known as Back Row, ran at right angles to Lanark Road for a few hundred yards and then turned sharply to the left to meet Inglis Green Road, near the aqueduct. All the old houses, including the Railway Inn, between the Bowling Green and Inglis Green Road, have been demolished and replaced by modern dwellings.

The south side of Lanark Road is equally interesting, albeit dwarfed, at its east end, by the modern premises of British Telecommunications. The high ground on which the telephone exchange was built was formerly occupied by the stables and coachhouses of Craiglockhart House, and the lower ground was occupied by two rows of small cottages running at an angle to the main road. A row of more substantial houses, with stone walls and railings to Lanark Road, finished at the south-west corner of Craiglockhart Avenue. At the entrance to Craiglockhart Dell, before crossing the Water of Leith, the single-storey building, at present occupied by a veterinary surgeon, was the north lodge to Craiglockhart House.

Perhaps the most complete part of the old village is on the south side of Lanark Road, to the west of the Water of Leith. The yard, previously belonging to Buchan the builder, is now used for car sales, and beside it is the eighteenth-century Cross Keys Inn. The castellated gateway leads to the former Secession church and manse which date from 1785. The congregation was formed in 1782 primarily from parishioners from Corstorphine who objected to the introduction of the Paraphrases. For a time they met at Sighthill before acquiring the Slateford site as their permanent home. In 1783 the congregation was augmented by a group from Colinton, and later by a contingent of the Cameronian congregation from Old Pentland. The first minister was the Rev. John Dick, son of a Burgher minister of Aberdeen, who was ordained in October 1786. In 1800 he preached a series of sermons which were later published as the *Essay on Inspiration*. A year later he was translated to Greyfriars, Glasgow and in 1820 he became Professor of Divinity at Glasgow. The Rev. John Dick was succeeded, in 1802, by the Rev. John Belfrage who spent his whole ministry in the parish. His great intellect and bearing led Dr John Brown to observe that 'his strong will and authority, his capacious, clear, and beneficent intellect, dwelt in its petty sphere like an oak in a flower pot'. He died in 1833 and was buried in Colinton churchyard. The Secession church at Slateford took part in the various church unions in Scotland, becoming first United Presbyterian, and then United Free, before finally becoming a parish church of the Church of Scotland in 1929. The congregation moved in 1955 to the new Slateford-Longstone Parish Church in Kingsknowe Road North. At the present day the old Secession church building is in commercial use and the two-storey manse, with dormer windows and a stone porch, is a private house.

To the west of the castellated gateway is the Chalmers Memorial Hall, designed by the architect James Jerdan. The ornamental stonework above the doorway contains the initials D C for David Chalmers, and the date 1899, the year of his death. The hall, which communicates with the much older Slateford House to the west, was built by David Chalmers' widow Isabella Grace Grant-Chalmers, for

Craiglockhart Hydropathic in Colinton Road—a giant Italian villa—by Peddie and Kinnear between 1877 and 1880. It was used as a military hospital during the First World War and is now part of Napier College. From *Picturesque Views of Colinton and District*.

the purpose of carrying on 'home mission work in the village of Slateford and district in connection with the parish church of Craiglockhart'. Slateford House dates from around 1770, and is described in the Register of Sasines as 'that dwelling house consisting of two storeys or flats as presently possessed by the said Miss Margaret Inglis being the westmost house of the range of houses erected on the south side of the King's highway leading through Slateford from the bridge towards Currie'. Margaret Inglis was the eldest daughter of David Inglis, a prosperous linen manufacturer and clothier. She was born on 10th September 1739 and died unmarried on 27th February 1800, having lived for many years at Slateford House. Her father was elected to Edinburgh Town Council on 27th September 1739 and held positions as City Treasurer, and Director, Deputy Governor and Treasurer of the Bank of Scotland. When he died on 13th January 1767 his brother, George Inglis of Redhall House, became guardian to Margaret Inglis and her sister Katherine.

In January 1985 the Royal Society for the Prevention of Accidents moved its Scottish office into Slateford House, and made use of Chalmers Memorial Hall as a conference and training centre. The Society has an interesting history of its own, unconnected with the historic Slateford House. In the early years of the twentieth century the need for an accident prevention movement gave rise, in 1916, to the London 'Safety First' Council. This groundwork led to the formation of the London Accident Prevention Council, from which stemmed the Royal Society for the Prevention of Accidents. The Society is a completely independent professional body governed by an Executive Committee, which is able to draw on the vast reserves of experience in the various voluntary national committees. There is a staff of almost two hundred located at the head office in Birmingham and in various offices throughout Britain. Its annual budget of over four million pounds is derived from the Society's 20,000 subscribers, government grants, and the sale of its own material and services, in each of the main areas of Agricultural, Home, Leisure, Occupational, Road and Water Safety, and in Safety Education. One of the privileges enjoyed by the Society has been the support of the Royal Family through King George VI, Her Majesty Queen Elizabeth, and His Royal Highness the Duke of Edinburgh.

During the Slateford and Longstone road improvements of 1967 Inglis Green Road was widened to occupy two railway arches, and a roundabout was built at the junction with Lanark Road, almost opposite Slateford House. Prior to 1967 Inglis Green Road was very narrow and passed under only one of the railway arches. The village smiddy, and a group of small cottages in the form of a courtyard, stood on the west side between Lanark Road and the canal aqueduct. On the east side of the same section of roadway a row of similar cottages backed onto Back Row. Also on the east side, midway between the aqueduct and the viaduct, was a small group of buildings beside the mill lade.

To the north of the railway viaduct lay the huge complex of Macnab the dyers, drycleaners and laundry. Many of the employees occupied the small cottages lining both sides of the road. The cottages on the east side had short gardens running down to the lade, but those on the west side formed a double line with a small lane to allow access. The frontages were very plain and symmetrical, broken only by the projecting gable of the house at each end of the line, and in the centre. At the Longstone end of the cottages, on the west side, a substantial lodge house, with overhanging eaves, and railings, stood at the end of two long driveways which led to two substantial houses built for the Stevenson family who owned the Macnab works. In relation to modern development, Kingdom Hall, the home of the Jehovah's Witnesses, is built near to where the double row of cottages stood, and Longstone Hearts Social Club occupies one of the houses which belonged to the Stevensons.

For many years a large tract of land on the east side of Inglis Green Road has been given over to industrial use. Although it is several years since Macnab, the drycleaners, have operated at Inglis Green the name is perpetuated in Macnab's Cash and Carry in the same complex. Further north, Gray's Mill and Slateford Mill have disappeared, the Slateford Mill site being occupied by Pritchard House. Beside the garage, the Public Hall takes up a small section of ground bounded by privet hedges. In the past the hall has been used as additional school accommodation, for various community events, and as a masonic hall. In 1984 the interior was extensively damaged by fire but has now been renovated.

The heart of old Longstone village was between Longstone Inn and Longstone School. The Inn, with its grey-painted walls and wine-coloured shutters, occupies the small promontory between the Murray Burn and the Water of Leith, along with a few old houses. To the south-west of Longstone Road, the area of ground known as Angle Park was greatly altered when Kingsknowe Road North was developed. The school building bears the date 1877 but almost certainly replaced a smaller school from an earlier date.

Many of the Longstone inhabitants worked at Hailes Quarry or at the brickworks which were started in an endeavour to reduce the high cost of extraction by putting some of the quarry waste into the manufacture of bricks. The only remaining link with the brickworks is the manager's two-storey house with the date 1906 which stands near the roundabout at the junction of Longstone Road and Murrayburn Road. After the brickworks were demolished, part of the land was used in 1955 for the construction of Longstone bus garage to replace the tramcar and bus depot at Gorgie which was found to be unsuitable for further extension. At the present day Lothian Region Transport employ about four hundred staff at Longstone and operate approximately one hundred and eighty vehicles on various routes throughout the city.

One of the continuing links between the villages of Slateford and Longstone is the Slateford-Longstone Parish Church in Kingsknowe Road North, designed in 1954 by Leslie Grahame MacDougall, and described in the Edinburgh volume of *The Buildings of Scotland* as 'mildly Italian, the circular east tower seen as a light-flooded chancel from the portal-arched nave'. The opening and dedication of the new church took place at a special service conducted by The Very Reverend Charles L. Warr, Dean of the Thistle and Chapel Royal, on Monday 28th November 1955. At the present day the spiritual lead given by the church is complemented by the secular advice provided by LANCAS—Longstone and Neighbourhood Community Advisory Service—which operates from the church building. LANCAS was set up at a public meeting of local residents on 21st September 1982 when a constitution was adopted and a Management Committee formed, with the aims of 'advancing the education of the public in matters relating to mental, physical and social welfare, and of relieving poverty'. It is registered as a charity and provides practical advice on a wide range of topics including welfare, housing, employment, and legal aid.

Redhall House

Vehicular access to Redhall House is from Craiglockhart Drive South, but the more interesting route is on foot, following the line of the original approach to the house from Lanark Road. The pathway descends to the entrance bridge over the Water of Leith and then ascends steeply between rows of ancient trees. At the top, the achievement is tinged with disappointment by the present-day condition of Redhall House, dejected and boarded up against further attacks of vandalism.

The lands of Redhall, or Reidhall, and the Castle belonged to Sir Adam Otterburn, King's Advocate from 1524 to 1538, and Lord Provost of Edinburgh on numerous occasions, namely 1522, 1528-1532, 1543-4, and 1547-8. Sir Adam was a man of varied talents who undertook several diplomatic journeys as ambassador to England and to France. He was in office as Lord Provost shortly after the defeat of the Scots at the Battle of Pinkie in 1547, and was assassinated by a servant of Governor Arran, in the aftermath of the Earl of Hertford's invasions.

Redhall was purchased in 1755 by George Inglis of Auchendinny who commissioned James Robertson to design the present house in 1758. It was built as a five-bay block of two main storeys, attic and basement, with an advanced centre supporting a pediment enhanced by three large urns. The substantial west wing and the ornate front porch with Ionic pillars and balustrades were added in 1900 when most of the interior was redesigned. Fortunately, the bulky cantilever timber staircase has been left intact along with a good chimneypiece and some friezes. The outside of the house is devoid of dates, initials or other inscriptions except for some roughly hewn stones set into the south-west corner which may have been intended for some ornamental addition.

Nothing remains at the site of the former Redhall Castle which lay approximately one hundred yards north-west of the present house. Around the turn of the century an excavation of the site revealed only the footing of a small semicircular turret approximately seven feet in diameter. However, an interesting panel depicting the arms of the Otterburn family was removed from the castle and built into the north side of the hexagonal dovecot standing two hundred and fifty yards north-east of the house. It is said that the dovecot, the only one of its kind in Edinburgh, was built in 1756 by John Christy for the sum of forty pounds.

In 1945 A. Niven Robertson included Redhall in a most informative article entitled 'Old Dovecotes in and around Edinburgh' for Volume XXV of the *Book of the Old Edinburgh Club*. Each of the dovecot's six walls is ten feet wide and two feet thick, constructed of red sandstone on a slightly projecting plinth. The walls are divided by a single stringcourse midway between the plinth and the eaves. On the south side, which contains the door, there is an empty square recess below the stringcourse, and a blocked-up window above it. The roof was slated, with the pigeon holes arranged in three rows, each with landing boards and four holes, and the apex carried a pole on which sat a nine-point star. At the present day the entire roof has been destroyed. The north wall was more elaborate than the south wall. Below the stringcourse a large semicircular recess, which may have been intended for a statue, has been blocked up. Above the stringcourse is the Otterburn coat of arms containing a shield with a chevron and three otters' heads supported by two rampant wyverns with barbed tails intertwined and parrot-like beaks. The Otterburn motto DE VIR-TUTE IN VIRTUTEM is carved below the shield. The inside of the dovecot is now completely destroyed. Originally there were 757 nest holes in twenty tiers, all of which were made of wood except the two lowest tiers which were of stone. The stone nest holes were arranged in a circle but the wooden ones formed a dodecagon.

To the south-west of Redhall House, the stable block with the stone horse on the main gable dates from around 1758 but is at present in a poor state of repair. Two modern special schools, Graysmill and Cairnpark, both built of yellow brick, have recently been erected in the policies.

Craiglockhart Castle

Craiglockhart Castle must rank as one of the least-known castles in Edinburgh, fading into oblivion on the south side of Glenlockhart Road, whilst nearby private and public buildings enjoy a new lease of life. This small fifteenth-century tower or castle is nearly square in plan, measuring approximately twenty-eight feet north to south, and twenty-four feet east to west, with walls between five and six feet thick. It is interesting to trace the various descriptions of it over the last hundred years. Grant describes it as 'half hidden among trees and the buildings of a farm steading, the curious remains of a very ancient little fortalice which seems to be totally without a history'. J. Munro Bell in *Castles of the Lothians* records similar information and gives the height of the remaining walls in 1893 as fifteen feet. Perhaps the most comprehensive description is in the 10th Report of the Royal Commission on the Ancient Monuments of Scotland in 1929, in which the walls are described as being thirty feet in height, much higher than that recorded by Bell several years earlier. Originally the castle had four storeys, two of which were mezzanine floors within the barrel vaults, which protected the basement and upper floors. The entrance was on the north side with a semicircular head which opened at ground level into the basement chamber, measuring eighteen feet by fourteen feet, and lit by a narrow light in the south wall. The north-west angle contained a wheel stair to the mezzanine and upper floors lit by fairly large windows in the east and west walls. The Report also provides a brief historical note 'that in 1505 the King granted to Thomas Kincaid son of Thomas Kincaid burgess of Edinburgh on resignation by Patrick Kincaid of Craiglockhart, the lands of the same with tower and fortalice'.

Craiglockhart House

Craiglockhart House in Craiglockhart Dell Road is of more recent date than the castle, having been built for Dr Alexander Monro, Professor of Anatomy at Edinburgh University, who acquired the estate of Craiglockhart in 1817. Dr Monro was the third generation of his family to hold the Chair of Anatomy, but apparently he did not emulate the high standards achieved by his father and grandfather. Charles J. Smith, in Volume 2 of *Historic South Edinburgh*, records how the long 'Monro Dynasty' came to a sad ending in 1846 when Dr Monro eventually resigned amid growing criticism of his ability.

A later, and less controversial, owner of Craiglockhart was Sir Alexander Oliver Riddell, born in 1844, the third son of Alexander Oliver Riddell, civil engineer of Edinburgh. He was Deputy Lieutenant of the City and County of Edinburgh and a Justice of the Peace for Midlothian. His many other interests included Vice-President of the Liberal Unionist Association, the National Lifeboat Society, and the National Society for the Prevention of Cruelty to Children. He was also a generous benefactor of Craiglockhart Parish Church and of St. Cuthbert's Episcopal Church in Colinton. In business life he was a senior partner in the firm of Andrew Usher and Company, the Edinburgh distillers, and a director of the North British Distillery Company. He was married in 1880 to Jane Fazackerley, second daughter of Henry Hornby of Seaforth, near Liverpool.

The twenty-two room mansion was built in 1823 on the northern edge of the estate quite close to the Water of Leith and the older mansion of Redhall. Its two principal lodges were to the north, and to the east: the north lodge is presently occupied by a veterinary surgeon in Lanark Road at the entrance to the Dell; and the east lodge is in Craiglockhart Avenue at the entrance to the British Telecommunications building. Craiglockhart House is still in private ownership in much reduced policies surrounded by bungalow development built in the 1930s. The original two-storey house, with pedimented projection, has been given a semi-octagonal addition containing a new entrance hallway similar in style to that at Baberton House.

Craiglockhart Hydropathic

Some time after the death, in 1859, of Dr Monro of Craiglockhart House, plans were made for feuing out parts of Craiglockhart estate for building purposes. In 1873 much of the west part of the estate was sold to the Craiglockhart Estate Company who, in turn, feued thirteen acres, between Colinton Road and Wester Craiglockhart Hill, to the Craiglockhart Hydropathic Company. The feu charter required the Hydropathic Company to erect buildings within three years to a value of not less than £10,000, and stipulated that no factories or public houses were permitted. The old farmhouse and steadings of Craiglockhart Farm were demolished and 'a giant Italian villa' was erected by Peddie and Kinnear in a commanding position on the north side of Wester Craiglockhart Hill. In the late nineteenth century hydropathics were becoming very popular, and Craiglockhart, with its proximity to the city, was ideally placed to become an attractive resort. Outdoor facilities extended to tennis, archery, croquet and bowls, whilst indoor activities included billiards, reading and card rooms, and a large heated swimming pool. Despite these attractions the Hydropathic was not particularly profitable in its early years, and the directors found it necessary to raise a substantial loan of £25,000 in 1881, against the security of the property. Following further financial problems and difficulty in finding a prospective buyer, the Hydropathic was eventually sold in 1890 to James Bell of Dunblane Hydropathic Company Limited. Under Mr Bell's management, Craiglockhart operated successfully up to the time of the First World War when it was used as a military hospital for officers suffering from shellshock and related disorders.

After the First World War the Hydropathic reopened for a short while but it was sold in 1920 to the Society of the Sacred Heart to be used as a convent and training college for Roman Catholic teachers. Several additions were made to the property in later years: the convent chapel was opened in 1933 and extended in 1963; the Demonstration School was built in 1957; and in 1965 a six-storey hall of residence was added along with a new lecture block, hall and gymnasium, under the name of Craiglockhart College of Education. All the buildings were acquired in 1986 by Napier College of Commerce and Technology.

The Hydro's most poignant history, however, belongs to its short but memorable time as 'Dottyville' during the First World War. From 1917 to 1919 Craiglockhart Hydropathic was used as a military hospital for officers suffering from the trauma of war experience. They came in their hundreds, narrowly escaping the ignominy of courts-martial, to be rid of the horrible memories of the front line. But for the pioneering work of Dr W.H. Rivers, acting Captain in the Royal Army Medical Corps, and two of the hospital's most famous inmates, much of the fine work done at Craiglockhart might never have been recorded. Before the outbreak of war Dr Rivers had already earned himself an impressive reputation for his work in experimental psychology, with particular reference to the meaning and effect of dreams. At Craiglockhart he did not have far to look for his patients, many of whom suffered indescribably from the reality of war dreams, which Rivers maintained were quite different to any other form:

> A characteristic feature of this variety of dream is that it is accompanied by an effect of a peculiarly intense kind, often with a special quality described as different from any known in waking life. The dream ends suddenly by the patient waking in an acute state of terror directly continuous with the terror of the dream and with all the physical accompaniments of extreme fear, such as profuse sweating, shaking and violent beating of the heart. Often the dream recurs in exactly the same form night after night, and even several times in one night, and a sufferer will often keep himself from sleeping again after one experience, from dread of its repetition.

During these long bouts of self-inflicted insomnia two inmates fought to rearrange their shattered minds, in verse and in prose. For Siegfried Sassoon morning never came too soon:

> The place [Craiglockhart Military Hospital] had the melancholy atmosphere of a decayed hydro, redeemed only by its healthy situation and pleasant view of the Pentland Hills. By daylight the doctors dealt successfully with these disadvantages but by night they lost control and the hospital became sepulchral and oppressive with saturations of war experience. One lay awake and listened to feet padding along passages which smelt of stale cigarette smoke; for the nurses couldn't prevent insomnia-ridden officers from smoking half the night in their bedrooms though the locks had been removed from all doors.
> One became conscious that the place was full of men whose slumbers were morbid and terrifying—men muttering uneasily or crying out in their sleep. By night each man was back in his doomed sector of a horror-stricken front line where the panic and stampede of some ghastly experience was re-enacted among the livid faces of the dead.

Sassoon was a man of great bravery, serving in the Royal Welsh Fusiliers and winning the Military Cross as well as the nickname 'mad Jack'. He was wounded in April 1917 and returned to England where he began to consider whether the war of defence and liberation which he had entered had become a war of aggression and conquest. After making some ill-advised comments about the futility of war he came close to a court-martial, saved only by the strenuous intervention of a fellow-officer, Robert Graves, who arranged for him to be transferred, to the care of Dr Rivers at Craiglockhart. Here he met Wilfred Owen who had arrived at the hospital only a month before, as a traumatic casualty from Picardy. In the difficult days and nights which lay ahead Sassoon, Owen and Rivers forged a unique friendship, learning from one another's experience of the War.

Both Sassoon and Owen wrote extensively of their war experiences whilst recuperating at Craiglockhart. Sassoon's autobiographical fiction, *Sherston's Progress*, dwelt on life at the military hospital, and *Counter-Attack* (also by Sassoon) was a volume of poems dealing with the horrors of war. Whilst Owen was at Craiglockhart he edited the hospital journal *Hydra* which was elevated to a place in literature by the unique contributions of both Sassoon and Owen. Perhaps Owen's finest poem was *Anthem for Doomed Youth*:

> What passing bells for these who die as cattle?
> Only the monstrous anger of the guns.
> Only the stuttering rifles' rapid rattle
> Can patter out their hasty orisons.
> No mockeries for them; no prayers nor bells,
> Nor any voice of mourning save the choirs—
> The shrill, demented choirs of wailing shells;
> And bugles calling for them from sad shires.
> What candles may be held to speed them all?
> Not in the hands of boys but in their eyes
> Shall shine the holy glimmers of goodbyes.
> The pallor of girls' brows shall be their pall;
> Their flowers the tenderness of patient minds,
> And each slow dusk a drawing-down of blinds.

Owen went back to the front line in November 1917. Sassoon left Craiglockhart and returned to England. He waited anxiously to hear from Owen, but he waited in vain. Owen fell a week before Armistice amid 'the monstrous anger of the guns'.

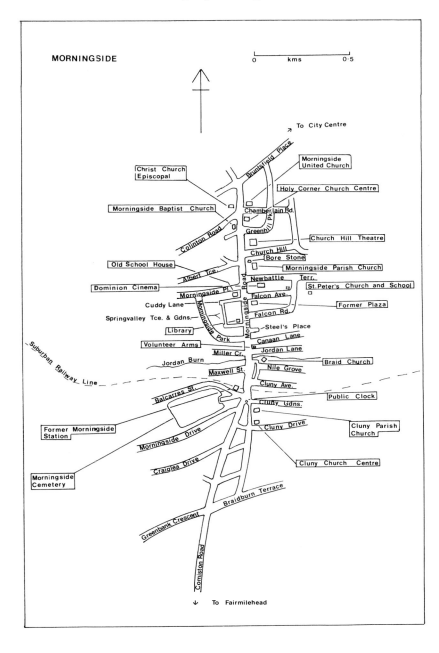

MORNINGSIDE

0   kms   0·5

To City Centre

Bruntsfield Place

Morningside United Church

Christ Church Episcopal

Holy Corner Church Centre

Morningside Baptist Church

Chamberlain Rd.

Greenh

Church Hill Theatre

Colinton Road

Church Hill

Bore Stone

Old School House

Morningside Parish Church

Albert Tce.

Newbattle Terr.

Dominion Cinema

St. Peter's Church and School

Morningside Pl.

Falcon Ave.

Cuddy Lane

Falcon Rd.

Former Plaza

Springvalley Tce. & Gdns.

Morningside Road

Morningside Park

Steel's Place

Library

Canaan Lane

Volunteer Arms

Jordan Lane

Miller Cr.

Jordan Burn

Braid Church

Maxwell St.

Nile Grove

Suburban Railway Line

Cluny Ave.

Balcarres St.

Cluny Gdns.

Public Clock

Former Morningside Station

Cluny Drive

Morningside Drive

Cluny Parish Church

Craiglea Drive

Cluny Church Centre

Morningside Cemetery

Braidburn Terrace

Greenbank Crescent

Comiston Road

↓   To Fairmilehead

CHAPTER 7

Morningside

Morningside, as the name may infer, lies on a south-sloping aspect to the south of Church Hill, on the old road from Tollcross to Biggar. Its origins are undoubtedly agricultural, when it served as a centre of population to the many neighbouring farms, Plewlands, the Grange of St. Giles, Oxgangs, Braid and Comiston, and the biblically-named Canaan and Egypt. The first map to show Morningside is Richard Cooper's Plan of the City of Edinburgh and Adjacent Grounds (1759), on which the village is represented by only three houses. By the 1880s Grant, in *Old and New Edinburgh*, was able to say that Morningside was 'once a secluded village, consisting of little more than a row of thatched cottages, a line of trees, and a blacksmith's forge, from which it gradually grew to become an agreeable environ and summer resort of the citizens, with the fame of being the 'Montpellier' of the east of Scotland, alluring invalids to its precincts for the benefit of its mild salubrious air'. A century later, whilst the climate may not have altered very much, the appearance of Morningside Road has altered completely from that of the main street of a quiet country village. Although the transformation from village to suburb was gradual, at least two factors combined to precipitate the change: in 1885 the Edinburgh Suburban and South Side Junction Railway was opened with a goods yard at the west end of Maxwell Street; and simultaneously a proliferation of villas and mansions was increasing the population dramatically. Around the same time, many of the old cottages which had lined each side of the main street were demolished for the construction of four-storey tenement buildings which completely dwarfed the remaining houses. The main part of the village lay to the west of Morningside Road between the Old Schoolhouse and what is now Morningside Library. In the first half of the twentieth century the centre of commercial activity tended to move south towards Morningside Station but in recent years that trend has been arrested, if not reversed.

The story of Morningside and its fascinating anecdotes, characters and buildings is related with great panache by its local author and historian, Charles J. Smith, in *Historic South Edinburgh*. Towards the

The Old Schoolhouse, Morningside Road, dating from 1823, which served the village population until 1892 when South Morningside School was opened. Since 1906 the Old Schoolhouse has been used by the Christian Brethren.
Courtesy of N.B. Traction Group Collection.

end of his account of Morningside, Mr Smith concludes that 'In the chronological sequence of smiddy, inn, village school and Parish Church can be traced the development of the community'.

Schools

The Old Schoolhouse in Morningside Road, opposite the junction with Falcon Avenue, is one of the district's best-known landmarks. Dating from 1823, it provided adequate, if not palatial, accommodation for many years before the growth in Morningside's population at the end of the nineteenth century. Whilst there are no figures available to show the increases in attendance, it is virtually certain that St. Cuthbert's and Dean School Board had a major problem with accommodation before South Morningside School was opened in 1892. In researching for Volume 1 of *Historic South Edinburgh*, Charles J. Smith was fortunate to trace the charter dated 27th March 1823, by which James Robertson, factor of William Deuchar, owner of Morningside estate, conveyed a small portion of land for the building of Morningside's village school. Four eminent citizens were closely involved in its formation: George Ross of Woodburn House; Alexander Falconar of Falcon Hall; James Evans of Canaan Park; and Henry Hare of Newgrange. It was George Ross, the distinguished judge, whose interest and financial backing ensured the continuation of the school, which became known as the Ross School. Although little is known of the masters and assistants when the school first opened, one name has survived several generations. Until recently there were a few senior citizens who could recall the most famous of all the village schoolmasters, Andrew Myrtle Cockburn, known to pupils and parents alike (though perhaps not in his presence) as 'Cocky' Cockburn. He came to the village school in 1873 from Redding, near Polmont, and transferred to South Morningside School as First Assistant in 1892.

The school roll diminished significantly shortly after 1843 when many parents, who supported the new Free Church, withdrew their children from the village school and sent them to the Free Church School which was built on a site near the present public library.

In addition to the village school under the control of St. Cuthbert's and Dean School Board, and the Free Church School, there were a few private schools in various locations. The most important of these was Morningside College, which operated from several addresses before closing in 1892. The College was established in Morningside Drive in 1882; it transferred to Rockville House in Napier Road in 1889; and in 1890 it set up in Falcon Hall on the east side of Morningside Road. Whilst at Morningside Drive it occupied a handsome building previously used as a Hydropathic, surrounded by grounds and parkland extending to about thirteen acres. The ground floor contained the dining room, museum, gymnasium and swimming baths, and, on the floor above, a long corridor opened onto the classrooms, exhibition hall, concert hall and theatre. This corridor, one hundred and forty feet long and twelve feet wide, was an important architectural feature containing several stained glass windows depicting the College arms, the arms of the City of Edinburgh, and the Scottish shield. The three upper storeys were occupied by individual bedrooms for pupils, and masters, with additional sick rooms under the supervision of a trained nurse who reported to the school matron. All the resident masters were graduates of Oxford or Cambridge, the 1888 report stating that 'the very competent and ample staff are evidently enthusiasts in the cause of education and earnestly devoted to their duties in their several departments'.

Left: Thomas Chalmers, leader of the Disruption in 1843, lived at No 1
Church Hill where Free Church services were held
Photograph from *Disruption Worthies*.
Right: Andrew Myrtle Cockburn ('Cocky' Cockburn), one-time 'maister'
of the Old Schoolhouse.
Courtesy of his daughter, the late Mrs M. Wilson, and Charles Skilton Ltd.

The curriculum paid particular attention to preparing pupils for the
Indian and the Home Civil Service, an objective which was vigorously
pursued by the principal, Dr Fearon Ranking, when the College
transferred to Falcon Hall. An educational article of the day, under
the title 'Schools—Private and Public', focused public attention on Dr
Ranking's aims:

> But while Scottish students have distinguished themselves in every other
> department of learning, the melancholy fact remains that comparatively
> few of them have taken high places in the entrance examinations to the
> Indian Civil Service and Sandhurst and Woolwich . . .

At Falcon Hall the school had two departments, preparatory and
senior. In the preparatory department the pupils were 'prepared on
the lines of the great English schools', with particular attention being
paid to those subjects which were required for the public services
examinations. In the senior classes relevant branches of the civil law
were taught by Dr Ranking personally, as well as military law, and
tactics.

Left: Eric Liddell, the runner and missionary known to the world through the film *Chariots of Fire*. His name is remembered in the new Eric Liddell Centre at Holy Corner.
Courtesy of *The Scotsman* Publications Ltd.
Right: Charles J. Smith, lecturer and author of *Historic South Edinburgh*, lifelong resident of Morningside.
Photograph by C.P. Smith.

Towards the end of the nineteenth century, the population of Morningside was growing rapidly, as tenement properties were constructed in Morningside Road and Comiston Road. A new school in Comiston Road was designed by the architect, Robert Wilson, in 1891, and on 5th September 1892 South Morningside School was opened, under the control of St. Cuthbert's and Dean School Board. Within the first few days the enrolment reached 572, made up of pupils from the Old Schoolhouse, Gorgie School, James Gillespie's School, and numerous small private schools in the district. The school was officially opened on 3rd October 1892 by Professor Masson of Edinburgh University, who contrasted the new accommodation with the elementary schools of sixty years previously. The official programme listed several separate events:

ST. CUTHBERTS AND DEAN SCHOOL BOARD
FORMAL OPENING OF
SOUTH MORNINGSIDE PUBLIC SCHOOL
3RD OCTOBER 1892

PROGRAMME
JUVENILE DEPARTMENT
PSALM – OLD HUNDRED
PRAYER – REV. W.D. MACKENZIE
SONG   *SCOTS WHA HAE*
SONG   *BONNIE WOOD O' CRAIGIELEA*

REMARKS – HEW MORRISON, ESQ.,
CHAIRMAN OF THE BOARD

ADDRESS PROFESSOR MASSON
VOTES OF THANKS

INFANT DEPARTMENT
HYMN   *FATHER, HEAR THY CHILDREN*
THE LORD'S PRAYER
NURSERY RHYMES
SONG   *WHAT DOES LITTLE BIRDIE SAY?*

KINDERGARTEN GAMES
THE HEN AND HER CHICKENS   *THE SNAIL*

INSPECTION OF CLASSROOMS
NATIONAL ANTHEM

Mr Hew Morrison, Chairman of the Board, made a lengthy speech in which he drew attention to some of the important educational issues of the day. He announced that no fees would be charged for pupils between the ages of five and fourteen, and pointed out that, in his opinion, a free education was just as valuable as one which had been paid for. The school was designed for a total of 1200 pupils but, until the extension was completed, only half of that number was enrolled. With expansion in mind, Mr Morrison was reported as follows: 'It might be that when the whole was finished they might find room for the teaching of laundry work without a knowledge of which he thought a girl's education could hardly be complete'. A shorter speech was made by Andrew Carnegie, whose business interests, in the iron and steel industries of America, later financed his vast philanthropic programme in his native Scotland.

In the first few years at South Morningside there were acute difficulties with accommodation. Within a fortnight of the official opening Miss Mathison had a class of eighty in Standard 2, and Miss Aitchison 'with 105 beginners is, of course, unable to make any satisfactory progress'. Some improvement was achieved when the cookery class was removed to a shop at 143 Comiston Road, and a temporary corrugated iron hut was erected in the playground. On 15th May 1895 control of the school was transferred to Edinburgh School Board and the new wing was opened in the autumn of 1896.

In common with other similar schools South Morningside has maintained a daily log of events since it opened. Whilst these logs contain many transient items, they also contain interesting examples of everyday reaction to events of national importance. A fairly lengthy entry for 22nd January 1901 reads: 'A feeling of deep sadness pervaded the school on Tuesday morning. Our beloved Queen had passed away on the previous evening. The school flag was hoisted half mast high. A few words appropriate to the occasion were said to the children by the Headmaster and other teachers, and then the children in deep solemnity marched slowly out of the school—one of the Senior girls meantime played the Dead March in Saul. It was a touching and never to be forgotten sight'. That high sense of patriotism returned again on 25th January on the day of the Proclamation in Edinburgh of Edward VII, but this time the children were absent on holiday.

Lengthy entries in the school logs cover the First World War 1914-1919, the General Strike in 1926 and the Second World War 1939-1945. The post-war progress of the school was under the able direction of three eminent headmasters, Forbes MacGregor from 1951 to 1965 followed by John L. Sloss from 1965 to 1971 and George Mutch from 1971 to 1982. Mr Mutch was succeeded in 1982 by the first female head teacher, Mrs Jeanette Perry. The school roll for the Session 1986-87 was 546.

The foundation stone for St. Peter's School in Falcon Gardens was laid in 1909 by the Most Reverend James Augustine Smith, Archbishop of St. Andrews and Edinburgh, and the school was opened on 4th April 1910. The colourful and imaginative Father John Gray of St. Peter's Church in Falcon Avenue was appointed as the school manager, and Sister Agnes McMullen, a Sister of Charity, acted as head teacher. The two-storey building of stone and harl is built round a central hall with balconies on three sides. The fourth, or south wall, contains an interesting mural, dated 1912, by the artist John Duncan, but unfortunately no further information on it is available, except that many of the figures on the mural were sketched from pupils attending the school at that time.

The management of the school was transferred from the Church to the Education Authority in 1919, at the end of the First World War. To mark the celebration of peace the children assembled in the hall on 16th July 1919 in the presence of Father Gray and his curate Father Bruce. The proceedings opened with 'Rule Britannia', after which Father Gray addressed the pupils to explain the meaning of the assembly. After singing 'Hearts of Oak', the pupils saluted The Flag and sang the National Anthem. According to the head teacher's logbook entry the school Roll of Honour was then read out 'and the children cheered each one'. Three logbook entries in the 1930s make interesting reading: '3.2.1930 Yesterday the Education Authority kindly granted permission to use the school for the presentation of his new robes to the Very Rev. John Canon Gray on his promotion to the Cathedral Chapter; 3.2.1933 Dr Park visited the school and examined the children on the Free Food List; 11.11.1937 In honour of the Coronation the children had a special dinner consisting of sausages and potatoes and a fruit jelly, while those on the Free Food List had an extra bottle of milk. After Grace was said I [the headteacher] reminded the children of the generosity of the Corporation of the City for whom three cheers were given'.

In more recent years the school has been subject to a number of administrative changes to rationalise the use of various buildings. In April 1966 St. Ignatius Primary School at Glen Street and Chalmers Street was discontinued as a separate school and incorporated in St. Peter's, and in August 1967 a new infant wing was opened at Falcon Gardens. It was not until 1975, however, that the Chalmers Street building was closed and all pupils were taught at St. Peter's. In 1979 an inter-denominational nursery class was opened.

Today the administrative offices of the school are located in a large detached house immediately to the north of the main school building. This house was occupied as a convent by the Sisters of Charity until 1969. The present head teacher is Miss M.T. Dunne, assisted by Miss C.J.S. Knowles; there are fourteen permanent staff in addition to specialist visiting staff; and the roll is 226 plus fifty pupils in the nursery.

Ecclesiastical Morningside

In 1947 William Mair devoted a separate section of *Historic Morningside* to the many churches established in and around the district. Forty

Morningside Parish Church on the corner of Newbattle Terrace and
Morningside Road, opened on 29th July 1838.

years later, whilst the number of separate churches has been reduced
slightly, the capacity for innovative change has not abated. Morningside's first parish church was opened in 1838 in the heart of the old
village but, as the population increased, churches of various denominations were established, firstly at Holy Corner, and later around
Morningside Station. The story of their evolution and involvement in
the community, through periods of unity and disunity, presents an
interesting microcosm of church history.

Morningside Parish Church

Morningside's oldest permanent church building dates from 1837. Before that, Sunday services were held in the Old Schoolhouse in Morningside Road, as the nearest church was St Cuthbert's at the West End. A lengthy circular letter, dated 19th June 1837, was distributed in Morningside drawing people's attention to the fact that there was no parish church, and that 'no efforts [had] hitherto been made to supply the deficiency'. The response was excellent. A long list of subscribers, headed by Alexander Falconar of Falcon Hall and his five daughters, pledged the sum of £2,037: 16s—well in excess of the estimated cost at £1,600. The architect, John Henderson, provided plans for 634 sittings, including a front gallery, with provision for two side galleries when required. A plot of land on the north corner of Morningside Road and Newbattle Terrace was gifted by Sir John Stuart Forbes, Bart., of Pitsligo and Fettercairn, proprietor of the lands of Greenhill, and within a very short time Morningside Parish Church was completed. The opening services, on Sunday 29th July 1838, were taken by Dr Thomas Chalmers in the morning, and the Rev. James Begg of Liberton in the afternoon. Subsequent services were conducted by the Rev. David Davidson and the Rev. Dr John Paul of St. Cuthbert's before the Rev. George Smeaton was appointed as the first permanent minister on 14th March 1839. After a short incumbency he was followed by the Rev. Dr Thomas Addis who joined the Disruption in 1843 and became the first minister of Morningside's first Free Church.

The fabric of the church has been altered from time to time over the years, frequently in response to increased membership. Although the bell was originally provided from Whitechapel Foundry at a cost of £27: 16: 11, Mr Henderson's drawings did not allow for a clock within the slender spire. In 1840 the congregation bought the mechanism of the clock from the Old Schoolhouse across the road, and transferred it to the church. It remained there until 1929, by which time it was probably more than a century old, and was replaced at a cost of £64. Shortly after the Rev. John M. Lang's appointment in 1868, the church was enlarged by the addition of an apse to the east, and transepts to the north and south, designed by Peddie and Kinnear. Further expansion was planned in the 1880s to meet the demands of an ever-increasing population, particularly to the south around Morningside Station. Instead of extending the parent church again, a decision was taken to erect a temporary iron church in 1884 on a piece of ground now occupied by the house at 2 Cluny Avenue. The 1868 apse was replaced in 1888 by a chancel, designed by Hardy and Wight, and in 1914 a proposal to demolish the church completely and rebuild it was thwarted by lack of money at the outbreak of the First World War.

In modern times the most significant event was the reunion in 1960 with Morningside High Church, built in 1894 as the last building used by Morningside Free Church (now occupied as the Church Hill Theatre).

Morningside Free Church

Morningside's involvement in the Free Church is equally interesting, particularly when it is remembered that the leader of the Disruption, Dr Thomas Chalmers, lived at 1 Church Hill, a few hundred yards from Morningside Parish Church. The Rev. Thomas Addis had been minister at the Parish Church for only a short time when he 'came out' in 1843 and led most of the congregation in their opposition to the principle of patronage. Having made their protest against a system which prevented the congregation from having a say in the selection of its own minister, the Morningside Disruptionists found themselves faced with some practical problems. They had no church—and very little money. Not surprisingly, they were threatened with expulsion if they remained in the Parish Church building, and when they applied to use the Old Schoolhouse, they met with equal opposition. Fortunately Dr Chalmers was at hand with a large, conveniently situated villa, in which services were held for the first few weeks. Thereafter, the congregation secured the use of a large circular tent pitched at the south corner of Abbotsford Park, but when it collapsed, the managers of the Old Schoolhouse seem to have had a change of heart and offered them the use of the Schoolhouse until a more permanent home was found.

Between 1844 and 1929 when the United Free Church and the Established Church were reunited, Morningside Free Church occupied three separate buildings. The first was built in 1844, apparently as a replica of Tanfield Hall at Canonmills where the Disruptionists first met. The site (now occupied by the house at 74 Morningside Road) was gifted by Mrs Steel of Grangebank House, Burghmuirhead but

Morningside Baptist Church at Holy Corner, formed in 1894, in the building originally designed by MacGibbon & Ross in 1872 for the Free Church.
Photograph by Graham C. Cant.

unfortunately the church was demolished shortly after 1874. The second church, designed in 1872 by MacGibbon and Ross, was opened in 1874 a few hundred yards to the north of the first church, opposite the junction of Morningside Road and Greenhill Park. The congregation remained there until 1894 when the Free Church made its last move to the red sandstone church designed by Hippolyte J. Blanc, now occupied as the Church Hill Theatre. As Morningside High Church, it eventually united with Morningside Parish Church in 1960.

Morningside Baptist Church

Morningside Baptist Church was formed in 1894 when the Free Church vacated their former building at Holy Corner. The potential for a Baptist Church, in the heart of ecclesiastical Morningside, was realised by the Rev. J. Cumming Brown, then minister of Leith Baptist Church, who arranged purchase of the former Free Church building for the sum of £3,000. A meeting of interested parties was held in Torrance's Tea Rooms on the corner of Comiston Road and Belhaven Terrace, at which it was decided to form a church, initially with only nineteen members. The opening services were held at the beginning of December 1894.

By the end of the century the total membership was sixty-two. The first minister resigned in 1899 and was succeeded in the following year by the Rev. Ernest G. Lovell under whose ministry numbers rose to over two hundred. One of the longest ministries was that of the Rev. F.M. Hirst from 1924 to 1942 who led open-air services on Bruntsfield Links.The church sustained a serious setback in 1973 when fire destroyed part of the building, but after rebuilding it was reopened with a much increased membership. Today, Morningside Baptist Church is involved, with other churches, in the development of Holy Corner Church Centre in the building formerly used by North Morningside Parish Church.

Baptist churches differ from other denominations in certain important respects, notably in the practice of baptism of believers by immersion. Some Baptist churches restrict membership to those who have been baptised in this way, whilst others, like Morningside, accept members who believe in Jesus Christ as Saviour and Lord, whatever the form of their baptism. Although a Baptist church is self-governing through the church meetings of its members, some centralisation of administration is inevitable. The Baptist Union of Scotland co-ordinates the efforts of individual churches in Scotland in matters which cannot easily be undertaken by a single church, and Edinburgh and Lothians Baptist Association deals with similar matters at a more local level.

Christ Church Episcopal at Holy Corner, on the north corner of Colinton Road and Morningside Road, designed in 1875 by Hippolyte J. Blanc. Photograph by Phyllis Margaret Cant..

Christ Church, Morningside

The Episcopal Church is also represented at Holy Corner on the north corner of Colinton Road and Morningside Road. The nucleus of the first congregation met in the drill hall of Merchiston Castle School on 30th August 1874 under the convenorship of Dr Bruce Bremner who had already secured the voluntary services of the Rev. Francis E. Belcombe. When attendances at subsequent meetings reached about a hundred and fifty a decision was taken to build a permanent church. In 1875 the architect Hippolyte J. Blanc, himself a member of the congregation, drew up plans for a church in the French-Gothic style of architecture. The builders were W. & J. Kirkwood who had completed sufficient of the work for the church to be opened on 4th June 1876. Work on the chancel, tower and spire was completed later by a gift from Miss Falconar of Falcon Hall, in memory of her father, a founder member of Morningside Parish Church. On completion the church was dedicated by Bishop Cotterill on 12th March 1878 'in the presence of a vast assemblage of clergy and laymen'. When the Rev. Francis E. Belcombe resigned due to ill-health in 1885 he was succeeded by the Rev. C.M. Black who remained Rector for the next thirty-five years.

In the closing years of the nineteenth century Christ Church, like the other denominations, found that a lot of the new population lived further south, round Morningside Station. To meet their needs an iron church was erected in 1896 on the south corner of Braid Road and Comiston Terrace. This small Mission Station, St. Fillan's, eventually gathered a congregation of nearly three hundred, but was closed in 1906 when the ground was required for building purposes. Many years later, in 1937, a second St. Fillan's came into being at Buckstone Drive, and became independent of Christ Church in June 1971.

At the centenary in 1976 a most informative booklet, *Christ Church Morningside 1876-1976*, was written by N.J. Littlefair, outlining the early history of the church and its involvement with the community over the years. Christ Church has joined with the Morningside Baptist Church and Morningside United Church in establishing and administering Holy Corner Church Centre.

Morningside United Church: Holy Corner Church Centre

Two other church buildings at Holy Corner have a particularly interesting, and sometimes confusing, history. One is Morningside United Church on the north corner of Chamberlain Road and Morningside Road, and the other is Holy Corner Church Centre on the south corner. Their present-day use can be traced back to the year 1860.

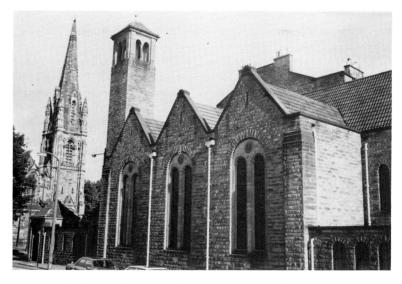

Morningside United Church at Chamberlain Road, Holy Corner, in which the congregation is both part of the Church of Scotland and of the Congregational Union of Scotland.
Photograph by Phyllis Margaret Cant.

In that year a nucleus of people interested in establishing a United Presbyterian Church in Morningside met in a classroom at Merchiston Castle School. By July 1862 they had sufficient support to engage the architect R. Paterson to draw up plans for a modest church to hold 450 people. The site of the completed building was the north corner of Chamberlain Road and Morningside Road, and on 5th November 1863 Dr John Cairns preached the opening sermon. Although a gallery was added in 1874, it was clear by 1879 that accommodation would become increasingly inadequate. A decision was taken to build a new church on the south corner to seat one thousand, and the foundation stone was laid on 28th February 1880 by Dr Calderwood. At the inaugural service on 16th October 1881 the collection amounted to £1,813, which included one particularly poignant offering of a shilling, wrapped in a piece of paper on which was written 'The small gift of a dead child'. North Morningside United Presbyterian Church became United Free in 1900 and part of the reunited Church of Scotland in 1929.

When the United Presbyterian Church moved from their original site on the north corner of Chamberlain Road and Morningside Road in 1880, the old church was bought for £2,000 by Morningside Athenaeum Club who provided a library, lecture theatre and concert hall for members. On 6th November 1887 the hall was let to a small group of Congregationalists for their inaugural service taken by the Rev. W. Douglas Mackenzie, and in January 1890 Morningside Congregational Church bought the building from the Athenaeum Club for £2,300. By the turn of the century serious thought was given to demolishing the old building, and erecting a new church on the same site. It was not, however, until 1927 that any real progress was made. A large church hall was erected in 1927 which was used for Sunday services until the old church was demolished and the new one built. The new church was designed by James McLachlan in 1927; the foundation stone was laid on 16th June 1928 by Charles Price J.P; and the service of dedication was held on 5th October 1929.

For many years churches of very different denominations have been represented in Morningside, but in the late 1950s a wind of change was blowing round Holy Corner. The various denominations were still there, but the differences were looking less important than the similarities. A series of initiatives began to break down some of the apparent barriers: in 1958 the First United District Services were held among the four Holy Corner churches; in 1962 the idea was taken up by the Bruntsfield churches; and on 4th February 1968 a joint service took place between North Morningside Church and Morningside Congregational Church. Further progress might well have been delayed but for the fact that both churches found themselves without a minister in 1973. A document on linking was drawn up, approved by both churches and formalised on 9th June 1974. A new minister, the Rev. J. Stewart Miller of Mortlach and Cabrach, was inducted on 20th March 1975 and services were held in alternate churches, linking the congregations spiritually but not financially. It was not until 12th June 1980 that North Morningside Church and Morningside Congregational Church joined to form Morningside United Church, a unique union in which the congregation is both part of the Church of Scotland and part of the Congregational Union of Scotland.

The former North Morningside Church building is now the home of the Holy Corner Church Centre, administered jointly by members of

The former North Morningside Church, now Holy Corner Church Centre, is being redeveloped as the Eric Liddell Centre.
Photograph by Phyllis Margaret Cant.

Morningside United Church, Christ Church and Morningside Baptist Church. The ancillary accommodation is already in use for the lunch club, Napier Club for senior citizens, and the Christian Fellowship of Healing. A recent addition is the Sycomore restaurant which takes its name from the biblical story of Zacchaeus who climbed into a sycomore tree to get a better view of Jesus. By far the most ambitious scheme, however, is the recent appeal for one million pounds to create a major community centre on four separate floors in the old church. A recent competition for the best design has been won by the architect John Forbes of Nicholas Groves-Raines. The building has been named the Eric Liddell Centre, in memory of Eric Liddell, the former runner and missionary known to the world through the film *Chariots of Fire*, who was a member of Morningside Congregational Church.

St. Peter's Church

St. Peter's Church in Falcon Avenue owes much to the chance meeting of two men from completely different backgrounds. John Gray, the eldest of nine children, was born at Woolwich in 1866 into a fairly poor

St. Peter's Roman Catholic Church in Falcon Avenue, designed in 1905 by Sir Robert Lorimer, and opened on 25th April 1907.

background. He started work as a metal worker at the age of thirteen to assist the family finances, but later he studied languages at evening classes and attended London University. He entered the Civil Service and became librarian to the Foreign Office. In 1888, when he was deeply involved in literary circles in London, he met André Raffalovitch whose family were Russian Jews who had escaped from anti-Jewish pressures in Paris in 1863. Towards the end of the nineteenth century Gray's writing and poetry took on an increasingly religious theme, which was obviously beginning to redirect his life. He resigned from his job as librarian and went to Rome to study for the Catholic priesthood. He was ordained in Rome on 21st December 1901 and was appointed curate at St. Patrick's Church in the Cowgate in Edinburgh. His friendship with Raffalovitch continued and was greatly strengthened, in 1905, when Raffalovitch moved to Edinburgh, and took up residence at 9 Whitehouse Terrace. In that same year the two men resolved to build a new Roman Catholic church in Morningside, mainly from a generous donation by Raffalovitch. The site on the north corner of Falcon Avenue and Falcon Gardens was purchased from the Merchant Company in May 1905, and Sir Robert Lorimer was commissioned to draw the plans. The foundation stone was laid on

17th April 1906 by Archbishop James Augustine Smith, who returned on 25th April 1907 to bless the church, when Mass was celebrated for the first time.

St. Peter's Church is considered to be one of Sir Robert Lorimer's greatest achievements, although much of the interior work has been altered from the original. Fortunately, in 1957, several photographs were taken of the interior by Paul Shillabeer and reproduced in *St. Peter's Edinburgh Golden Jubilee Brochure 1907-1957*. The nave is lit by tall arched windows between shallow buttresses on top of which perch two carved beasts used as rainwater heads. The masonry is coursed rubble with Prudham dressings. The Presbytery and former school on the south-west corner form an interesting forecourt, reached through an ornamental iron gateway supporting crossed keys. In the north-east angle of the courtyard is a tall campanile with a bell chamber below the Chinese-style roof. Internally, the lofty nave is flanked by narrow aisles, the tie-rods being anchored by wrought-iron monograms high up on the arched walls. Of the many stained-glass windows the most recent, in 1963, is in the north-east chapel, in memory of Canon John Gray.

The Christian Brethren

When the Old Schoolhouse in Morningside Road was closed in 1892, the owner, Peter Cowieson, let the accommodation for various purposes, but in 1906 he rented it to the Christian Brethren as a place of worship. In 1946 the building was sold to them subject to the express condition 'that it would continue as a place of Christian witness in the locality'.

For many years this small church has been a centre of evangelical activity, with particular emphasis on concern for children. Immediately after the Second World War the Sunday School had more than one hundred children on the roll, most of whom came from families living in the neighbouring streets of Springvalley. Whilst that high level of attendance at Sunday School has not been maintained in recent years, there is instead, greater emphasis on children's clubs and other activities during the week. In the early years after the Disruption Dr Chalmers preached in the Schoolhouse, and the present congregation is acutely aware of its long tradition. Many members of the congregation have dedicated their lives to overseas mission service in different parts of the world, particularly in Zaire, formerly the Belgian Congo.

The Rev. Angus W. Morrison, minister at Braid Church, with William R. Smith, chairman of the Congregational Board, at the unveiling of the plaque erected to mark the centenary of the church.
Courtesy of *The Scotsman* Publications Ltd.

The Old Schoolhouse is a very distinctive building of one storey, the central bay of which is slightly advanced to support the masonry of the clock tower. The clock has recently been given a complete overhaul—for many years the hands remained at 3.40! However, on New Year's Eve 1980 the movement was set going again. The work involved in the renovation was done by a member of the congregation, most of the parts being handmade. In 1980 the fairly modest accommodation was greatly improved by the addition of small single-storey wings to the north and to the south.

Braid Church

Although a United Presbyterian church was established at Holy Corner as early as 1863, almost twenty years elapsed before the population at the south end of Morningside Road was sufficient to , sustain another congregation. A temporary iron building for Braid United Presbyterian Church was erected at the north end of Braid Road and Comiston Road on or near ground now occupied by the red sandstone building above the Hermitage Bar. With financial assistance from Dr John Kerr the church was opened on 27th January 1883 by the Rev. Professor Calderwood. The members were formed into a congregation on 15th October 1883 and the Rev. Walter Brown of Galashiels was appointed as the first minister. Two years later the building fund had reached £1,140, which enabled the congregation to give serious thought to building a permanent church. A site at the west end of Nile Grove was purchased and the architect George Washington Browne was employed to draw up plans for a church to seat 750, at a total cost of £5,000. The foundation stone was laid on Saturday 9th October 1886 by the Rev. Professor Duff, Moderator of the United Presbyterian Church, but before the building was completed a small divergence of funds was required: the sum of fifty pounds was spent to extend the old iron church by twelve and a half feet to provide five more rows of seats. The stone church was opened for public worship on 10th July 1887, by which time many of the organisations had been established, including the Young Women's Guild, Band of Hope, Literary Society and a Home Mission Station at Swanston.

The completed building is very different to any other church in Morningside. The simple octagonal shape is enhanced by a half-round portico entrance, supported by pairs of Ionic pillars, above which is a steep-sided pediment, flanked by two open conical towers. Internally the octagonal shape created an interesting auditorium in which the congregation was arranged around the pulpit, the organ and the choir. The chancel area was greatly improved during extensive renovation work in 1952 by re-siting the organ and choir on the east side.

In the Centenary book, the second fifty years contains, among other things, two interesting contributions by ministers of the parish. The lengthier one is by the Rev. Roderick Smith, minister of the parish from 1948 to 1976, in which he highlights the church's increasingly strong financial position despite an alarming decrease in members. The second contribution is by the present incumbent, the Rev. Angus W. Morrison, who concludes the chapter with a confident blend of realism and optimism expressed by the hope that there is 'perhaps the faintest hint that nationally a time for return to religion, both evangelical and ecumenical, is to be discerned'.

Recently Braid Church has marked another of its important dates by the erection of a small granite stone, and plaque, in the church grounds. Below an engraving of the old iron church is the following inscription:

> From 27 January 1883 Braid
> (U.P.) Church worshipped in an iron
> building, shown above, some 300 yards
> south of this site.
> The present church, designed by
> George Washington Browne was
> opened on 10th July 1887
> We praise thee, O Lord
>
> 10 July 1987

The idea of the stone, erected to mark the church centenary, was given financial support from the Smith family of Morningside in honour of their parents, who were lifelong members of the congregation.

Cluny Parish Church

Cluny Parish Church, on the south corner of Cluny Gardens and Braid Road, was formed in 1974 from the union of St. Matthew's Parish Church and South Morningside Parish Church, both of which date from the end of the nineteenth century.

St. Matthew's Church might never have been built at all if it had not been for a decision taken in 1883 by Morningside Parish Church to erect an iron church in Cluny Avenue, rather than extend the church at the corner of Morningside Road and Newbattle Terrace. An iron church, under its first minister the Rev. George Milligan, was opened on 11th November 1883 at a cost of £650 to cater for the increased population living to the south of the original parish church. In October 1886 Hippolyte J. Blanc, the great church architect of the day, was employed to draw up plans for a permanent building; the foundation stone was laid on 1st June 1888 by the Lord High Commissioner to the General Assembly of the Church of Scotland, the Earl of Hopetoun; and the opening service was held on 4th May 1890. The eventual cost was £20,000, from which there was a small saving from the transfer of the old iron church to Bruntsfield Gardens for the new church of St. Mark's, later renamed St. Oswald's.

About the same time the Free Church was planning to establish a church near Morningside Station. A preliminary meeting was held on

14th January 1889 in the house of the Rev. Alexander Martin of the Free Church at 4 Nile Grove, when it was resolved to hold services in the hall at South Morningside Drive (now known as the Dunedin Hall in Morningside Drive). A site for a permanent church on the north corner of Cluny Drive and Braid Road (opposite the Pentland Tennis Club) was purchased from the Gordon of Cluny Trustees, and Rowand Anderson was appointed as the architect. The foundation stone was laid on 22nd January 1891 for a church to seat eight hundred people, estimated at £8,500 but costing over £11,000 on completion. At the opening service the church was called Braid Road Free Church, but shortly afterwards it was renamed South Morningside Free Church. In 1929 it became South Morningside Parish Church on the union of the Free Church with the Established Church.

After the 1929 union St. Matthew's and South Morningside continued as parish churches, taking their members from a cross-section of the population of Morningside and beyond. In 1974, however, the Rev. Dr R.C.M. Mathers stood down as minister of St. Matthew's after thirty-two years, in the interests of an impending union between the two churches. This was completed slightly later, St Matthew's Church being used for worship under the new minister, the Rev. George Munro, and South Morningside Church being redeveloped as Cluny Church Centre in 1976.

Although some compromise is frequently necessary in the rationalisation of the use of church buildings, it is generally considered that the architecture of St. Matthew's Church was more worthy of retention in its original form. Its red sandstone Gothic exterior commands an excellent position on the raised grassy bank, obscured only by mature trees within its own grounds. The high-roofed nave, measuring eighty feet by forty-two feet, is flanked by side aisles and transepts. The chancel, added later by Hippolyte J. Blanc, has a marble floor and oak furnishings in keeping with the organ by Henry Willis & Sons in 1901 and rebuilt by Rushworth and Dreaper in 1929. The finest stained-glass work is a group of four lights on the east wall depicting the Evangelists.

Entertainment

Morningside, like any other village or suburb, has always had its own places of entertainment, which have catered for the needs of the community through various changes in social patterns. Several clubs and halls, private and public, offered billiards, snooker, dancing and film entertainment, in addition to the many social gatherings held by the churches. One of the earliest venues, for billiards, was in Millar Crescent, in premises now occupied as a photographic repair centre, but much more modern facilities for the game are now available at the Angle Club in Jordan Lane. Weddings, dances and other social functions were held almost every Saturday at the Dunedin Halls in Morningside Drive and also at the Abbotsford Hall at Church Hill. In addition to purely local facilities, however, Morningside has been, and in some cases still is, in the forefront of cinema, ballroom dancing and theatre in Edinburgh.

According to *The Last Picture Shows: Edinburgh* by Brendon Thomas Morningside's earliest known picture house opened prior to the First World War in what was previously known as Morningside Hall in Springvalley Gardens. The hall was built at the end of the nineteenth century on the site of cow byres belonging to a local dairy. The cinema continued until 1938, during which time it had several names, including Morningside Photoplay House, the Ritz Kinema, Evans Picture House, Cine Playhouse and finally Springvalley Cinema. Between 1914 and 1938 it had three owners, R.M. Ireland in 1914, followed by Thomas Butt, and then George Murray in the last few years of its existence. In the late 1930s the proprietor decided to close the cinema, perhaps on account of the opening of its main competitor, the Dominion. After 1939, the Springvalley Cinema became the Silver Slipper Ballroom. Today the building is in commercial use: nothing remains of the cinema's interior fittings, but the facade is still obviously that of a hall or cinema.

As Springvalley closed, the Dominion opened, on 31st January 1938. After serving in the 1914-1918 War, Captain W.M. Cameron opened the Lyceum cinema in Slateford Road in 1926, and later he decided that his next cinema should be in Morningside. Fortunately, he already had the material, a pink-coloured artificial stone manufactured as Craighall Cast Stone by one of his other business interests. He acquired a site in Newbattle Terrace to the east of Morningside Parish Church Hall, and instructed the famous cinema architect, T. Bowhill Gibson, to draw up plans in the flamboyant Art Deco style of the period. The cinema was completed in only three months.

The Dominion Cinema, built by Capt. W.M. Cameron and opened on 31st January 1938, is still privately owned by the Cameron family. Photograph by Phyllis Margaret Cant.

Throughout the Second World War and into the period of declining cinema audiences, the Dominion maintained a family atmosphere both in its management and its patrons. Complete independence from the film distribution organisations enabled it to control the type and duration of its film programme, in a way which was not open to many of its competitors. Large-scale alterations were undertaken in 1972, when two separate cinemas were constructed within the original building. The occasion was marked by a reopening by Moira Shearer on 25th May 1972 when the programme was *Cold Turkey* and *On a Clear Day You Can See Forever*. Eight years later, in 1980, further expansion took place to provide a third cinema built into the roof space above the reception area. This commitment to expansion and renovation paid dividends recently when the Dominion won First Prize out of 1,242 entries in the United Kingdom, in the category 'Comfort and Decor' of the Cinema 1987 Awards.

The Dominion is still very much a family business: Mrs J.M. Cameron, widow of Captain W.M. Cameron, is the Chairman; her son Derek M. Cameron is the Managing Director; and Mr Cameron's two sons recently came into the business as the third generation of the Cameron family involved in the Dominion. In addition to the three

cinemas there is a bar, coffee lounge and The Spool Room restaurant—ample evidence that the Dominion still has an appetite for
expansion as it nears its half-century in 1988.

In 1926, when large areas of Britain were paralysed by the General
Strike, Morningside was visited by another entrepreneur, keen to try
ideas beyond his garage business. The story has been expertly re-
searched by Elizabeth Casciani, and reproduced, in part, in the *Scots
Magazine* for March 1980 under the evocative title 'The Plaza was the
Place'.

Charles Jones started in the motor business in Peebles but he later
moved to Edinburgh where he set up a garage in Lothian Road, before
coming to Morningside. He acquired the site on the corner of Falcon
Avenue and Morningside Road for Jones Motor House, a spacious
complex to include workshops, service areas, filling station, showroom
and public hall. It was this latter accommodation which proved to be a
tentative step in the right direction, as reported in the *Motor Trader and
Review* for August 1926:

> One day early last spring when I went down to see the progress of the work
> I found Mr Jones full of enthusiasm about a new scheme for making the
> hall a palais de danse. Three months later when I saw the main buildings I
> found that the dance hall idea had been carried out and that the 'Plaza
> Salon de Danse and Cafe' was to open in September.

It opened amid fierce competition from Maximes and the Marine
Gardens, and attendance was so poor that Mr Jones frequently
returned entrance money to his patrons when he felt that the low
attendance had spoiled the evening. This frank acceptance of the
difficulties, which did not affect the success of the garage business, may
well have been instrumental in increasing popularity. Within a short
time attendances began to increase substantially. A high standard of
music, dancing and formal dress, combined with the loyalty of the staff
under Miss Tweedie, eventually brought success.

The main ballroom was on an upper floor with the restaurant
between it and the smaller east ballroom on a lower floor. In the main
ballroom the male fraternity took up a position on the slightly elevated
balcony to survey the flock of city belles, whose only escape was a curt
refusal to dance. As the evening developed, couples progressed to the
restaurant and then to the east ballroom where the standard of
dancing was much higher. For those without a sense of rhythm, the

Church Hill Theatre during the Edinburgh Festival 1987, built as a Free Church in 1892 and converted in 1965 to a theatre, primarily for the use of amateur groups.
Photograph by Phyllis Margaret Cant.

intimate atmosphere and the euphoria of the moment appeared to compensate for the lack of basic skills.

Over the years, several well-known bands have played at the Plaza, including Lionel Murrey's London Dance Band in the 1920s, Joe Smith and The Uterpians after 1945, and the Colorado under the leadership of George McIntosh. Their repertoire reflected the many changes in dance styles up to the mid-1970s, when ballroom dancing ceased to draw large crowds. The Plaza closed after the last waltz on Saturday 1st March 1975, and the building was demolished in 1980.

The large supermarket built on the site in 1981 has a bronze plaque with the following inscription:

> This Safeway Superstore
> Now stands on the site of
> The Jones Motor House
> and
> The Plaza Ballroom

When Morningside High Church united with Morningside Parish Church in 1960 there was considerable controversy over the future of the red sandstone building at Church Hill, designed by Blanc in 1892. Fortunately, a proposal to demolish the church and construct flats was averted by the intervention of Edinburgh Corporation, who bought the former church in 1962 for £6,000. The idea at the time, which won the support of the Lord Provost, Sir John G. Dunbar, was to convert the building into a theatre, primarily for the use of amateur drama groups, who had lost the use of the Little Theatre in the Pleasance. The church interior was gutted and a new auditorium to seat 380 was constructed in the nave, with the seats steeply raked from the new stage at the east end to the original balcony at the west end. A coffee lounge, dressing room and scenery store were also provided, in addition to the small hall at the rear intended to be used for rehearsals. The total capital expenditure was £63,000.

The Church Hill Theatre was opened on 25th September 1965 by Tom Fleming, director of the Royal Lyceum Company, the first production being *The Importance of Being Ernest* with a cast drawn from various local groups. During the first week the small hall was used for an exhibition of art by the Edinburgh Sketching Club, Holyrood Art Club and the Edinburgh Photographic Society. More than twenty years later the theatre is still the home of amateur drama in Edinburgh, although professional groups do use the facilities at the Edinburgh International Festival. The administration of the theatre is in the hands of the Church Hill Theatre Users Association, whose members are elected from Edinburgh District Council and the various drama and music groups involved. The theatre is used by a wide variety of interests: drama groups include the Makars, Onstage 66, Davidson's Mains, Mercators, Edinburgh People's Theatre and Leitheatre; music is represented by the Southern Light Opera Group, the Bohemian Lyric Opera Company and Allegro; and several local schools use the facilities for their end-of-term concerts. Old-time dancing and highland dancing groups are regularly held in the small hall, in addition to local dance schools and ballet schools.

Morningside Road and the Old Village

In 1586 the Burgh Muir was divided into four lots, one of which was Morningside Estate, consisting of twenty-six acres to the west of what is now Morningside Road. It was bounded on the north by Albert Terrace, on the south by the Jordan Burn, and on the west by

Morningside Station in the early twentieth century before the clock was erected in 1910, with the single-storey station building on the left and a cab stance on the right, outside the small coal office.
Courtesy of W.B. Grubb.

Myreside. Within this large tract of land there were three separate villages, Morningside, Myreside and Tipperlinn, of which only Morningside has survived. Although the first Ordnance Survey Map of 1852 clearly shows the position of Morningside Road, it was not until 1885 that its designation and house numbering were applied continuously from Holy Corner to Morningside Station. Prior to that, Morningside Road consisted of a series of short sections, each of which had its own name. Starting at Church Hill and going south, the names were Waverley Terrace, Marmion Terrace, Banner Place, Morningside Bank, Esplin Place, Blackford Place, Falcon Place, Reid's Buildings, Morningside Terrace and Morningside Village.

As the Old Schoolhouse is one of the oldest and most distinctive buildings in Morningside Road, it is a convenient point to begin a study of the old village. When the school was built in 1823 Morningside was very much a rural community, the village lying mainly to the west of the main road between Cuddy Lane and Morningside Park. On the east side of the main street, intermittent groups of cottages stretched from the junction with Falcon Avenue down to Briggs o' Braid at the Jordan Burn, where the post office is now situated.

Time has not stood still: a busy road junction sits above the railway line which no longer provides a passenger service.
Photograph by Phyllis Margaret Cant.

Although the tenement building era of the late nineteenth century completely altered the rural scene, it is possible to reconstruct some of the village atmosphere from the small areas which remain.

Cuddy Lane, formerly known as Rosewood Lane, led to Springvalley House, a fine old mansion set in its own grounds, once the home of James Grant, author of *Old and New Edinburgh*, and many other works. The house was demolished in 1907 but is commemorated by a stone plaque set into the tenement of Nos. 43 and 45 Springvalley Terrace. In Cuddy Lane two buildings date from at least 1823. Rosewood Cottage (now No. 6 Cuddy Lane) was built for Miss Ann Henderson but was divided into two dwellings around 1944, the east section retaining the name Rosewood Cottage and the west section being named The Cottage. In the back garden of The Cottage (No. 4) is a deep well of fresh spring water, providing a tantalising clue to the significance of the name Springvalley. Immediately to the west of The Cottage is a larger two-storey building, Viewhill Cottage (now No. 2), dating from the same period as Rosewood Cottage. From about 1900 to 1920 Viewhill Cottage was occupied by Austin's Family Laundry, first established in 1890 at 4 Jordan Lane.

The tenement building immediately to the south of Cuddy Lane was built on an open piece of ground, and against its south gable is a short row of two-storey shops and houses. These formed part of the old village, along with another group to the rear, entered through a pend at No. 160. In the forecourt of the Merlin Public House a plain two-storey building was the site of Dick Wright's smiddy which closed around 1900. Afterwards it was occupied by a sculptor and tombstone maker on the ground floor. The upper storey was formerly the Blackford Press which took its name from the short section of Morningside Road in front of the Merlin, known as Blackford Place. The two-storey building and the sculptor's yard were removed when the Merlin was built.

Morningside Public Library was opened on 9th November 1904 by John Harrison, the second son of Lord Provost George Harrison. It is described in the Edinburgh volume of *The Buildings of Scotland* as having 'a hard officious frontage of Blackpastures (Northumberland) Stone with pedimented ends, the carving by Joseph Hayes', quite different in style to Denholm's Smiddy and cottage which previously stood on the site. Adjacent to Denholm's Smiddy, at the north corner of Springvalley Gardens and Morningside Road, was the Free Church of Scotland School, the site now occupied by 190-196 Morningside Road. To the south of the Free Church School was Reid Lane leading to Reid's Cottage and a dairy farm owned for many years by John Reid. The cottages are still there, but the byres were demolished in 1899 for the construction of Springvalley Gardens and Terrace.

One of the principal mansions of the district was Morningside House, which stood in its own grounds, set back from Morningside Road on land now occupied by a supermarket on the north corner of Morningside Park and Morningside Road. It is difficult to date Morningside House because some reports confuse it with the much grander Falcon Hall to the east. The best-informed opinion is that Morningside House was probably built around 1780 for Lord Gardenstone, the somewhat eccentric Senator of the College of Justice who came to live in Morningside in 1789. Kay's *Original Portraits* portrays Lord Gardenstone, 'distinguished as a man of some talent and much eccentricity', riding into town on horseback with a young boy in Highland dress running behind. The boy was employed to look after the horse during the time that the court was in session, and then to run all the way back to Morningside in the evening. The judge's affection for animals was not confined to the equine species. Even if the law was not an ass, at least it was close to a pig! Before retiring to bed in the

The Canny Man's or the Volunteer Arms, a favourite Morningside hostelry in the hands of the Kerr family for more than a century. Photograph by Phyllis Margaret Cant.

winter, his lordship allowed one of his favourite pigs to sleep in his bed to warm it up, and then to spend the rest of the night lying on his clothes to make them warm and comfortable for the morning. Later in life Lord Gardenstone was deeply involved in improving the living conditions of the inhabitants of Laurencekirk near his estate of Johnstone, and in the erection of St. Bernard's Well at Stockbridge. After he died in 1793 Morningside House and estate passed to his nephew, who sold to David Deuchar the distinguished etcher and engraver. The Deuchar family remained there until the early 1870s when Morningside House was occupied by John Reid, the dairyman, until it was demolished in 1895. The tenement which now stands on the site contains a sculptured panel commemorating the Diamond Jubilee of Queen Victoria in 1897.

At the beginning of the nineteenth century, land to the south of Morningside House was not developed, but in 1813 Morningside's first asylum was built 'for the cure or relief of mental derangement', to replace the Edinburgh Bedlam, at Bristo, where Robert Fergusson, the distinguished poet, died, ravaged by mental disorder, on 16th October 1774 at the age of twenty-four.

On the east side of Morningside Road, immediately south of the

Jordan Burn on what is now the front lawn of Braid Church, was the toll-house at Briggs o' Braid. It was erected shortly after 1752 when the previous toll at Wright's Houses, near the Barclay Church, was abolished. Not unnaturally, this extra financial burden was disliked by those residents of Morningside who lived south of the Jordan Burn, and, for many years, its existence seriously restricted the growth of housing to the south. After road tolls were abolished completely in 1883, Sir John Skelton of the Hermitage of Braid bought the toll-house in 1888 and had it demolished and re-erected as a lodge house at the entrance to the Hermitage where it still stands. Once the toll had been abolished, Morningside developed rapidly to the south with Maxwell Street being one of the first streets to be built. In 1884, when Morningside Station opened for passenger traffic, it became the natural focal point of the neighbourhood. Much of the planning for the successful suburban line was undertaken by Thomas Bouch, designer of the ill-fated Tay Bridge, which collapsed with the loss of many lives on 28th December 1879. Thomas Bouch died in October 1880 before the suburban line opened, and was buried in Dean Cemetery.

When the station opened, a group of Edinburgh businessmen, headed by Colonel Trotter of Mortonhall, decided to build an hotel on the corner of Braid Road and Comiston Road, but when the work was finished there were insufficient funds to complete the enterprise, and the building was converted into tenement flats. A less ambitious scheme, which nevertheless provided the district with its most distinctive landmark, was completed in 1910 when the station clock was presented to the people of Morningside by three local Town Councillors, R.K. Inches, William Inman and William Torrance. The Torrance family owned Torrance's Tea Room, a popular venue on the corner of Comiston Road and Belhaven Terrace. At the west end of Belhaven Terrace, Morningside Cemetery was laid out in 1878 and is the burial place of several eminent persons, including William Cowan, a past President of the Old Edinburgh Club who bequeathed a valuable collection of books and papers on Edinburgh to the City Library; Alison Cunningham, 'Cummy', Robert Louis Stevenson's nurse; and in much more recent times Sir Edward Appleton, Principal and Vice-Chancellor of Edinburgh University who died in 1965. In 1981 a detailed Survey of Monumental Inscriptions in Morningside Cemetery was compiled by members of the Morningside Association headed by Mrs Sheila B. Durham who did much of the early research. This invaluable source of genealogical information, in two volumes,

On the wall of Morningside Parish Church, the Bore Stone, said to have held the Royal Standard for the muster of the Scottish Army on the Borough Muir before the Battle of Flodden, 1513.
Photograph by Phyllis Margaret Cant.

copies of which have been lodged with the National Library of Scotland and the Edinburgh City Library, records all headstones between 1878 and 1981, indexed, and divided into categories by occupation, qualification, sculpture etc.

Much of the early development of Morningside village was on the west side of Morningside Road. On the east side lay the Lands of

Cabs compete with cable cars at Morningside Station, 1903, with St.
Matthew's Church and South Morningside Church on the left, the
intended hotel in the centre, and Torrance's Tea Room on the right.
Courtesy of W.B. Grubb.

Canaan, delineated in an interesting Plan of Cannaan dated 1802,
now in Register House. The plan, surveyed by Thomas Johnston, was
probably drawn up in connection with a lawsuit between William
Mossman of Canaan and Major Archibald Mossman. It shows the
Lands of Canaan divided into twenty-two lots, mainly of three acres
each, bounded on the north by the Road to Grange, now Newbattle
Terrace; on the south by the Burn of Jordan and the Lands of Braid; on
the west by the road from Edinburgh to Biggar, now Morningside
Road; and on the east by the Lands of Blackford. The original feuars
included several names which constantly reappear in the early history
of Morningside: Alex Adie, James Belfrage, William Coulter and John
Ross, followed later by Lady Oswald and the Falconar family.

There is some confusion about the mansions of Falcon Hall and
Morningside Lodge. Around 1780 William Coulter (later Lord Provost of Edinburgh in 1808) built a house on the Canaan estate which
was probably called Morningside Lodge. In 1815 Alexander Falconar
built the much grander Falcon Hall, possibly by extending the original
Morningside Lodge. When completed, Falcon Hall was a very grand
building of two principal storeys with a facade of twelve monolithic
pillars. Four pillars created an imposing entrance, and above these
were eight pillars, in pairs, supporting a broad pediment. On the

214

The same junction in 1987—the churches are united into Cluny Parish Church, the hotel is a block of flats and Torrance's Tea Room is occupied by offices.
Photograph by Phyllis Margaret Cant.

ground floor the pillars were flanked by statues of Nelson and Wellington. Despite their apparently opulent lifestyle, the Falconars were generous benefactors to the community and in particular to Morningside Parish Church and Christ Church Episcopal. A few years after the last of the five Falconar daughters died in 1887, Falcon Hall became a boarding school for boys.

According to *Plans and Notes of the Landed Estates of the Merchant Company Institutions* 1891, eighteen acres of land between Church Lane (Newbattle Terrace) and Canaan Lane were purchased by George Watson's Hospital from the Trustees of the Misses Falconar and Mrs Craigie in 1889 for £33,000. Strips of ground were also sold to the City for £1,195 to widen Newbattle Terrace and Morningside Road. Reference to the Minute Books of George Watson's Hospital for 1894 and 1895 suggest that the Governors were beginning to consider some form of development of the house and grounds. On 13th December 1894 they adopted a suggestion by the architects MacGibbon and Ross that the entrance gates and pillars should be advertised for sale by private bargain, and that the purchaser was to remove the material at his own expense. A few weeks later, on 3rd January 1895, the Committee authorised the sale of the gates and pillars to John White, the Builder, of 79 Craiglea Drive, for £25. The Minutes do not record whether Mr White proceeded with the job immediately but it was not until December 1906 that the Governors asked if the present occupier of Falcon Hall, John George Bartholomew, wished to renew the lease which expired at Whitsunday 1907. Mr Bartholomew confirmed on 14th March 1907 that he would not be renewing and, after several abortive ideas, the builder J.M. Cruickshank suggested in July 1907 that the mansion should be demolished. The Committee agreed, subject to ten items of historical interest being preserved, which included the statues of Wellington and Nelson, several falcons, marble door-jambs and tinted glass from the circular room. These items have never been traced, nor has a report dated 10th August 1907 from Mr Birnie Rhind R.S.A. on the statues which were to be presented to the City 'for the Art Gallery or the front of the new Art School'. Fortunately, when Falcon Hall was eventually demolished in 1909 the pillared facade was removed at the instigation of John George Bartholomew and rebuilt at the headquarters of Bartholomews, the cartographers, in Duncan Street. The gates and pillars with the falcons, for which Mr White agreed to pay £25, now stand at the entrance to Edinburgh Zoo at Corstorphine.

The village inn, probably dating from before Falcon Hall, stood on the south corner of Canaan Lane and Morningside Road. Originally known as The Volunteers' Rest, or The Rifleman, it later changed its name to The Volunteer Arms or The Canny Man's. At the end of the eighteenth century it was a small single-storey building resembling a cottage, which was purchased by James Kerr in 1871. He succeeded in building up a substantial clientèle consisting of local people, the carters and labourers from surrounding farms, and the men of the Edinburgh Volunteers who practised shooting in a field near Blackford Hill. The present building, under the name of the Volunteer Arms or the Canny Man's, is still in the hands of the Kerr family. A few yards east of the Volunteer Arms, in Canaan Lane, the former police station and fire station is still extant, although no longer used for these purposes. It was built in 1893 on two storeys, to provide three cells, a muster room, witness room and charge room, in addition to a fireman's room and fire engine house. Two flats were provided on the second floor, consisting of a living room, bedroom, bedcloset and W.C. Each flat shared a wash house and a drying area built on the roof of the cells.

Going north from Canaan Lane, the line of tenement buildings on the east side of Morningside Road is almost unbroken except for the supermarket built on the site of the old Plaza Ballroom. The piece of waste ground on the north corner of Falcon Avenue has only recently been developed as flats in a warm rustic brick with shop units at ground level. Further north, two important stones flank the main road. On the east side, built into the boudary wall of Morningside Parish Church, is the Bore Stone 'In which the Royal Standard was last pitched for the muster of the Scottish Army on the Borough Muir before the Battle of Flodden 1513'. Romantic and stirring as the inscription might be, the authenticity of the stone is seriously challenged in a very scholarly article by Henry M. Paton in Volume XXIV of the *Book of the Old Edinburgh Club*. On the opposite side of the road, the second stone offers little scope for challenge, with the inscription:

ONE MILE FROM TOLLCROSS.

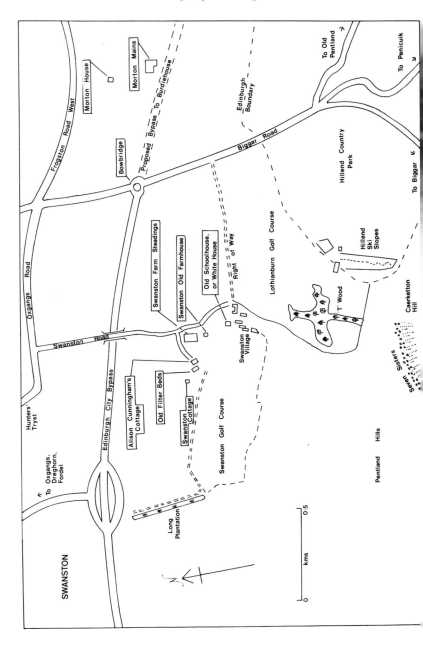

CHAPTER 8

Swanston

Swanston lies close to the southern boundary of Edinburgh, at the base of Caerketton Hill, surrounded by small wooded areas and open farmland. It is one of Edinburgh's most picturesque villages, and is the only one to remain largely unaffected by the spread of suburban development. Ironically, Swanston does not have many of the traditional essentials of village life: there is no church; there has been no school for more than fifty years; there are no shops, pubs or buses; and there is no village street. Despite this, or perhaps because of this, Swanston exudes the old-world charm of a quiet country village, with whitewashed thatched cottages, one or two larger dwellings, and the old steadings of Swanston Farm.

Swanston has played an important part in the development of Edinburgh, and in its reputation abroad. Following lengthy litigation with the local landowner, the springs at Swanston were piped in 1761 to augment Edinburgh's first water supply from Comiston. In the late nineteenth century Swanston Cottage was the summer retreat of Robert Louis Stevenson before his departure to Samoa, and Hunters Tryst, nearby, was the meeting place of the Six Foot Club. The club was formed in 1826 for the promotion of athletics and gymnastics, with membership restricted to persons of at least six feet in height, although exceptions were made for honorary members. Among the many famous literary members were Sir Walter Scott, James Hogg (the Ettrick Shepherd) and J.G. Lockhart (son-in-law and biographer of Sir Walter Scott).

More recently, Lothianburn Golf Club and Swanston Golf Club have extended their hold on the lower slopes of the Pentland Hills, and further afield, Hillend Ski Centre is one of the largest artificial slopes in Europe.

About half a mile to the north of the village the Edinburgh Bypass creates an obvious barrier between the city and the open countryside beyond. It is possible that the Bypass will halt, or slow, the rate of suburban housing on the south-facing slopes from Oxgangs Road. If this can be achieved, the unique character of Swanston, in a Conservation Area, will be protected well into the twenty-first century.

In and Around the Old Village

Swanston village is reached by Swanston Road, which runs south from Oxgangs Road, near Hunters Tryst. The old Swanston Road, formerly little more than a cart track, formed the boundary between what was Easter and Wester Swanston. Easter Swanston belonged to the Ross family from the fifteenth century and passed to Henry Trotter of Mortonhall in 1749. Wester Swanston belonged to Sir John Cockburn in 1462, thereafter to the Foulis family of Colinton in 1538, and finally to the Trotters of Mortonhall in 1670. In addition to Easter and Wester Swanston there were the small, but important, Temple Lands, the exact location of which is now uncertain. Charles J. Smith in *Historic South Edinburgh* states that 'the name is believed to have originated with the Templars, or Knights of the Temple, an association of men whose vows united those of monks with those of knights, and whose object was to protect pilgrims on visits to the Holy Land'. They settled at Temple in Midlothian in the twelfth century. Their association with Swanston is confirmed in a charter by James VI dated 1614, in which all the Templars' possessions in Scotland are listed, including a reference to 'terras templarias de Swainstoun possessas'.

Today Swanston Road follows approximately the same line as the earlier road but has been greatly widened on the section between Oxgangs Road and the new bridge across the Bypass. On the south side of the bridge the road continues down into the hollow where the Swanston Burn has been realigned, before rising again towards the steadings of Swanston Farm. Immediately past the square courtyard and grieve's cottage there is a modern bungalow, built in 1948 for the greenkeeper at Swanston Golf Club. The house was named Rathillet by the founder of the Club, Miss Margaret Carswell, whose family came from a farm near the village of Rathillet in Fife. Swanston Golf Clubhouse lies to the right, beside the car park built in part of the garden ground of the former Swanston farmhouse. This L-plan house, dating from the early eighteenth century, has not always been maintained to the standard expected of a category B listed building. After its use as a farmhouse was discontinued in 1959 it provided accommodation for casual farm labourers at the harvest and potato-lifting seasons. During this period its condition deteriorated greatly despite protests by the Cockburn Association. Following a serious fire in 1984 the property was acquired by a firm of builders who renovated the entire property and formed three distinctive houses around a U-

A view of Swanston from below Oxgangs Road, 1949, with the Pentland
Hills in the background before the ski-slope was constructed. Swanston
farmhouse is in the centre of the picture and the line of trees in the
foreground now marks the position of the City Bypass.
Courtesy of *The Scotsman* Publications Ltd.

shaped courtyard. The general character of the surrounding policies
was maintained, albeit at some temporary cost to lawns and shrubs.
The main part of the old farmhouse with the crowstepped gables was
completely refurbished to create an elegant modern house on three
floors without losing the character of the eighteenth-century stonework.
Similar renovation was completed on the smaller adjacent house to the
south, and the original cottage, which formed the east wing, was
extended to create a larger house.

To the south of the farmhouse a half-square of stone cottages with
slated roofs and ornamental chimney pots looks onto a small commu-
nal green. The cottages were originally built for farm workers in the
late nineteenth century. Some of the residents still recall when water
was first installed in 1934 and electricity in 1949. About fifteen men
were employed to work a thousand acres of sheep, cattle and arable
farming. Wages were around twenty-five shillings per week depending

The Whitehouse, an elegant private dwelling in its own grounds, formerly the schoolhouse for children travelling from Bowbridge, Lothianburn, Fordel and Dreghorn.

upon seniority, with the 'first man' receiving an extra shilling per week for the responsibility of ensuring that the others got out of their beds and into the fields by the appointed hour. Nine Clydesdale or Belgian horses were used on the land, each of the four pairs kept by an experienced hand, and the single horse was looked after by the apprentice, who did all the fetching and carrying. The first man usually drove a pair of white horses which, when working in the fields early in the morning, were more easily seen by the farmer from his vantage point in the farmhouse.

The White House, or Schoolhouse, frequently mistaken for Swanston Cottage, lies a hundred yards to the west of the farm cottages, surrounded by a large country garden through which flows the Swanston Burn. This large, two-storey house of uncertain date was formerly the village schoolhouse for children travelling as far afield as Bowbridge, Lothianburn, Comiston House, Fordel and Dreghorn. Children from ages five to fourteen were divided into separate age groups rather than classes, which posed particular problems for the teachers, Miss Graham and later Mrs Boyd. When the school closed in 1931 the property was bought by Mr and Mrs Boyd and the old schoolroom became a fashionable dining room.

Slightly further up the hill from the White House the rough pathway opens out onto a well-tended undulating green, with Lothian-burn Golf Course to the east, and Swanston Golf Course to the west. At the end of the Second World War this part of Swanston consisted of very basic early eighteenth-century cottages with earth floors and no water or electricity. A particularly bad winter in 1947 left forty villagers virtually cut off by huge snowdrifts, bread and other supplies being brought in by a horse-drawn snow plough from Oxgangs Road. Although high-voltage electricity pylons hummed almost overhead the houses were dependent upon oil for heating and cooking. In May 1949 a petition was directed to the South East of Scotland Electricity Board on behalf of Swanston Farm, Swanston Cottage, the Schoolhouse and Swanston Golf Club, and this resulted in electricity being installed in the village. By 1954, however, the thatched cottages at the top end of the village had fallen into a serious state of disrepair, and many of those which were habitable were used only as holiday cottages. In 1956 an ambitious scheme, originally estimated at £17,000, was put forward by the City Architect for conversion of nine old cottages into seven renovated dwellings, and associated landscaping. Work progressed slowly, the specialised job of thatching being done by John Brough of Auchtermuchty. By 1960 the eventual cost of renovation was nearer to £26,000: rents were between £150 and £200 per annum; and Edinburgh Corporation set about the difficult task of allocating a handful of houses among ninety eager applicants. The successful few (some of whom have subsequently bought their cottage under recent legislation) secured a beautifully restored eighteenth-century cottage on a three-year lease, the conditions of which prohibited the use of external television aerials, and the sale or display of souvenirs, postcards or refreshments. After several years of neglect Swanston once again earned Stevenson's description of almost a century earlier—though perhaps without the qualification in parenthesis:

> The hamlet...consists of a few cottages on a green beside a burn. Some of them (a strange thing in Scotland) are models of internal neatness; the beds adorned with patch, the shelves arrayed with willow-pattern plates, the floors and tables bright with scrubbing or pipe-clay, and the very kettle polished like silver.

Bleaching clothes outside the old thatched cottages at Swanston, 1908.
According to the *Topographical Dictionary of Scotland*, 1846, 'the washing of
clothes for families residing in the city is carried on to a large extent here'.
Courtesy of Miss Nan Melville.

The same view in 1987 showing the cottages beautifully restored in a
quiet rural setting, with washing greens discreetly placed at the rear of the
houses.
Photograph by Phyllis Margaret Cant.

At the highest point of the green there is a teak bench with the following inscription to a less well-known poet and novelist:

> To the memory of Edwin Muir 1887-1959
> Poet, Novelist, Essayist, Teacher.
> This seat is given by his friends to
> the village of Swanston where the poet
> liked to linger and meditate.

In May 1962 the seat was handed over by Lord Guthrie, Senator of the College of Justice, and chairman of the Committee of Trustees of the Edwin Muir Memorial Fund, and accepted by Lord Provost Sir John Greig Dunbar.

From the gate at the top of the green the pathway rises steeply towards the distinctive scree slopes of the Seven Sisters on Caerketton Hill. To the east is the T wood laid out by Henry Trotter of Mortonhall in 1766. Although seen as T-shaped from Edinburgh, it is actually in the form of a Maltese cross, which takes away from the argument that the wood was planted by Trotter ('T' for Trotter?) to assert dominion over his land after the unsuccessful legal dispute over water rights. An Act of Parliament in 1758 permitted Edinburgh Corporation to use spring water from Swanston to increase the public water supply from Comiston. The Act provided for compensation and procedures for potential disputes. As anticipated, Henry Trotter objected, saying that he required the water for his own use, and that in any case the water would hardly be needed if the Comiston pipes did not leak so badly. As the matter could not be resolved, the case went to the Sheriff Court, which ruled in favour of Edinburgh Corporation. Trotter appealed, firstly to the Court of Session, and then to the House of Lords in May 1760, when he was again unsuccessful. Edinburgh Corporation proceeded with the work of tapping the fresh clear water from numerous springs, and a water-house was constructed in 1761, a few hundred yards to the west of the village. The inscription on the lintel stone, giving the date and the name of the Lord Provost, can still be seen:

> EDINBURGH
> GEORGIUS LIND PRAEFECTUS
> ANNO MD CC LXI

Three slow sand filter beds were later constructed of brick with slated roofs to collect and purify the water from several sources. A system of stopcocks allowed the supply to be switched between each of the three beds to allow for cleaning the sand. This was brought out

Swanston Cottage, 1987, the summer residence of R.L.S. from 1867 to 1880, setting for *St. Ives* and the inspiration for many of Stevenson's verses.

manually and washed in a separate pond with the water flow reversed in order to float the impurities to the surface. Nearby is the water engineer's cottage. Its curious lintel stone with the inscription 1880 AC 1893 opens another chapter in the history of Swanston.

Swanston Cottage and R.L.S.

After the water-house was constructed in 1761 the city fathers decided that additional accommodation was needed as a general meeting place. The small single-storey thatched cottage which they built to the north-west is described by Robert Louis Stevenson in *Edinburgh: Picturesque Notes:*

> After they had built their water-house and laid their pipes, it occurred to them that the place was suitable for junketing. Once entertained, with jovial magistrates and public funds, the idea led speedily to accomplishment; and Edinburgh could soon boast of a municipal Pleasure House. The cell was turned into a garden; and on the knoll that shelters it from the plain and the sea winds, they built a cottage looking to the hills.

The Cottage was greatly enlarged around 1835 when the magistrates added a second storey and replaced the thatch with slate. Bow

Robert Louis Stevenson, born 13th November 1850, qualified as an advocate in 1875, but instead of going into practice he followed his first ambition to become an author.
Photograph from *Robert Louis Stevenson's Edinburgh Days*.

windows were built out at the front and a single-storey addition was constructed to the east. Fothergill, in *Stones and Curiosities of Edinburgh and Neighbourhood*, describes and illustrates several gargoyles and finials brought to Swanston Cottage from St. Giles Cathedral during the extensive alterations by Burn the architect in 1830. These were used to embellish the roof of the east extension and the high stone wall beside the quarry garden. By far the most interesting era, however, began at Whitsunday 1867 when Thomas Stevenson, father of Robert Louis Stevenson, took the tenancy of the house as a summer retreat. Little did he know that Swanston Cottage was to become the romantic setting and inspiration for so many of Robert Louis Stevenson's poems and novels.

Robert Lewis Balfour Stevenson was born in Edinburgh on 13th November 1850. On his father's side the family had a long tradition as highly specialised engineers. Louis' grandfather, Robert Stevenson, had built the Bell Rock Lighthouse and Louis' father had continued the family tradition. Louis' mother was Margaret Balfour of the Balfours of Pilrig, whose father was the Rev. Lewis Balfour of Colinton Parish Church. When the Stevensons married on 28th August 1848 they set up house at 8 Howard Place. After a short stay at 1 Inverleith Terrace (now renumbered 9) they moved to 17 Heriot Row which was their main residence during the tenancy of Swanston Cottage. Early in Stevenson's life the name Balfour was dropped and the spelling was altered from Lewis to Louis apparently on account of his father's aversion to a Radical politician named Lewis. As a young child, and throughout his short life, Louis was dogged by ill health which eventually hastened his departure from Edinburgh. His sleepless nights and anxious days would have seemed infinitely longer, however, had it not been for the endless support and encouragement given by his nurse Alison Cunningham. Cummy, as she became known, looked after Stevenson from an early age and undoubtedly played a very important and influential role in his life. In gratitude, and in recalling these early days, Stevenson dedicated to her *A Child's Garden of Verses*, published in 1884:

> For the long nights you lay awake
> And watched for my unworthy sake;
> For your most comfortable hand
> That led me through the uneven land:
> For all the story books you read:
> For all the pains you comforted:
> For all you pitied, for all you bore,
> In sad and happy days of yore:-
> My second Mother, my first Wife,
> The angel of my infant life—
> From the sick child now well and old,
> Take, nurse, the little book you hold.

Although ill health was certainly a factor in Stevenson's life, it did not confine him to a life of inaction. It was his father's forlorn hope that he would follow in the family footsteps and become an eminent civil engineer, but after a period of study at Edinburgh University, it was clear that no bridges would be built. Stevenson's one ambition was to become a writer. In a final bid to provide his son with a 'respectable' profession, Mr Stevenson persuaded Louis to study law, in which he qualified as an advocate in 1875. Instead of going into practice he went to France, a journey which provided the inspiration for *An Inland Voyage* and *Travels with a Donkey*. By then Stevenson knew what Cummy had probably always known—that 'her boy' would become a famous author.

Stevenson's parents held the tenancy of Swanston Cottage from 1867 to 1880 during which time Stevenson made frequent use of this quiet country retreat. Whilst at Swanston he formed a lasting friendship with John Todd, the 'Roarin' Shepherd', and Robert Young, the gardener, both of whom unconsciously provided inspiration and dialogue for later novels. In *St. Ives* Stevenson's description of the drovers owes much to his long conversations with John Todd, and Swanston Cottage is the place of safety in which the French prisoner found shelter after his escape from Edinburgh Castle. From his bedroom window on the upper storey, Stevenson looked out over Caerketton and Allermuir which inspired so many of his verses and poems.

These timeless days were numbered. In 1880 the Stevensons gave up their tenancy of the Cottage and on 19th May Stevenson was married in America. He returned to Edinburgh in August of that year when his father was instrumental in persuading him to try for the Chair of Constitutional Law and Constitutional History at Edinburgh University, but he was unsuccessful. He spent the following years in the Riviera and in Bournemouth but when his father died in May 1887 Stevenson visited Edinburgh for the last time. Soon after, he left for America and later settled in Samoa where his recollections of Swanston were never far from his thoughts:

> I gang nae mair where aince I gaed,
> By Buckstane, Fairmilehead or Braid,
> But far frae Kirk and Toon,
> Oh, still ayont the muckle sea,
> Still are ye dear, and dear to me,
> Auld Reekie, still and on.

Stevenson died at Vailima, Samoa on 3rd December 1894 at the age of forty-four. His mother was devastated 'to weep the eyes that should have wept for me'. Cummy, his second mother, first wife and only nurse, was heartbroken. She had remained at Swanston

Stevenson's nurse Alison Cunningham, or 'Cummy', to whom he dedicated *A Child's Garden of Verse*:
My second Mother, my first Wife,
The angel of my infant life.

with her brother who was the waterman, after the Stevensons had left in 1880, and had corresponded with Louis for several years. In 1893 she left for 23 Balcarres Street in Morningside. Towards the end of her lifetime she lived with her cousin at Comiston Place where she died on 21st July 1913 at the age of ninety-one, and was buried in Morningside Cemetery.

After the Stevenson era, Swanston Cottage was occupied for a time by Dr Taylor of Edinburgh and later by Lord Guthrie, Senator of the College of Justice. Today the Cottage is privately owned, but there are numerous links with earlier days. On the central upper window-sill is chiselled '1867 RLS 1880', and on the waterman's cottage the lintel,

Tommy Armour, the Edinburgh golfer, winner of the British Open, the United States Open and the P.G.A. titles in the 1920s and 1930s. Courtesy of *The Scotsman* Publications Ltd.

already referred to, commemorates occupation by Alison Cunningham, or Cummy, '1880 AC 1893'.

Lothianburn Golf Club

Lothianburn Golf Course occupies several acres of ground on the lower slopes of Caerketton Hill, bounded on the north by the right of way to Swanston, on the south by Hillend Park, on the east by Biggar Road, and on the west by Swanston Burn. On that hilly terrain the first nine-hole course was laid out in 1893 when Lothianburn appeared to be very much further out of town than it is now. Intimation of the club's first competition stated on the specially prepared postcards that 'brakes would leave Morningside Station at certain hours and that refreshments could be obtained on the ground'. A steel and timber clubhouse was built three years after the club opened, and in May 1899 the course was extended to eighteen holes, played over 3844 yards. In 1907 ladies were admitted as temporary members, an experiment which appears to have gained universal approval, as two years later fifty ladies were given full membership. The club's early heyday was between the First and Second World Wars. In 1928 the course was extensively altered by James Braid to take in ground towards Swanston and the T wood, and in 1931 the club's most renowned player, Tommy Armour, won the British Open Championship at Carnoustie.

In keeping with its proximity to Swanston, Lothianburn has given some of the holes names associated with Stevenson, namely Seven Sisters, Swanston and St. Ives. In 1982 the club had four hundred and fifty male members, seventy-five lady members, and seventy-five juniors. In addition, there is a special 'over 65' membership of about forty, who play twelve holes only (i.e. the first eight and the last four), cutting out the holes at the highest part of the course, which can be snowbound for lengthy periods in the winter. Until recently, the oldest member was Jimmy Anderson who attended the annual general meetings although he had ceased to play even on the shorter course.

Swanston Golf Club: Miss Margaret Carswell

Swanston Golf Club is also laid out on the lower slopes of Caerketton Hill, to the west of the village, the first hole, appropriately named R.L.S., running parallel to the garden of Swanston Cottage. The club was formed in 1927 by Miss Margaret Carswell who was also a prominent member of the Edinburgh Women's Athletic Club. Finding it almost impossible to obtain sufficient places for ladies in local golf clubs (presumably including Lothianburn), Miss Carswell decided to found and construct her own course, solely for the use of female members. Her commitment to a ladies-only club did not, however, influence her choice of employee. Following an earlier meeting with Herbert More at the Merchants' Golf Club at Craiglockhart, Miss Carswell succeeded in engaging him for the job of greenkeeper. A lease of land was obtained from Mr Jack of Swanston Farm and Miss Carswell, assisted by Herbert More, proceeded to lay out a nine-hole

Miss Margaret Carswell of Swanston Golf Club prepares to drive off on her tour of inspection of the course, which she founded and laid out in 1927.
Courtesy of Jim and Ellen McLagan.

course. True to her original concept, Miss Carswell insisted that membership be confined to ladies only, but she eventually came under pressure from her own membership to relax the rule in favour of their own male acquaintances, who also happened to be interested in the game of golf. It was a decision she came to regret, although the increased membership and income enabled the club to extend to eighteen holes in the late 1920s, and to build a pavilion in 1935 to replace the rather rudimentary accommodation in one of the old thatched cottages in the village. By 1947 the total membership had risen to four hundred, with men outnumbering ladies by three to one.

The club celebrated its Silver Jubilee on 13th October 1952 when Miss Carswell presented a teak seat (now in the garden of Rathillet in Swanston) to Herbert More to mark his long service as greenkeeper. In many ways, however, the 1950s and 1960s were dominated by constant clashes between Miss Carswell's original ideals for the club, and the aspirations of the younger male-orientated committee. As owner and founder of the club she dominated committee meetings, and even in advancing years her control of the club never waned. When well over eighty years of age she purchased a mini tractor and trailer and was driven around the course by a lady member to inspect the fairways and the condition of the greens.

Today Swanston Golf Club has approximately three hundred and thirty members in which the men outnumber the ladies by about twelve to one. The club has moved away from its original concept, remembered now by only a few senior members. There is, however, a move to recognise, in some tangible way, the memory of Miss Margaret Carswell, whose vision and determination created Swanston Golf Club.

Margaret Carswell was obviously a person of considerable ambition and energy whose interests extended far beyond Swanston Golf Club. In her own characteristically blunt words, 'I was feeling rather bored with the world in general and myself in particular so I answered an advertisement in a newspaper'. The advertisement had been inserted by Mr Stuart Morrow, an American, who was looking for someone to start a Soroptimist Club in Edinburgh, similar to the many existing clubs in the United States. Miss Carswell called together several professional and business women, and the first meeting of the club was held on 29th November 1927 with twenty-six members. Ethel de la Cour was elected President, an honour which was bestowed on many able successors, including Miss C. Fraser Lee, headmistress of St. Trinneans School at St. Leonards House in Park Road. One of the Soroptimists' most interesting rules—subsequently relaxed—was to admit only new members whose profession or occupation was not already represented, Miss Carswell being admitted as a Golf Club Proprietrix.

The Soroptimist Club of Edinburgh under its motto 'Looking Further' is part of the worldwide Soroptimists International and has been involved in a great variety of charitable works and links of friendship. A small booklet, giving details of the club and its activities, was published in 1977 at the time of the Golden Jubilee.

Hillend Country Park and Ski-Slope

Hillend Park was gifted to the city by John White, an Edinburgh builder, and was opened for the public by Lord Provost Sir William Sleigh in July 1924. However, the growth of Edinburgh in the last few decades has brought the southern suburbs almost to the base of the Pentland Hills, with the result that Hillend, and its surrounding area,

The largest artificial ski-slope in Europe, at Hillend, a popular venue for all ages, first established in 1964 and extended on numerous occasions since.
Photograph by Phyllis Margaret Cant.

is visited to a much greater extent than previously. Inevitably, that has led to an increase in control of the land and facilities for a wider range of interests. Hillend was designated as a Country Park in 1981 by Lothian Regional Council under the powers of the Countryside (Scotland) Act of 1967. A much larger geographical area, Pentland Regional Park, was also designated by Lothian Regional Council in 1984 under similar legislation, and confirmed by the Secretary of State for Scotland after a public enquiry in 1986. The idea behind a Regional Park is to allow the traditional land uses to continue within its boundaries yet provide for conservation of landscape and wildlife as well as creating recreational facilities where necessary.

As early as 1972 the Pentland Hills Conservation and Recreation Report recommended the introduction of a Ranger Service in the Pentland Hills, but it was not until 1976 that the proposals were implemented. Initially, two rangers were employed to cover all the territory owned by Lothian Regional Council, and the rights of way. The number of rangers was subsequently increased to eight, and they work a three-shift system to provide the maximum coverage and availability to the public. With such a wide area to be covered by Landrover, bicycle or on foot, great use is made of the two-way radio system which links the rangers with their base at Hillend. The Ranger Service has no compulsory powers, but its powers of recommendation and persuasion are frequently stretched to the limit in reconciling the conflicting interests of the public. The hill-walker and ornithologist seek the minimum of control except, perhaps, when their favourite haunt is threatened by the sound of motor cycle engines, whilst conservationists and landowners frequently have legitimate interests which conflict with several other groups.

Despite these obvious difficulties, progress has been made in recent years on several projects. In 1983 Lothian Regional Council entered into an agreement with the owner of Swanston Farm for the upkeep and continued protection of the T wood. A twenty-year programme was established, divided into four phases of five years each, the object of which is to replace dead and broken timber with new underplanting. The wood is predominantly beech with a mixture of Scots pine, oak and sycamore, many of which require to be fenced to prevent damage by grazing sheep. Another area which has attracted new planting is on the west, or wind side, of the ski-slope. Fast-growing lodge-pole pine has been planted to break the force of the wind and to protect later plantings of larch and Scots pine. A recent, but less successful, experiment was the fish farm, housed at the old filter station at Swanston village. This idea was eventually abandoned after several attempts failed to maintain a consistently high volume of water.

In addition, the Ranger Service has an interest in the woodland areas around regional reservoirs, and it manages the Flotterstone Countryside Information Centre and Bavelaw Marsh Nature Reserve. One of its most important roles is in relation to the enjoyment and education of visitors to the Park. This is particularly so for schoolchildren who are taught to observe the Country Code, and to have a sympathetic attitude towards the countryside. From its base at Hillend, the Ranger Service administers several courses, visits and guided walks, including fishing for rainbow trout at Loganlea Reservoir and sailing on Harperrig Reservoir at Balerno.

Of all the outdoor activities at Hillend, ski-ing is undoubtedly the most popular. The potential for success was recognised as long ago as 1964 by G. Boyd Anderson, an Edinburgh businessman, whose enthusiasm and financial backing brought ski-ing to Hillend. The original fifty-metre experimental slope, laid in 1964, was resited and extended in 1965, and, in the following year, a double chairlift of three hundred and sixty metres was installed. The complex, which cost £40,000, was officially opened on 1st October 1966 by Herbert Brechin, Lord Provost, followed by a special open slalom competition for the Dendix Snowslope Trophy. This competition was the first held on an artificial slope in Scotland and opened the Scottish ski-ing season for that year. Before the end of the decade additional facilities had been provided, including a short nursery slope, permanent floodlighting, and closed-circuit television for teaching purposes. The 1970s saw further expansion financed by Lothian Regional Council. A two-hundred-metre ski tow was built in 1974 and between 1977 and 1980 a tow slope was laid and extended to two hundred and sixty metres long by thirteen metres wide. A permanent two-storey building to accommodate equipment, administration, changing rooms and first-aid room was officially opened on 26 April 1984 by Councillor Brian Meek.

Today, Hillend Ski Centre has about fifteen permanent staff and almost fifty part-time staff most of whom are engaged in ski instruction for the many visitors each year. There is a particularly strong involvement with the schools of Lothian Region who have special facilities and competitions. As a fitting tribute to one of the founders, schoolchildren still compete for the Boyd Anderson Trophy designed by Ian A.R. Davidson of Edinburgh College of Art.

Comiston House

Comiston House stands in extensive grounds at the west end of Camus Avenue, a little more than a mile to the north of Swanston village. The name Comiston has a derivation of great antiquity and is cited in various forms by Dixon in *Place Names of Midlothian* as Colmanstone 1336, Cumyngstoun 1484, Comestoun 1531, and Coimistoun 1647. The earliest recorded owner of the lands of Colmanstone was Alexander de Meignes in 1335 who was succeeded by William Cunynghame of Kilmaurs. Comiston was owned by James Foulis of Colinton in 1531, followed by John Fairlie at the end of the sixteenth century and then by Andrew Creich and his wife Margaret Dick in 1608. Their son was also Andrew Creich, whose daughter Catherine Creich acquired the estate in 1631 with her husband John Cant of the Grange of St. Giles. The property came to the Porterfield family on the marriage of John Cant's daughter, Catherine Cant, to William Porterfield, and

Comiston House in Camus Avenue, built in 1815 for Sir James Forrest,
1st Baronet, Lord Provost of Edinburgh from 1838 to 1843.
Photograph by Joyce M. Wallace, from *Historic Houses of Edinburgh*.

remained in the family until 1715 when Comiston entered one of its
most interesting phases.

The long and distinguished association of the Forrest family with
Comiston began in 1715 when the property was bought by James
Forrest. The family came to prominence in the middle of the nineteenth century on the birth of a later James Forrest, who became a
Writer to the Signet. When he married his cousin Catherine, only
daughter and heir to the estate of Comiston, his future as a prominent
landowner was assured. On his death in 1820 the estate passed to his
heir, also James, who became Lord Provost of Edinburgh.

Sir James Forrest, 1st Baronet, born in 1780, was admitted as an advocate to the Scottish Bar in 1803. It was he who built the present Comiston House in 1815 towards the end of his father's life. He was an ambitious and able man who held a number of public and private appointments, including Grand Master Mason for Scotland from 1838 to 1840, and Lord Provost from 1838 to 1843. Being Lord Provost at the time of Queen Victoria's coronation, he was made a baronet in honour of that occasion. During his term of office he was deeply involved in many of the important issues of the day. Shortly after his election he called a meeting to petition Parliament for the adoption of voting by ballot to prevent intimidation. He became involved in pressure groups for the repeal of the Corn Laws (which imposed duty on imported cereals), and the abolition of patronage, as well as being instrumental in setting up various schemes under the Poor Laws. His dislike of patronage made him an obvious choice to lead the many members of the Town Council who joined the Free Church in 1843.

Despite his otherwise impeccable conduct, and a long list of civic accomplishments, few writers have been able to resist the temptation to recount his most inglorious moment. In 1842 Queen Victoria and Prince Albert visited Scotland shortly after her coronation. It was an occasion of great public jubilation with bonfires lit at various vantage points as the Royal Fleet made its way up the Forth. The following morning the Queen left the royal yacht a few minutes before nine o'clock to come ashore, but the Provost and his Town Council were under the impression that their presence would not be required until more than an hour later. Undaunted and unescorted, the young Queen proceeded with her itinerary, meeting the people and His Grace the Duke of Buccleuch who was one of the few dignitaries present. Needless to say, this unintentional *faux pas* created great merriment which was quickly set to verse in a parody of the Jacobite song *Hey, Johnny Cope*, the new version being:

> Hey, Jamie Forrest, are ye waukin' yet?
> Or are your Baillies snoring' yet?
> If ye are waukin' I would wit
> Ye'd hae a merry, merry mornin'!
>
> The Queen she's come to Granton Pier,
> Nae Provost and nae Baillie here,
> They're in their beds I muckle fear,
> Sae early in the mornin'!

With characteristic Royal diplomacy the Queen announced that there had been a change in arrangements to accommodate a visit to Dalkeith Palace where the keys of the city were later presented to Her Majesty by Provost Forrest.

After the death of the Lord Provost in 1860 Comiston remained in the possession of the Forrest family for some years, but the Baronetcy became extinct in 1928 on the death of Sir Charles Forrest whose only son was killed in the First World War.

Until recently, Comiston House was occupied as the Pentland Hills Hotel but the house now lies empty with its elegant front doorway and windows bricked up against unauthorised entry. The grounds are overgrown and reduced to a state of almost complete desolation. Despite this the main fabric of the house is unaffected and it is still possible to trace various aspects of former ownership in the extensive grounds.

Comiston House is described by the Royal Commission on the Ancient Monuments of Scotland as 'a neat country villa typical of its time, consisting of an oblong main block with a circular bay projecting from its north side and a service wing from the east'. The main block has two main floors, the central front entrance being reached by a short flight of steps which span the half-sunk basement. The south-facing front is pedimented and has broad Ionic pilasters, the angled volutes being repeated at the head of the pairs of unfluted Ionic columns on each side of the entrance doorway. The ground-floor windows have moulded architraves and cornices, and there is an elegant bow window on the north elevation which lit the drawing room. The groin-vaulted entrance hall led to the dining room on the east side and the library on the west side.

The remains of the stable block, also dating from around 1815, lie to the south-west of the main house. The block was built in U-shaped formation facing south, with an arched central doorway above which was a clock. The main building is still roofed and in reasonable condition but the buildings on the east and west, which flank the courtyard, are roofless and derelict. High up on the west side of the main south-facing block is an interesting old stone containing a coat of arms but no date. It is almost square with a raised perimeter band and is divided diagonally (bottom left to top right) by what appears to be a spear. The left-hand triangle contains two hunting horns, whilst the right-hand triangle contains two stars and a crescent. A sketch of the stone appears in Fothergill's *Stones and Curiosities of Edinburgh and*

Neighbourhood along with a well-researched explanation. Fothergill considers that the stone depicts the coats of arms of the Porterfield family (the hunting horns) and the Cant family (the stars and crescent), commemorating the marriage of William Porterfield and Catherine Cant in the seventeenth century. As the stone pre-dates the stable building by more than a century it is likely that it was transferred there from the much older Comiston House or Castle, a remnant of which remains at the south-east corner of the stable block. This consists of a single round tower about twenty-five feet high built of rubble with corbels near the top. It has a very small and narrow entrance to the north and at least two gun loops for protection. Its exact age is uncertain but it could be as early as the sixteenth century. At one time it was used as a dovecote, providing 161 nest holes, irregularly placed around the inside walls. The stables and old tower lie within a hundred yards of the back entrance to Comiston House which is still marked by two stone pillars and the remains of the iron gates. This entrance leads to the public right of way, Cockmylane, which runs from Greenbank to the former Comiston Farmhouse.

At the present day the houses in Camus Avenue come within a few hundred yards of Comiston House but at one time the driveway extended the whole length of Camus Avenue to the main road from Morningside to Fairmilehead. The entrance was marked by imposing gate pillars with urns, and a lodge house which contained another interesting stone from the original Comiston House. The stone, believed to have been part of a dormer in the old house, contained the date 1610 and the initials AC and MD for Andrew Creich and Margaret Dick. In 1937, when Braidburn Valley Park was being laid out, the gates and pillars were removed to the entrance in Greenbank Crescent, but the 1610 stone was lost after the lodge was demolished.

Morton House; Morton Mains

Morton House stands about a mile north-east of Swanston village in several acres of mature garden at the east end of Winton Loan. It was the principal building in a group of much more modest houses described by Good in *Liberton in Ancient and Modern Times* as the hamlet of Mounthooly or the Holy Mount. Adjacent modern housing now forms the more recent district of Winton, named after the younger daughter of the Earl of Eglinton and Winton, Lady Edith Mary Montgomerie, who married Colonel A.R. Trotter, a former owner of the estate.

Originally the lands of Morton (and Mortonhall which was discussed in Chapter 1) were granted to Sir Henry St. Clair of Rosslyn in 1317 by Robert the Bruce 'in free warren for the services of the tenth part of a Knight's fee', a Knight's fee being that area of land sufficient to maintain him. Subsequent owners, for several generations, owned both Morton House and Mortonhall, notably the families Rigg and Trotter.

Morton House dates from the early eighteenth century. It consists of two distinctly different styles of architecture, designed about a century apart, the L-plan east block being described by the Royal Commission on the Ancient Monuments of Scotland as 'a little country-house of Queen Anne's time which seems to be based on the remains of an older house'. The east elevation of two storeys and an attic has a central chimney gable flanked by half-dormers on each side. The south-most dormer bears the date 1702, being the year when this part of the house was built by Thomas Rigg, Deputy Sheriff of Edinburgh. A kitchen wing to the north-east was built shortly thereafter and contains a sundial with the date 1713, built into the south-east corner, almost at roof level. The kitchen has a large fireplace and oven at the east end, and a small stairway at the west end which originally gave access to a room above which has now been converted to a small gallery. A doorway in the north wall leads to the kitchen courtyard, bounded by old buildings previously used by domestic staff as living accommodation.

In 1806 a completely new block, of elegant Georgian symmetry, was built in polished ashlar, in orderly contrast with the rubble masonry of its vernacular predecessor. Its central Roman Doric doorway, with supporting small-pane windows, is flanked by much broader windows lighting the principal rooms. The whole facade is set off against a sweeping carriageway between square pavilions and rusticated gate piers with urns. The Georgian wing consists of six principal rooms grouped around a central vestibule and staircase lit from a round cupola. Several rooms retain original features. The ground-floor dining room to the south has a fine chimneypiece with intricate shell decor and the initials R and T (perhaps for Rigg and Trotter) alternating in the frieze.

The basic structure of the garden around Morton House remains substantially unaltered from that laid out by Thomas Rigg. Many of the original sycamore trees, lime trees, laurels and hollies survive, set off by extensive lawns, herbaceous borders and formal rose beds. The east boundary is marked by two pointed stone obelisks which frame a magnificent view of the farm lands of East Lothian and the Lammermuir Hills. The most significant garden structure is the Belvedere dating from the early eighteenth century and contemporary with the obelisks. It lies on a small hilltop a few hundred yards to the south-east of the house and has recently undergone extensive renovation of its roof and external stonework. It is two storeys in height with a pitched slated roof, large windows in the upper storey and a recessed doorway to the south-east. Although the interior is now empty, at one time it contained a fine painted and panelled upper room, reputedly used by the menfolk of the house as a retreat or escape from the mundane pressures of domestic life. Its ideal position, beside the former bowling green and beyond earshot of the house, may well have influenced the Rev. Thomas Whyte to conclude in 1792 that 'the Belvedere here is mightily well situated'.

The twin pavilions with ogee roofs, on either side of the west entrance gates, date from the same period as the Belvedere, and have also been renovated in recent years. One pavilion contains the original stable and the other is used as a garage. At the end of the Second World War the garden was overgrown with scrub but was renovated by the late Colonel Trotter and Mrs Trotter whose horticultural interests have been continued and extended by the present owners.

In keeping with its unique character, Morton House has been the home of several eminent persons, notably Lord Cunningham, a Court of Session judge, and Dr John Hill Burton the Historiographer Royal and author who died there in 1881. Among Dr Burton's many books are the *Life of David Hume*, *Narratives of the Criminal Law of Scotland*, *The Scot Abroad*, and *The Book Hunter*. The present owners of Morton House are the Hon. Lord Elliott and Lady Elliott.

Morton Mains lies a few hundred yards to the south of Morton House on a south-sloping aspect facing the Pentland Hills. The handsome square farmhouse dates from around 1840, but parts of the surrounding steadings give the impression of being at least a century earlier. Its position, exposed to the prevailing wind, induced the builders to construct the steadings in such a way as to give maximum shelter to the farmhouse, and to create open courtyards between the main buildings.

The farmhouse is situated on the east side and connects with a smaller but much older building, to the north, which was probably the original farmhouse. The large walled garden contains formal lawns and a tennis court but the original vegetable garden is now used as a practice paddock for horse riding. Built into the extreme south-east corner of the garden wall and commanding extensive views across East Lothian are the remains of a raised outlook post, which was part of the city's defences during the Second World War. To the west of the farmhouse is the start of the steadings and the smallest of the three courtyards, enclosed by Rose Cottage on the south side and a range of stone buildings on the west side. This was the coachman's domain which provided living accommodation, stables, tack room and coach house all within convenient distance of the house.

To the west of the coachman's area is a much bigger courtyard bounded on three sides by farm buildings, its north entrance narrowed by the garden of a cottage which abuts Rose Cottage. This courtyard is obviously very old and contains several interesting features. The east side consists of stables, now partly demolished, which provided space for fourteen Clydesdale horses before the days of mechanisation. Above the door of one of the existing stables is an interesting lintel which has probably been brought from an earlier building:

THE STORM BLEW DOWN BOTH OUR ROOFS
14TH JANUARY 1739
EARLY SUNDAY MORNING AFTER AN
ECLIPSE OF THE MOON

—a windy spot, then as now! The south side of the courtyard has a long low building previously used as a piggery but now converted for livery horses. At its east end a flight of stone steps leads to a small bothy used in connection with the stables. The buildings on the west side form part of the third courtyard which is not as complete as the others. Stables form the south boundary and part only of the west side which is otherwise open to the prevailing wind. The courtyard contains the most interesting and possibly the oldest building which has been greatly altered from the original. It is a hexagonal-shaped horsemill in which the stone roof-supports have been linked by additional stone-work of a slightly different colour to form a solid-sided building of unusual shape. The slated conical roof, supported by a labyrinth of roof timbers, appears to be unaltered, but the interior contains no evidence of the central grinding wheels or machinery to which the horse would have been harnessed. The hexagonal-shaped wall on the

The Scottish vernacular architecture of Morton House in Winton Loan,
built in 1702 for Thomas Rigg, Deputy Sheriff of Edinburgh.

In 1806 a completely new block, of elegant Georgian symmetry, was built
in polished ashlar at Morton House, in orderly contrast with the rubble
masonry of its vernacular predecessor.
Photograph by Phyllis Margaret Cant.

south side has also been altered by the addition of a squat, round chimney and a blackened vent which may have been used at one time as a forge.

To the west of the farm steadings several cottages remain which were once tenanted by farm labourers. At the back of these cottages is the former Church Hall, a small single-storey brick building of uncertain date, in which services were held every second Sunday. The building is now used as a stable, but in recent years the fireplace at the east end, the pews and the tiny vestry were still in evidence. Perhaps the most picturesque cottage is beside the north entrance pavilion to Morton House, in the vicinity of Good's hamlet of Mounthooly. The whitewashed cottage was once thatched and stands in an attractive country garden with several old stone outhouses.

The fields which lie between Morton Mains farm steadings and the Lothian Burn have recently been shortened to allow the construction of the Swanston to Straiton section of the City Bypass, and the farm steadings of Bowbridge have been demolished to make way for the complicated intersection being constructed beside the Fairmile Inn. The line of the Bypass also passes close to Broomhills Farm House and steadings which lie in a more sheltered position to the east of Morton Mains. The steadings are not as old as at Morton Mains but, being close to the Lothian Burn, had the advantage of water power to drive the mill machinery. Broomhills and Morton Mains have been farmed by the Brass family since 1949.

Suggestions for Further Reading

General Author	Title	Year of Publication
Anon	The Lord Provosts of Edinburgh 1296-1932	1932
Birrell, J.F.	An Edinburgh Alphabet	1980
Colston, James	Edinburgh & District Water Supply	1890
Fothergill, George A.	Stones & Curiosities of Edinburgh and Neighbourhood	1910
Geddie, John	The Fringes of Edinburgh	1926
Gifford, John, McWilliam, Colin and Walker, David	The Buildings of Scotland: Edinburgh	1984
Grant, James	Old & New Edinburgh	1882
Hunter, D.L.G.	Edinburgh's Transport	1964
McKean, Charles	Edinburgh: An Illustrated Architectural Guide	1982
Royal Commission on the Ancient Monuments of Scotland	The City of Edinburgh	1951
Thomas, Brendon	The Last Picture Shows: Edinburgh	1984
Turnbull, Michael	Edinburgh Portraits	1987
Wallace, Joyce M.	Historic Houses of Edinburgh	1987
Various	Book of the Old Edinburgh Club	1908 to date
Various	The Streets of Edinburgh	1984
Warrender, Margaret	Walks near Edinburgh	1895

Burdiehouse; Straiton; Old Pentland

Aitchison, C.	Lasswade Parish and Loanhead in the Olden Time	1892
Conacher, H.R.J.	The Oil-Shales of the Lothians	1927
Geddie, J.	The Fringes of Edinburgh	1926
Gibsone, J.C.H.	The Gibsones: A Family History	1984
Good, G.	Liberton in Ancient and Modern Times	1893
Speedy, T.	Craigmillar and its Environs	1892
Sutherland, R.	Loanhead: The Development of a Scottish Burgh	1974

Author	*Title*	*Year of Publication*
Colinton		
Colinton Amenity Association	Colinton: Seven Walks	1985
Geddie, John	The Home Country of R.L. Stevenson	1898
McKay, Margaret M.	The Rev. John Walker's Report on the Hebrides	1980
Murray, Thomas	Biographical Annals of the Parish of Colinton	1863
Shankie, David	The Parish of Colinton	1902
Steuart, James	Notes for a History of Colinton Parish	1938
Various	Colinton Parish Church	1986
Various	Portrait of a Parish	1968
Gilmerton		
Geddie, J.	The Fringes of Edinburgh	1926
Good, G.	Liberton in Ancient and Modern Times	1893
Skinner, Rev. Donald M.	Historic Gilmerton	1964
Speedy, T.	Craigmillar and its Environs	1892
Juniper Green		
Geddie, John	The Home Country of R.L. Stevenson	1898
Jamieson, Stanley (Editor)	The Water of Leith	1984
Scottish Women's Rural Institute	Village History Book	1966
Shankie, David	Parish of Colinton	1902
Tweedie, John	A Water of Leith Walk	1974
Liberton		
Ferenbach, Rev. Campbell	Annals of Liberton	1975
Finlayson, Charles P.	Clement Litill and his Library	1980
Fothergill, George A.	Stones & Curiosities of Edinburgh and Neighbourhood	1910
Good, George	Liberton in Ancient and Modern Times	1893
Goodfellow, James	The Print of his Shoe	1906
Speedy, Tom	Craigmillar and its Environs	1892
Speedy, Tom	The Election of a Minister at Liberton	1898

Author	*Title*	*Year of Publication*
Longstone; Slateford		
Baird, Hugh	Report on the Proposed Edinburgh and Glasgow Union Canal	1813
Bell, J. Munro	The Castles of the Lothians	1893
Craig, George	Building stones used in Edinburgh	1892
Geddie, John	The Home Country of R.L. Stevenson	1898
Harris, Stuart L.	Parish in the Past	1971
Jamieson, Stanley (Editor)	The Water of Leith	1984
Stevenson, Drummond	Memories	1962
Tweedie, John	A Water of Leith Walk	1974
Various	A. & J. Macnab, A Company History	1960
Various	City of Edinburgh New Markets and Slaughterhouses	1910
Morningside		
Cochrane, Robert	Memories of Morningside: About St. Matthew's Morningside	1906
Davies, Rev. Roderick G. and Pollock, Rev. Alex.	Morningside Congregational Church 1887-1937	1937
Durham, Sheila B., and others	Survey of Monumental Inscriptions: Morningside Cemetery Edinburgh	1981
Eddington, Alexander	North Morningside Church	1930
Findlay, H.J.	South Morningside Church of Scotland: A Jubilee Retrospect 1889-1939	1939
Gowans, John Stuart	Morningside Parish Church	1912
Gray, John G.	The South Side Story	1962
Littlefair, N.J.	Christ Church Morningside 1876-1976	1976
Mair, William	Historic Morningside	1947
Mitchell, Alexander	The Story of Braid Church 1883-1933	1933
Skelton, Harold	History of Christ Church Morningside	1955
Smith, Charles J	Historic South Edinburgh	
	Vol 1	1978
	Vol 2	1979
	Vol 3	1986

Author	*Title*	*Year of Publication*
Morningside		
Various	The Story of Braid Church 1883-1983	1983
	Morningside Parish Church	1907
	Congregational Reports 1901-07 and 1908-15	1915
	Plans and Notes of the Landed Estates of the Merchant Company Institutions	1891
	St. Peter's Edinburgh Golden Jubilee Brochure 1907-1957	1957
Swanston		
Balfour, Graham	The Life of Robert Louis Stevenson	1913
Fort, Nicholas (Edinburgh City Planning Officer)	Swanston Village Conservation	1973
Fothergill, George A.	Stones & Curiosities of Edinburgh and Neighbourhood	1910
Simpson, E. Blantyre	Robert Louis Stevenson's Edinburgh Days	1914
Smith, Charles J	Historic South Edinburgh Vol	1979
Stevenson, Robert Louis	Edinburgh: Picturesque Notes	1910
Various	Soroptimist International of Edinburgh 1927-1977	1977
Watt, Lachlan Maclean	The Hills of Home	1913

Index